The Allotment Keeper's Handbook

The Allotment Keeper's Handbook

A down-to-earth guide to growing your own food

Jane Perrone

theguardian

ATLANTIC BOOKS
LONDON

First published in 2007 in Great Britain by Atlantic Books
on behalf of Guardian Newspapers Ltd.
Atlantic Books is an imprint of Grove Atlantic Ltd.

The author and publisher would like to thank Organic Catalogue for
permission to reproduce images of purple sprouting broccoli and
beetroot choggia on pages 131 and 157. All other photos reproduced
by permission of the author.

ISBN 978 1 84354 548 4

A CIP catalogue record for this book is available from the British Library.

9 8 7 6 5 4

Printed and bound in Slovenia by MKT Print on behalf of Compass Press

Atlantic Books
An imprint of Grove Atlantic Ltd.
Ormond House
26–27 Boswell Street
London
WC1N 3JZ

For Rick

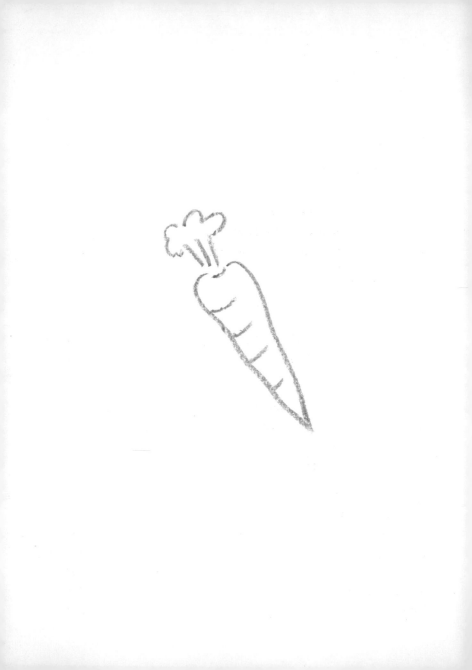

Contents

Introduction

For less than the cost of an annual television licence, my allotment – a parcel of land roughly half the size of a tennis court – is a source of fresh, local, organic food, a refuge from the stresses of modern living, a wildlife haven, and a lifestyle statement. It's helped me make new friends, keep fit and learn more about my community.

I can't imagine life now without the pleasure of watching the sun set over the electric blue blooms of cardoons and cornflowers while munching on mangetout and pottering about pulling weeds or picking lettuces. Or a time when I am no longer able to widen my culinary horizons and embrace a world beyond the limits set by the local supermarket, a world in which peas can be purple, carrots white and potatoes pink, black or red. Nor would I ever want to forego the thrill of watching my friends' eyes widen as they pop a ripe raspberry or sugarsnap pea in their mouth and let their tastebuds reel at the flavour that only just-picked, organically grown produce can offer.

I got an early taste of allotment life as a child, when I remember playing happily in the tall grass around my dad's plot as he sowed and dug. I was such an enthusiast for all things green and growing that I ended up with the nickname Botany at school, and had a bedroom full of house plants rather than a pile of copies of *Just Seventeen* or *Smash Hits*. My initial foray into gardening as a child involved sowing parsley and little red radishes, then a few vegetables here and there in my back garden. It was only when I settled into my first permanent home with my partner Rick that I decided to see whether there was an allotment close by.

I signed up to rent a plot, but it clearly hadn't seen a spade for quite a while. In fact it was a rectangle choked with thistles, couch grass and dock plants. It was really hard graft at first – as soon as I'd cleared a patch to plant a few beans the weeds began to fight back and retake the territory they'd won during years of neglect. Then Rick was seduced into getting involved by the taste of the single strawberry from our first plants and a new partnership was born. With two of us digging, pulling out thistle roots and cutting back brambles, the work remained as hard, but we progressed twice as fast. Over the past few seasons we've carved out a productive plot that supports a wide selection of soft fruit, flowers for cutting, and lots of interesting vegetables – from the unusual, such as cardoons, Jerusalem artichokes and white carrots, to staples like lettuce, potatoes, beetroot, pumpkins and leeks – all grown according to organic principles and providing some home-grown ingredients for our meals pretty much all year round.

In March 2004 I decided to start writing an online journal, or blog, about my allotment exploits, called *Horticultural* (http://perrone.blogs.com). I soon discovered that there was a whole online community of fellow plot holders keen to exchange ideas and tips with me and offer words of encouragement when things went wrong; even to swap recipes. I'm a journalist by training, not a gardener, and I've learned everything I know from sharing ideas with other growers and family members, as well as from reading countless seed catalogues, magazines and books, and by simply finding out for myself through trial and error.

This book is my attempt to continue the conversation started through my blog, to get you hooked on allotments too, or to reinvigorate your enthusiasm if you're already an allotmenteer. With the help of extracts from my online diary, examples of my own mistakes and successes, and tips and quotes from real allotmenteers, I explain how to go about finding your first allotment and choosing a plot, what you'll need to do to get started, and how to plan, sow, nurture and harvest your first crops. The glossary at the back of the book will help you cut through the jargon, and the guide to what you can sow, plant and harvest each month will steer you through your first year on the plot.

Whether you've never picked up a trowel before or you're an experienced gardener who has run out of space for vegetables in your own garden, I hope this book will inspire you to plot your path to a productive allotment.

Getting started

One

Whys and wherefores

My chosen mission statement is 'Grow what we eat, not eat what we grow'. I don't like radish. I don't eat radish. So I'm not going to grow them, even if it's pretty easy to.

Phillip Cook, *Our Allotment's Blog*

My allotment isn't one of those picture-perfect plots you see in glossy gardening programmes, filled with neat rows of burnished cabbages, beanpoles standing to attention and not a lettuce leaf out of place. No: it's an unedited-for-TV slice of land, the occasional weed and all. At times it's lush and full of flowers, fruits and a wisp of bindweed; at other times, when work, holidays or family commitments intervene, it's a bedraggled rectangle, weeds choking the crops and snails taking chunks out of everything that's green. It's also littered with evidence of my past mistakes: the ramshackle storage box, lid held in place with a plank, testament to my poor construction skills; the half-built raised bed; and the straggly raspberry canes that really should have been pruned several months ago.

Before you close this book in disgust, let me say this: unless you are lucky enough to consider tending an allotment your full-time job, your personal battle against the twin gods of time and nature is likely to be the one constant in your bid to grow your own food. Don't worry about it – revel in it! Having an allotment is all about getting to know a patch of earth, tracing out its foibles, and taking what you can from it amid the hubbub of modern life. That might mean feeding a family of four all year round with a cornucopia of fresh fruit and vegetables, or, perhaps more realistically, furnishing your household with an erratic but valued supply of each season's specialities. So what if your plot doesn't look as if it's been tended by the hands of Alan Titchmarsh or Monty Don: you don't have a film crew and a team of paid-for assistants on hand to polish your potatoes and cast out every last weed. Growing vegetables for your kitchen isn't difficult. That's just a myth perpetuated by those gardeners who resist the expansion of their cosy club. Anyone can make a go of an allotment, given a small amount of time, money and know-how. The resulting crops may not win any prizes, but who cares so long as they taste good and give you the option of ignoring the vacuum-packed cucumbers, bagged lettuces and tasteless tomatoes on your supermarket shelves?

Having an allotment has converted me from a passive consumer to an active and informed producer, making me more aware of the effort that goes into growing our food. It has taught me that organic vegetables don't come out of the ground as scrubbed, machine-graded, shrink-wrapped commodities, but as mud-encrusted, pest-nibbled, delicious ingredients. I now find a perfectly hole-free lettuce deeply unnatural and worrying. An allotment makes you aware not only of where you are but also of the time of year. Seasons matter on the plot in a way they don't in our daily lives. The first strawberry is greeted with cries of delight and a small ceremony involving slicing the succulent fruit and sharing the slivers around. And the pumpkin season is one of the consolations of the end of summer, heralding hearty soups and creamy risottos made from the stack of squash glowing in the dusk amid the fading leaves.

Back in 1998, the government select committee report on *The Future for Allotments* found that around three quarters of allotmenteers said they had a plot because they wanted to grow fresh food. But let's be clear: very few allotmenteers are trying to emulate the self-sufficiency of Hugh Fearnley-Whittingstall or Tom and Barbara Good in the seventies' sitcom *The Good Life*. Total self-sufficiency is a pipe dream for anyone with one, two or even three allotment plots, even if chickens or goats are permitted. But the smallest of plots will allow you to grow a significant amount of ultra local veg and slacken the grip of the supermarkets on the contents of your kitchen cupboards. The only produce I never need to buy is blackcurrants. My freezer is always full of plastic boxes of them, ready to be defrosted and made into sorbet, ice cream,

Allotment diary

November 2004

One of the great things you learn when allotmenteering is that everything you think you know about veg is up for grabs: a carrot isn't necessarily orange, or carrot-shaped; an apple isn't always a Granny Smith or a Gala; and beetroots can be red, white, yellow, or striped like a bull's-eye.

jam or a crumble. I also eat my own onions, shallots, potatoes, garlic, and winter squash for about three quarters of the year, and salads and herbs almost all year round. And the money I save on my grocery bill goes on buying more exotic Fairtrade organic fruit and vegetables that I'll never be able to grow myself.

Is an allotment right for you?

I'm passionate about my plot: I can't envisage life without the rhythm of regular visits to the patch, enjoying home-grown seasonal produce and a green space to experiment on. Research has shown that physical exercise and time spent in green places can ease depression, and I can understand why. For me, the best possible fix for a stressful week in the office is to retreat to the allotment, lifting mental if not meteorological storm clouds. It's my outdoor gym, too: why pump away at a machine in front of a television screen when I could be outside, digging and watering and weeding and generally giving my body an all-round workout?

But allotmenteering is not for everyone. There are many reasons why taking on an allotment might not work for you. The sight of a newly rented patch of weeds can be overwhelming. A certain level of physical fitness is required, particularly if you take on a plot that will need a considerable amount of work to overhaul. You need to be strong enough to handle a spade and turn over a heap of compost, and flexible enough to bend over for planting and weeding. If you're not, you will need to find a friend or family member who will commit to helping you with the heavier tasks, or at least get you started by building raised beds that will allow you to tend your crops more easily. You will also need to be prepared for some exposure to the elements – both winter cold and summer sun – the occasional bee or nettle sting, and the inevitable blisters, scratches and bruises that come from working outside.

It's also worth weighing up how much spare time you have to devote to your allotment. I didn't realise the amount of work involved when I first took on my plot. Even if your new land is well cultivated, I'd estimate you need to devote a minimum of five to ten hours a week to keep a small or medium plot in good order during the busy spring and summer months, perhaps more if you want to grow demanding, thirsty crops such as tomatoes. This drops off in winter, of course, when a couple of hours a week is just about enough.

An allotment can become a love–hate relationship if you begin to wilt under the pressure of trying to answer the continuous call to weed, sow and water while attempting to get on with the rest of your life. Many people give up their allotments in the first year because they have taken on too much or been too ambitious in their plans. But there are ways around the time commitment issue. Don't feel pressured into taking on a large plot: try negotiating to rent a 'half plot' at first if you can, with the option of taking on more land once you are up and running. This will be easier to do on a site without a lengthy waiting list, as is often the case in London.

Many people take on a single plot with a best friend, work colleague, or group of friends or family, sharing responsibility for its maintenance and enjoying the resulting harvest together. It's a great way of spreading the workload and turning the plot into a social venue where you can get together on sunny summer evenings to potter about picking lettuces and chatting. I've even heard of groups of pub regulars renting allotments as a form of exercise and fresh air, and pairs of families getting together to work on a plot while their children learn about the outdoors and make new friends. It's worth remembering, though, that only one of you can sign the allotment agreement, and that person will be the one receiving written warnings threatening eviction from the site if you fail to keep the plot up to the required standard. Try to share your plot with like-minded allotmenteers, as arguments can brew about what to grow and how to grow it, particularly if one of you is a keen organic gardener whereas the others want to throw weedkiller on everything. It's also sensible to lay out some firm ground rules before you begin, clarifying how expenses such as seeds and compost will be shared, who has the right to which crops come the harvest and how much time each individual or group will be expected to put in on the plot.

Money is one thing that shouldn't hold you back, as the cost implications are generally small. Allotment rents vary between roughly £5 and £100 a year, with discounts commonly offered for students, retirees and the unwaged, and you can get by with a small outlay on a few essential tools and half a dozen packets of seeds when you start out. Some sites try to encourage new plot holders by offering smaller, cheaper, 'beginners' plots' for rent, with the option of taking on more land after the first year, while others will waive the first few months or years of rent on particularly overgrown plots.

If, after careful consideration, you don't think you can spare the time for your own plot, you can still bring the allotment spirit into your own home, whether you have a lone windowsill, a balcony or a garden to play with. The three projects described towards the end of the next chapter should help you start growing your own food on a small scale. These will also be useful if you want to gain some growing experience before you dive in to full-scale allotmenteering, or you are biding time while your name is on a waiting list for a plot in an area where vacant allotments are scarce.

A plotted history and an uncertain future

The history of allotments as we know them begins with a series of enclosure laws enacted over two hundred years ago. Common land that had been accessible to all was closed off, resulting in a crisis for rural people, who no longer had anywhere to graze their livestock or grow vegetables. The ensuing outcry led to further legislation in the 1800s, requiring landowners to provide allotments (literally, 'portions') for rural labourers. In the 1900s, as the Industrial Revolution took hold and rural workers increasingly shifted to the cities in search of employment, factory owners also began to provide allotments for their workers in the belief that this would keep them fit and healthy. But it was the food shortages of the First and Second World Wars that prompted the biggest boom in allotments. Parks, playgrounds and other 'empty' pieces of land were requisitioned for vegetable growing, and rationing meant demand for plots soared as families tried to find ways to supplement their meagre food allowance. In their book *The Allotment: Its Landscape and Culture*, David Crouch and Colin Ward estimate that the number of allotments trebled and

13

quadrupled in towns and cities during the First World War. Much of the requisitioned land was returned to its original use once the conflict was over, but the enthusiasm for growing food did not wane, and demand for plots remained high. A couple of decades later, after the onset of the Second World War, the government was back to calling for more allotment land with its Dig for Victory campaign.

My grandfather was a model allotmenteer and doubtless a product of the war-era imperative to grow your own fruit and veg. When not at work, John Admiral Byng was to be found on one of his five plots, toiling to supply his wife and five children with every crop imaginable, from asparagus to loganberries; it was his only hobby, if you can call it that. John Byng's plots were razed along with the rest of the huge site to make way for a new shopping precinct in 1966, by which time my grandfather was in his sixties and too old to take on a new plot elsewhere. I was not yet born when he gave up his allotment, but I do remember the vegetable patch in the garden of his retirement bungalow, the plump beefsteak tomatoes and the giant runner beans – the last vestiges of a much grander growing scheme. The fate of his allotment site echoes a story repeated across Britain from the end of the Second World War until the present day: the erosion of allotment land. In the mid-forties there were 1.4 million allotment sites, according to government figures; by the nineties, that figure had dipped to below 400,000, and the National Society of Allotment and Leisure Gardening (NSALG) estimates that there are now around 330,000 plot holders. The reasons for this decline are varied, with the post-war housing boom, the rise of the supermarket as a source of cheap food, the prevalence of houses with gardens, and rising standards of living all playing a part. And although there was a burst of interest in allotments in the seventies, and again at the start of the new millennium, sparking articles in newspapers and magazines and features on radio and television – cabbage chic, you might call it – this hasn't been matched by a boom in the number of allotment sites available for rent.

Around three quarters of all existing allotments are 'statutory' sites, which means that they are protected by law from being sold off without the consent of the government. Before seeking permission to dispose of a site, the allotment owner must also consult with plot holders, and must be able to prove to the government's satisfaction that the use of the land as an allotment site is not necessary or that the land is surplus to requirements, and that the owner has actively promoted the availability of allotment sites to the community. The other 25 per cent of allotments are a hotchpotch of temporary sites, which are again owned by local authorities but don't have the same protection as statutory sites, and allotments in private ownership. Temporary and private allotments can be disposed of or converted to another use by the landowner at any time, although 12 months' notice to quit should be issued to plot holders. The owners can be private individuals, or large organisations such as Universities, the Church of England and Railtrack, which has inherited allotments next to railway tracks provided for railway workers in the early 1900s as a place to grow their vegetables. Many private sites have been sold off in recent years to reap the rewards of the ever-increasing demand for land in towns and cities.

You don't need me to tell you that you are much better off finding a statutory site, if you can, as there is less risk of being evicted at short notice. That doesn't mean that statutory sites are completely protected from developers, however. A 1998 government report noted that such sites are under threat from increasingly cash-starved councils who see the opportunity to make a profit by selling land that, because of its location in the centre of urban and suburban areas, will command a high price. Sites can be at risk from everything from park-and-ride schemes and cemeteries to supermarkets and housing. According to the NSALG, there were more than fifty applications from local councils to dispose of allotment land in 2004–5 alone, ranging from a three-metre strip for a cycle path to three sites for housing. Although the law insists that alternative land must be found for displaced plot holders, the idea of giving up land nurtured for many years is, not surprisingly, heartbreaking to many allotmenteers. Prior to a sell-off, a downward spiral often occurs, where local councils mismanage sites by failing to advertise vacant plots or carry out repairs on fences that keep out vandals. Once rumours begin that a site has been earmarked for development, people are discouraged from taking up plots and the site becomes overgrown – at which point it's easy for the local council to argue that it's not wanted by the local community.

If you want to find out more about the history of allotments, or if your plot is blighted by developers, there are plenty of sources of information and help. The Allotments Regeneration Initiative publishes useful factsheets on how to find new tenants for abandoned plots and how to restore derelict sites, and also runs seminars on how to get started in allotment regeneration in your area. The NSALG offers advice to members faced with the closure of their site. See the directory for contact details.

Allotment community

Just like any community, allotments are a mixed bag. There are friendly people and people who resent newcomers; people who immerse themselves in the social life and those who prefer to turn up, tend their plot and leave. It can become depressing if the only contact you have with your landlord or fellow plot holders is paying your rent, or even worse, a letter chiding you for having an untidy plot. But it's up to you to find your own place within the allotment community and decide how involved you want to get in the social life of the site. Don't be afraid to wander up to someone who seems to have a well-established plot and strike up a conversation: most people will be delighted that you're taking an interest, and more than willing to fill you in on all the site gossip.

If you're a weekend visitor and everyone else on your site turns up during the week, or vice versa, this may not be easy, but it pays off. Most statutory allotments are either directly run by the local council or are what is known as 'self-managed'. In the case of the latter, allotment associations usually lease the site from the local council and collect the rent, carry out repairs and maintain waiting lists. This means that those running the site have a vested interest in it, and problems are likely to be dealt with more quickly, but it does rely on a core of plot holders taking on the responsibility of managing the site rather than leaving the work to council officers.

Either way, as a plot holder you should be able to attend meetings of either your allotment association or, if your site is run by a local council or other organisation, the AGM or plot holders' liaison committee. This may seem like a drag but it's one way of getting to know your neighbours and learning about matters that may impact on you, be it the arrival of a help-yourself pile of manure or reports of vandalism or theft. If your site is dominated by an old guard of retired men, your attendance at a meeting may be greeted by a moment of silence, but once the shock fades, chances are they'll appreciate you bothering to show up, particularly if you're

Allotment diary

October 2005

A few nights ago I spent a rainy evening attending the annual allotment committee meeting for the two sites in my small corner of the Home Counties. The demographic of the attendees broadly matched that of the wider group of allotmenteers I see around the site, and that of the area I live in – sixteen men, four women, all white, average age fifty-odd – although I think it was skewed towards those plot holders who have been renting for years rather than relative newcomers like me. There weren't any of the other newbies who tend plots near mine, for instance.

The main topics for discussion were ones that will be familiar to anyone who has ever had an allotment: how to improve security on the site, complaints about rubbish tipping (asbestos, of all things), and worries about the erosion of allotment land, in this case via the erection of a mobile telephone mast (one plot holder joked that the new, bigger mast would help him grow an even larger pumpkin next year).

prepared to get involved in the running of the site by doing the accounts, helping to keep communal areas tidy or typing up newsletters. And make yourself heard: there is no rule stating that someone who has had an allotment for twenty years should have any more say in the running of the site than a brand new plot holder. If you can't make the meeting, most sites should have a number of site representatives or officers you can contact.

It can be easy to fall into the trap of sizing up your neighbours' work and becoming crestfallen that their sweetcorn is twice the size of yours, or because they seem to have some kind of weed-excluding force field around their plot. Even if you never glance at your neighbours' work, know this: they will be checking out yours. But try to resist becoming envious at what others have achieved. It has taken me several years to stop wishing for the golden day that my plot will be 'finished', and learn instead to enjoy the ceaseless activity of sowing, weeding and watering for what it is, rather than as part of a single great goal. To employ an old adage, it's all about revelling in the journey, not endlessly peering ahead to a final destination.

Why an organic allotment?

Ladybirds. Ladybirds everywhere: crawling up my arms and down my legs, nestling in every lettuce leaf, shooting the breeze with the other 'birds in a huddle on the waxy shards of a globe artichoke head. It's a sight I come across every spring on my allotment. The temperature gauge rises to ladybird level and the next generation of the most blessed of the beetle family emerge from their pupae. Granted, there's always an abundance of other, perhaps less welcome insect life, too: the blackfly on broad beans, the cloud of

19

whitefly rising from the purple sprouting broccoli and the aphids clustered on the fresh new growth of salad leaves. But to an organic gardener, that's all part of nature's balancing act: without the aphids, there would be no ladybirds.

It's what's known as biodiversity, and it's at the core of what it means to grow organically. Biodiversity simply means nurturing the staggering range of creatures that will exist on your handkerchief of earth. At the sexier end of the biodiversity scale, there's the ladybird explosion, the grass snake sunning itself on the wood pile, and the robin dithering on a beanpole, watching your spade unearth a breakfast of worms. Getting literally a bit more down to earth, biodiversity encompasses those worms, and also slugs. Often the villain of the allotment, slugs do however play a crucial role in breaking down dead plant material and providing dinner for other creatures like frogs, toads and birds. By allowing a balance to be maintained, there's never an opportunity for a single pest to get out of hand.

So that's biodiversity: but what exactly is organic gardening? It's more than just chucking out the synthetic pesticide bottles. The British organic gardening organisation Garden Organic (formerly known as the Henry Doubleday Research Association or HDRA) provides the clearest definition: 'Organic gardeners focus their energy into increasing the natural health of their soil, choosing appropriate plant varieties, and working with nature to produce a healthy and productive garden.' I'd like to claim that I thought hard about the pros and cons of growing organically on my allotment, but that simply wasn't the case. It never even entered my head to go about it any other way once I'd signed the lease for my plot. I had bought synthetic pesticides and weedkillers before, but when I'd used them, I'd found the experience deeply unsatisfying. They were expensive to buy, tricky to use, and only ever seemed to be a temporary fix. The alternative made much more sense to me: learning to encourage biodiversity and to feed and nurture the soil so it could support healthy plants that could weather attack by pests and diseases. And it seemed deeply perverse to sweat away growing my own fruit and vegetables, only to dose them up with the same chemicals I'd find in produce on the supermarket shelves.

To apply a bit of hindsight, I can say I made the right decision. Since the mid-nineties, organic gardening has shifted from the margins to the mainstream, on allotments as well as in back gardens. It's not hard to see why: as we've all become more aware of where our food comes from and how it is produced, the imperative to seize back a portion of control over our fruit and veg has become ever more urgent. It's a small contribution, admittedly, but an allotment helps people to trim their 'footprint' on the earth by encouraging recycling and a little slice of self-sufficiency. Allotments also play a particularly powerful role in helping to maintain biodiversity in urban centres: the NSALG reports that allotment sites have up to a third more species diversity than urban parks, for instance. And they act as green lungs in the centre of towns and cities across Britain, allowing anyone, regardless of means or background, to grow their own food.

Have I convinced you of the value of allotments yet? I hope so, because in the next chapter I'll explain how to find an allotment site and choose a plot of your own.

Spotlight on...

RAINBOW CHARD

I first became passionate about rainbow chard during a visit to the botanical gardens of the University of British Columbia in Vancouver. In their beautifully maintained vegetable garden, I was captivated by the plant's puckered, glossy leaves, held aloft on thick-ribbed stems coloured brash yellow, magenta, creamy white, acid orange and a dozen shades in between. A close relative of the beetroot, Swiss chard is truly an ancient vegetable, mentioned by both Aristotle and Pliny, but it is the leaves and stems, rather than the roots, that are

prized for the kitchen. The stems can be chopped up for use in stir-fries, baked into a gratin with cheese, or mixed into stews, while the leaves can be used in frittatas, hearty soups, tarts, stir fries and much more.

Seed packets and gardening books may refer to Swiss chard as spinach beet, leaf beet, seakale beet or simply as chard: the names are interchangeable, although leaf beet generally refers to Perpetual Spinach, a variety with thin, tender stems and smaller leaves that is used as an easier-to-grow substitute for real spinach and is particularly useful for salads.

Rainbow chard goes under a range of names, including Bright Lights. This variety has been around for hundreds of years and is thought to have been cited by the Elizabethan physician John Gerard in his 1597 *Herball*, in which he describes seeds taken from a 'beet' that 'doth bring forth plants of many and variable colours'.

Since I raised my first crop I've become a rampant evangelist for this beautiful, easy-to-grow all-rounder, not least because it is almost impossible to buy in the UK, aside from at the occasional farmers' market. It is attractive enough to be used in an ornamental planting scheme, and with a twice-yearly sowing in spring and early autumn and some protection from a cold frame during the depths of winter, it can be available for harvest pretty much all year round.

Other popular chard varieties include Rhubarb chard, which has ruby red stems like its namesake, and Lucullus, which has stunning white stems, but if you want a riot of colour, rainbow chard really does live up to its name.

Seed sources: Available from all major seed suppliers.

Two
Choosing a plot

Error is a hardy plant; it flourishes in every soil.
Martin Tupper, *Proverbial Philosophy*, 1842

When I chose my plot, I did just about everything wrong. It was a misjudgement on such a grand scale that I am still paying the price for it. I hope that the lessons I have learned will put me in an excellent position to point out all the potential pitfalls of allotment selection, because I fell into every damn pit there was.

There are two allotment sites in the small town where I live, both managed by the town council. I chose the one just four minutes' walk from my front door; that was my first and only wise move. If an allotment site is not within walking or cycling distance, for the vast majority of your visits you'll be offsetting all your ethical Brownie points earned from growing your own food by polluting the environment with your car. It's also a hassle to drive to your plot, unless you are delivering heavy equipment or manure: on-site parking may be a problem and you'll probably have to fiddle about getting in and out of the car to unlock gates. There were maybe half a dozen available plots scattered around my chosen site, in varying states of abandonment. I chose one right in the corner, bordered by neglected plots on two sides; on the third, there was an overgrown, bramble and bindweed-wreathed hedgerow that was home to several flocks of sparrows constantly bickering and twittering in the trees, and on the final side there was a stretch of rough land long left to the weeds. Looking back I remember my thought process: I cherished the idea of isolation. I wanted to withdraw to my plot like some Romantic poet and lean on my spade, staring out over open fields, away from the judgemental eyes of other allotmenteers who might balk at my naive attempts at cultivation.

Wrong move. In seeking a quiet corner, I also hid myself away from the very people who could have provided encouragement, tips and maybe a few surplus seedlings to get me started. My catalogue of errors in plot selection didn't end there: the hedge posed a problem too. While bramble and bindweed rambled above ground, below the surface their roots were spreading huge distances under my patch, popping up when least expected, sapping the soil of its nutrients and strangling my first efforts at cultivation. I also failed to notice that I had picked a plot at the lowest level of the site, which slopes gently down to the northeast: if I'd bothered speaking to any of the existing plot holders I would have realised that during winter my chosen corner would be boggy at best – underwater at worst. So much for the romance of isolation: it was more puddle than potager. Nor did I think about how far it was from the gate, or how easy access was, what the soil was like, or just how long ago it had last seen a spade. As I quickly discovered, my plot hadn't been cultivated for some time, so the surface of the soil was covered with a thick mat of couch grass and other weeds.

That first winter and spring were a slog. Whatever I did, great lakes of water collected around the straggly, newly planted blackcurrant bushes that constituted my first effort at cultivation, and any attempts to clear the weed-infested ground quickly turned it into a slippery mud bath. Things did improve, slowly, and after much toil, though I did myself no favours by choosing a plot that was probably the most challenging on the site. But the wondrous thing is, despite making a complete hash of the process of selection, and despite the fact that my parcel of land was sub-par, to say the least, I've still managed to turn it into a productive patch, and had a lot of fun in the process. So don't be put off if the only plot you're offered looks like an industrial wasteland:

Allotment diary

August 2005

Perhaps I should go back to why I got an allotment in the first place. I guess at the heart of it was my sheer wonder at the fact that a seed – with some sunshine, soil, toil and water added – can be transformed into a tomato, a pumpkin, or a radish. I also wanted to grow vegetables and fruit that you simply can't buy in the supermarket (at least, not in the ones where I live): globe artichokes, Jerusalem artichokes, black-berries, Physalis Cape gooseberries, yellow tomatoes, rainbow chard, black potatoes, pink banana-shaped squash, white carrots, yellow beetroots...

Now, several years on, the idea of sticking with the dull inventory of vacuum-packed produce on offer in the shops fills me with horror. That's why my allotment brings me so much pleasure.

even the gloomiest rectangles of suburbia can, with some hard work and over time, be turned into a green oasis. The following chapters will explain how I did it, and, I hope, encourage you to follow suit.

How to find an allotment

Allotments are often tucked away in the least likely of places, and even if you have lived somewhere for a while, you may not know where your local ones are. They are often located near railway tracks, so you may have seen them from a passing train, but they may not be visible from the road. My patch is tucked away between playing fields, the back of a housing estate and some tennis courts, and is only accessible via a long track; I only learned of its existence by contacting my local council, and that should probably be your first move when looking for a site, too. Town, borough and district councils are required by law to publicise their statutory sites, but if that doesn't turn up any suitable plots, don't give up. You may be able to find a private or temporary allotment on a site run by private landowners. These can be a little trickier to identify: ask around in your street, check local maps, visit the library and try an internet search, as many sites have their own webpages. If you have found a site but there are no signs indicating who owns it, you may have to ambush a plot holder on their way in or out to extract some more information. It's worth doing this regardless, as it's an excellent way of finding out the lie of the land, literally and metaphorically. If I'd done that before choosing my plot, I am sure I'd have been talked out of picking the godforsaken corner I plumped for.

There are also a number of questions you should be asking the site owner or manager when weighing up whether a particular site is right for you. Find out if there is an area reserved for organic growers; whether there is any prohibition on sheds or other structures; whether hosepipes for watering, bonfires, and coldframes or polytunnels are allowed or restricted; and whether there are any extra charges for water, maintenance and so on. If you hope to keep livestock such as hens, rabbits or bees, you will also need to find out whether this is permitted, and whether there are rules on the size of pens or number of animals. There may also be restrictions on planting fruit trees, which are worth noting if you plan to turn your plot into a mini-orchard. You should also ask if there's a trading shed where you can buy cheap gardening supplies. They're usually staffed by volunteer plot holders and open a few hours a week, selling everything from seeds and tools to manure and netting. Many gardening supply companies offer special deals to allotment groups to buy in bulk at a discount, so you may find it's cheaper than your local garden centre, as well as closer to your plot. Volunteering to serve customers at your site's trading shed is a great way of getting to meet many of your neighbouring plot holders, too.

It's also worth asking whether there is a pool of equipment such as rotovators, strimmers and lawnmowers available to hire for a small sum; and whether there is an active allotment association that you can join to get the most out of the social life on your site. On-site toilets are also a plus if you plan to spend all day working on your plot. Some or all of these factors will help dictate which site you choose, but for many people, there may not be a choice:

if that's the case, you'll simply have to make the best of what's on offer.

But what if you're unlucky enough not to have any allotments in the vicinity, or they all have waiting lists several years long? There is something you can do. Everyone has a legal right to an allotment under the 1908 Smallholdings and Allotments Act. Under this law, local councils are obliged to meet local demand for plots. That means that if demand is outstripping supply and many people are waiting years for a plot to become available, more allotment land must be provided. The Act states that councils must respond to a request for more allotment land if six or more people who are on the electoral roll for that area and are waiting for a plot put their case forward to them. The only exception is for those who live in inner London, whose boroughs are not covered by this legal requirement.

It seems that this highly useful piece of legislation is little used, but it is still current law. Just point your council officials in the direction of the 1908 Act – section 23 to be precise – if they raise their eyebrows at your demands. Of course, the more people you can get to back your campaign, the better – 60 or even 600 will always pull more weight than six. Why not send a letter to your local newspaper asking people to join your crusade, or put notices up in pubs, leisure centres and other public places? You could find a whole group of people desperate for an allotment who just didn't know how to go about getting one.

For more information and advice on allotments and the law, Sophie Andrews' book *The Allotment Handbook* is an invaluable resource. See the bibliography for details.

Choosing a plot

Once you have narrowed down your choice to a single site with one or more empty plots, try to get a guided tour from the site manager, or failing that, a fellow plot holder or allotment association representative. You should be offered a numbered map of the site and a list of empty plot numbers. These maps are notoriously hard to read – often almost indecipherable, smeary documents that bear only passing resemblance to the physical reality of the site – which is why it's best to have someone on hand who can tell you what's what and point out empty plots. There are usually numbered plot markers on the actual allotment site, but sometimes these too are hard to read or are missing altogether.

On sites with a patchwork of overgrown plots between cultivated ones, managers may try to persuade you to take a particular plot simply because they want to fill in the gaps. Don't feel any compunction to make do with an inferior plot for the convenience of the site owner, however, and never say yes without seeing the plot in question first. Take a walk around the whole site, paying close attention to access, the state of paths, parking areas and drives, availability of water taps and security. More often than not, vacant allotments are overgrown. Allotment leases generally last for a year, so if someone moves away, loses interest or dies, their absence may not be picked up by the site manager for several months. By that time the plot could be choked with weeds. And on some sites where occupancy is low, some plots may not have been touched for years.

Once you've identified the vacant plots, there are a few ways of assessing which is the best. Find out from your guide which plots have been most recently tended, as these will probably be easier to revamp. Try to choose a plot that is close to a water tap, particularly if hosepipes aren't permitted; if you don't, you'll curse your choice every time you have to tramp back and forth with heavy watering cans during the summer. It's worth checking the tap too, if you can. They are not always well maintained, and even if they do work, water pressure might be painfully low, especially if your tap is at the end of the network of pipes serving the site. I know this from bitter experience: because I am in the far corner, every time someone closer to the mains supply turns a tap on, the flow from my standpipe slows to a pathetic dribble, making summer watering trips unbearably slow. And while I hope you won't be driving to your plot every time you visit, it's also crucial that you do have reasonable access: vehicles will need to get as close as possible for delivering manure and equipment, and solid paths between your neighbour's plot and yours are essential for wheelbarrows and trudging feet.

Level is better than sloping: a steep incline means work, as you'll have to terrace everything to prevent the soil slipping downhill. If your site of choice isn't completely flat (and many aren't), each of its plots will have an aspect – the compass direction of the slope from the highest point on your plot to the lowest. Aspect is important because it tells you how much sun your plot will get, and the more sloping the plot, the more important this becomes. A south-facing aspect is best, as that means the sun will be hitting your ground for the majority of the day; conversely, a north-facing aspect means not much direct sunlight. Before you ask, no, I didn't check this either: my plot's aspect is to the northeast. Take a compass along to check the aspect, unless there are several landmarks you can use to indicate which way your slope points.

Once you've narrowed your choice down to a couple of possibles, the final test is to check the state of the soil. Take a spade along so you can conduct a soil profile – that's digging a hole, to you and me. Garden Organic's *HDRA Encyclopedia of Organic Gardening* (my allotment bible) suggests a one metre by one metre hole that's at least one metre deep. That's a hell of a big hole, particularly if you're checking the soil on two or three plots. You can still get an idea of what's going on below the surface with something slightly less deep and wide: topsoil – the layer on the top, as the name suggests – can be anything from five to sixty centimetres deep, so if your topsoil is shallow, you'll have a fair idea of that well before you've dug a metre down. The depth of topsoil will depend on where you live, but it's also an indication of how fertile your plot is and so can vary from plot to plot, depending on how it's been cared for. A patch that's been nurtured year on year with plenty of compost or manure will have dark, rich topsoil that contains lots of organic material. As the layers of topsoil become paler, they turn into what's known as subsoil, which is far less fertile. If the subsoil contains clay, this will stop water draining away and could cause waterlogging in winter. If you're checking out the ground in wintertime, you'll be able to tell from the state of the earth underfoot whether there's a problem with waterlogging; if there is standing water on the surface, or your boots are squelching as you walk, there's probably a drainage problem that will take time and energy to fix. One other test you can do is to try plunging a fork into the ground. If the fork resists going into the ground up to the end of the tines (and assuming you haven't hit a stone or rock), the soil is probably compacted – in other words, it lacks air spaces between the soil particles. This is common on plots that haven't been worked for some time, or where livestock have been roaming, and can also signal drainage problems. If you want to know more about how to tell what kind of earth you're dealing with, consult chapter six which is all about soil.

It's also worth doing a careful visual survey of any plots you're interested in: are there useful structures such as fruit cages, sheds, raised beds or water butts you can make use of? Will you have to spend time removing rubbish from the site? Are there any established fruit bushes such as raspberries or blackcurrants that are worth keeping? These factors could help you choose between two similar plots: for instance, a solid shed is a big plus, while a tumbledown wreck that you'll need to spend time demolishing means more work at a time when you want to focus on the soil.

If you can, corner several plot holders and pump them for information; aside from anything else, it's a gauge of how approachable and friendly your neighbours are likely to be. Tell them you're thinking of renting a plot and ask for their opinion on the best areas of the site. They'll also be able to warn you about any problems with vandalism, theft, or pests such as rabbits and deer, and point out which areas are best avoided and how well the site is managed.

A matter of size

One of the more arcane aspects of renting an allotment is the way plots are measured. Most sites still subdivide the land into perches, poles or rods, usually in parcels of five or ten. Fortunately all three terms actually mean the same thing: a subdivision of a mile that covers a distance of sixteen and a half feet or five and a half yards (just over five metres). There are four poles (or rods, or perches) to the chain, ten chains to the furlong, and eight furlongs to the mile. All three names originate from medieval times and are derived from the concept of a measuring stick, itself believed to be an adaptation of the stick used to goad oxen with when ploughing. The Collins English Dictionary tells us that 'perch' comes from the Old French word 'perche', meaning stake, which in turn was derived from the Latin 'pertica', a long staff. A rod, perch or pole can also refer to an area of land, equalling thirty and a quarter square yards (just over twenty-five and a quarter square metres).

However confusing this may seem, what it means in practice to the plot holder boils down to this: the standard plot size on British allotments has traditionally been ten square poles (or rods, or perches), which is just over 300 square yards, or around 253 square metres. (If it helps you to visualise, a tennis court is just over 260 square metres.) However, many sites are now offering five-pole/rod/perch plots, sometimes referred to as 'half plots', as a standard rental size. In his 1980 book *Cowpasture: The Everyday Life of an English Allotment*, Roy Lacey dismisses five-pole plots as 'too small to be farmed properly'. My late grandfather, with his five plots, would probably have agreed. But since the mid-eighties this trend has been part of a wider cultural move towards making allotments more accessible to newcomers who might find a ten-pole plot too daunting. I have a five-pole plot, and know I would struggle to keep an area double that size cultivated. If your site only offers ten-pole plots, it's probably worth roping in a friend to help, or covering half the plot with weed suppressant material for the first year.

Bringing the allotment home

There are other ways of embracing the allotment ideal without renting a plot yourself. If you have children, you could join – or even start – a school garden project, and some sites run allotment projects for local children that you could help with. There may be charities or local organisations that would be delighted to have a volunteer willing to help elderly people tame their gardens. And if you fancy the idea of growing your own but don't have any outside space, there are still things you can do – even if all you have is a dark shelf at the back of a cupboard. Here are a few ideas.

Sprouting seeds

As a child, growing mustard and cress on a moist tissue was a fascinating introduction to the world of photosynthesis. There's no reason why you can't rediscover this pastime, as I did recently when my dad gave me a seventies-era 'cress hog', still in its original box. I filled the ceramic hedgehog-shaped pot with water and grew mustard and cress on his back. I've also invested in a seed sprouter: a nest of perforated plastic trays that can hold a considerable crop of sprouts. It takes up about the same room as a portable radio and, if kept topped up, will keep you in fresh sprouts for salads and sandwiches all year round. You can also make your own sprouter using a large, wide-mouthed glass jar with a piece of muslin spread tightly across the opening to allow water to drain in and out. Mung beans are the classic sprouting experiment, but there are many other possibilities, including chickpeas, alfalfa, raw peanuts, fenugreek, wheat, radishes and broccoli. The larger seeds should be soaked in water overnight to kickstart germination, then placed into the trays. You need to rinse them in fresh water twice a day, until the sprouts have reached their desired length. Some sprouts, such as mung beans, are best raised in the dark, while others, such as alfalfa, can be grown on a sunny windowsill. I tend to use my sprouter the most during the winter, adding sprouts to my salads of winter crops from the plot – chard leaves, winter lettuce and land cress – or sprinkling them on top of a slice of crusty brown bread slathered in home-made hummus.

Growing mushrooms

Another project you can embark on from the comfort of your own home is mushroom growing. You can buy the basic kits for growing button mushrooms from most garden centres, but it's possible to grow exotic fungi too, such as oyster mushrooms. Perhaps the best part about cultivating these is the fact that one of the suggested growing mediums is a damp toilet roll: the whole thing, not just the cardboard centre. The spongy paper provides ideal territory for the spores to grow, and is small enough to grow oyster mushrooms indoors.

Most mushrooms are best grown outdoors, however. You can buy a log already containing dowels impregnated with spores such as shiitake mushrooms, or buy the dowels to insert in your own log or tree stump. All you need to do is leave the log wrapped in a plastic bag in a cool, damp place – the base of a hedge partially covered by damp leaves is ideal – and wait for the wood to become fully colonised by the fungus. After a few months the log can be removed from the bag and stood upright with its base resting in a patch of shaded soil. There are a whole range of mushrooms to try, from the tasty Chicken of the Woods to the startling looking Lion's Mane Fungus. It can take months for the mushrooms to begin growing, but it's a fun experiment, and you never know, it might even encourage your children to start eating mushrooms.

Potatoes in a barrel – just in time for Christmas

There's something deeply satisfying about being able to serve your own potato crop for Christmas dinner. It may not be the most cost-effective way of growing, and the yield won't be as great as on an allotment, but you will get the satisfaction of watching the plants grow at close range, and your first potato harvest is thrilling: rather like an Easter egg hunt.

The fun begins in September, when you'll need to lay your hands on a barrel, plastic tub or other large container that has drainage holes in the base and is at least thirty centimetres deep and the same in diameter. You'll also need a small amount of sheltered outdoor space – a sunny patio or balcony is ideal – to keep the potato plants protected from frost; potatoes are unfortunately a strictly outdoor crop. To prepare the container, put some broken terracotta pots or a layer of gravel at the bottom to help with drainage. Then add about ten centimetres of soil or compost; assuming you can't use soil from a garden or allotment, buy some peat-free compost for containers. Next, arrange your

Spotlight on...

JERUSALEM ARTICHOKES

Jerusalem artichokes are easy-to-grow, seasonal vegetables that are worth trying because they're hard to find in the shops, and even when you can get hold of them they are expensive and no match for the crisp pearly flesh of a tuber straight from the ground. On his website, Jamie Oliver (www.jamieoliver.com) describes their knobbly appearance as making them look like 'new potatoes gone mad'.

I serve mine sliced thinly in stir-fries (get people to play 'guess the vegetable'); roasted with plenty of olive oil, halved lemons and thyme to accompany a Sunday roast; turned into the classic soup; or raw cut into little sticks for scooping up the classic Italian dip of anchovy, garlic and butter – bagna cauda. While you're eating, you can tell their fascinating backstory. As food writer Jane Grigson has written in her *Vegetable Book*, Jerusalem artichokes are 'none the worse for not being artichokes and having nothing at all to do with Jerusalem'. When French explorer Samuel de Champlain came across Native Americans growing Jerusalem artichokes – which they called sun roots – in the early 1600s, he decided they tasted like the globe artichoke, hence the misnomer. The 'Jerusalem' bit is said to be a corruption of the Italian word for sunflower, 'girasole', literally 'turning to the sun'.

The tubers are planted in the ground in the spring, and require very little care from then on. Fuseau is an excellent variety to choose as the tubers are not too knobbly, which makes for easy peeling. Once planted in a spot, they're hard to get rid of as you'll always miss a tuber or two and these will proliferate year after year. The plants are tall, so make a good windbreak or shade for other crops. They're in season in the autumn and winter: once the plant has died, cut it down to a few centimetres and leave the tubers in the ground until they're required. The only hitch with this tuber is

that, left in the open air, it goes soft within a day of harvest, so isn't suitable for storage in the same way as your potatoes. They'll keep a little longer stored in a plastic bag in the fridge, but I tend to yank the plants up one by one as I need them throughout the autumn and winter. The tubers usually cling to the stem, so you can pick them off individually. They need a good scrub, and peeling is optional, particularly if you plan to roast them.

One caveat about the Jerusalem artichoke that's important to mention is that it can cause an unpleasant side effect in some people in the form of excessive flatulence, particularly if eaten raw or whole. This is brought on by the presence of a carbohydrate called inulin in the 'chokes. In his book *Growing Unusual Vegetables*, vegetable expert Simon Hickmott says the more you eat them, the less this problem will trouble you; the addition of caraway or fennel seeds is reputed to lessen the side effects, too.

Tuber sources: Organic Gardening Catalogue, Mr Fothergill's, Marshalls Seeds, DT Brown Seeds.

tubers, no more than four or five to a container: you'll need to buy specially developed seed potatoes meant for autumn planting, which most specialist seed companies sell. Top up the compost until it's just short of the rim and water it well. Cover the tubers with another five centimetres of compost, then wait: once the plants have grown to about twelve centimetres, carefully surround them with more compost until just the tips of the shoots are showing. Allow the plants to continue growing, and keep adding compost at intervals until you reach the rim of the barrel. Water the compost regularly, and feed the plants with seaweed feed every couple of weeks.

If there's a cold snap and you can't move your potato barrel to a frost-free spot against the side of your home, protect the plants by covering them with an old sheet, or some horticultural fleece. The spuds should be ready to harvest in time for 25 December: just lift away the soil or turn the container on its side and pick out the potatoes. You should be able to harvest several pounds of potatoes using this method.

Three

Planning and preparation

I'm President of the United States and I'm not going
to eat any more broccoli.

George Bush Senior,
White House State Dinner, 1990

It's what you might call an allotment epiphany – that moment
when you closely inspect your plot, either as a brand new tenant,
or a lapsed allotmenteer with an overgrown patch. The enormity of
the task ahead begins to become clear: perhaps it's the huge pile
of rubble you're going to have to dispose of, a ramshackle fence or
greenhouse that could collapse at any minute, or ground that's
jungle-thick with weeds. Or perhaps all three, if you're really
unlucky. Getting hold of the plot was the easy bit; now comes the
fun – and the hard work. But don't be overcome with fear. Even the
most recalcitrant patch of land can, with time and determination,
be tamed and brought into productivity. The key is not to try to do
too much, too soon. And don't be discouraged when things don't
go quite as you planned.

I can't count the number of times I have felt like giving up,
particularly when I've looked over at my neighbours' finely tilled

earth, razor-sharp rows and lush vegetation, then back at my beds – which resemble nothing more than a dastardly experiment in mutant weed breeding. What keeps me going back for more? I am addicted. Addicted to the idea of growing my own vegetables; addicted to the annual blackcurrant harvest that heralds another batch of the best jam I have ever tasted; addicted to the thrill of bypassing the dull plastic-wrapped supermarket offerings; and addicted to the heady combination of fresh air, exercise and quiet companionship that comes from working the plot alongside my partner.

Allotment diary

August 2005

Despite the carefree attitude I (usually) display, there are times when having an allotment gets me down. I know other allotmenteers experience similar lows, and for some, these bad patches are enough to force them to give up. I'm always aware that I am only just keeping on top of everything: the harvesting, the sowing, and the weeding – my GOD the weeding… So what to do when you're feeling overwhelmed? Step back, take some deep breaths and relax: it's not the end of the world. In my experience the chard will grow pretty much whenever it's sown, the tomatoes will survive, and the potatoes can stay in the ground for several more weeks.

Getting the structure right

Whether your new allotment is overgrown or in prime condition, before you begin to lift a spade, it's worth thinking about the permanent features, or 'plot infrastructure', that will help to dictate its layout. It used to be considered essential to dig over your entire plot every winter or spring, in order to break up clods of soil, expose pests and allow soil improvers and fertilisers to be incorporated. And the received allotment wisdom was that crops should be grown in rows, between which you'd walk to water and weed. But this has changed in the last few decades, with the increasing popularity of the bed system.

The idea behind the bed system is that by setting up a series of permanent rectangular growing areas intersected by paths, the need to dig is hugely reduced because, as every centimetre of every bed is reachable from the paths, the soil in the beds is never walked upon. Beds should be at least fifteen centimetres deep and will typically measure 1 metre by 2 metres. For extra protection they may be raised up from the surface of the paths with edgings of wooden planks, stone, plastic, or anything you can lay your hands on that would make a low wall, such as old bricks or roof slates. More and more allotmenteers now use scaffolding boards, which can be bought cheaply and are made of untreated wood that's safe for use around edible crops, though be warned that untreated wood will rot within a few years. Another option is to buy ready-made raised bed kits made from recycled plastic, which are more expensive but much more durable than untreated wood.

The edgings should be a few centimetres higher than the soil level to prevent the soil from washing away when it's watered. You should allow paths of around 50cm wide between beds to make watering and harvesting easier. If you have a wheelbarrow, ensure that paths are wide enough to move it between beds.

The main disadvantages of the bed system are the initial outlay of time and expense required to set up the beds, particularly raised beds, in the first place, and the fact that the growing area may be slightly smaller, which can be a drawback if your plot is small and you wish to grow expansive crops such as squash or potatoes. In contrast, flat beds, or simple rows of vegetables, are simpler and quicker to create, and lend flexibility to your plot structure: if a flat bed is too large or the wrong shape, it's easy to remake it. But it doesn't have to be either/or when it comes to your planting scheme. I usually have some raised beds and some rows, depending on what I am growing and what materials I have to hand.

There are other features to consider too, including paths between beds, a shed or storage box, one or more compost bins or heaps, a manure or turf pile, and possibly even a pond, a wildlife area, or a polytunnel. Despite protestations to the contrary from some allotment writers, absolutely nothing is compulsory: there are no three-line whips in allotmenteering. After all, who needs a compost bin on a plot dotted with beehives? And cultivating a field of sunflowers requires no greenhouse. But it's worth scouring this checklist of the features you *could* include, as a way of helping you to plan:

- 🍅 **Compost bins or heaps:** if you plan to grow vegetables and fruit, a place to make compost is as close to a requirement as this list will get. See chapter six for more on compost.
- 🍅 **Permanent plantings:** you'll need to find a home for crops that stay where they are, year after year, such as rhubarb, or fruit trees, and you should also find a home for the organic allotmenteer's talisman of soil fertility, comfrey (about which, more in the next chapter).

- 🍅 **Shed:** very useful if you intend to spend whole days at your plot, and have a lot of equipment you wish to store on-site. Can be expensive to buy and install.

- 🍅 **Storage box:** a good alternative to the shed if you want to bring your tools with you, and leave a few basics; a wise choice if vandalism is a problem. The downsides are limited space for larger tools and nowhere to shelter in a downpour.

- 🍅 **Glass greenhouse:** it's worth the expense of putting up a greenhouse if you want to raise a lot of your crops from seed, or plan to grow tender plants such as tomatoes and peppers that benefit from being under glass. Can be bought second hand from the local classified ads if you are on a tight budget.

- 🍅 **Plastic-walled greenhouse:** a cheaper but less sturdy alternative to a glass greenhouse that can be invaluable for raising seedlings and protecting tender crops. These tend to mimic the glass greenhouse's tall shape, but lack their permanency, meaning they can be vulnerable to being blown away or ripped in high wind, so make sure you anchor it very securely.

- 🍅 **Polytunnel:** as the name suggests, a tunnel made of polythene stretched tight over a network of hoops that can be used in exactly the same way as a greenhouse, extending the growing season and allowing you to raise more tender crops with ease. Some are big enough to walk inside: others are small enough to place over a row of winter lettuce. Cheaper to buy, but harder to keep well ventilated than a greenhouse and not as attractive, and the plastic will need replacing every three to five years.

🍅 **Cold frames:** if a greenhouse or polytunnel is out of the question because of cost, time or space, you can still grow under glass by using cold frames – glass or clear plastic boxes with hinged lids that provide shelter for tender seedlings and winter crops. If you're into DIY these can be made for free from old windows scavenged from skips, or you can buy them for around £30 and up.

🍅 **Pond:** a great way of introducing wildlife to your plot, but may be a hazard to small children. Check whether your allotment agreement permits a pond.

🍅 **Wildlife area:** if you don't want a pond, you can still make a haven for all kinds of creatures with a little 'planned neglect' – it could be a patch of nettles, a pile of damp logs, a 'bog' garden or a toad house made of a large terracotta pot with a hole knocked out of the rim, placed upside down in a damp area.

🍅 **Water butt:** useful for collecting rainwater from the roof of your shed or greenhouse, if you have one.

🍅 **Fruit cage:** if you love raspberries, gooseberries and the like, a permanent, metal-framed cage to grow them in will be more successful at keeping pests out, but will be a large financial investment. Only bother if you plan to stay for more than a few years.

Planning what to grow

When I started an allotment, I vowed not to be bound by convention in my choice of crops, so I have eschewed some of the traditional choices: runner beans, Brussels sprouts and broad beans, for example. (I did cave in on the broad beans one year. They were an easy crop, though I still can't abide them.) When I scan the catalogues I am looking for the tasty, the unusual, and the downright weird: something to titillate my tastebuds, brighten up my meals and provide a talking point with my neighbours. I'm also a realist when it comes to the amount of time I am going to be able to devote to coaxing a crop into life, so I steer clear of fussy vegetables that demand a lot of hard work for little reward. Take celery: I've read scary warnings that this is one of those 'difficult' crops that requires constant cosseting, so, as I use it rarely in the kitchen, it doesn't really seem worth the bother or plot space. And I grow the poor relative of spinach, a variety of Swiss chard called Perpetual Spinach. It has a similar flavour but is less demanding to nurture and has a much longer growing season.

I start out each new growing year by making a list of the home-grown fruit and vegetables I'd like to eat, and work out which of these I can grow based on how much time and money I have to devote to my allotment. Your choices will also be based on how much experience you have, what state your allotment is in and how large it is. It may sound too obvious to mention, but personal taste should be top of your criteria for choosing crops. It's odd how many plot holders don't make this a priority – hence the quote at the top of the chapter. If you don't like broccoli, don't grow it! Some feel obliged to grow what's 'expected' of them, which is why you all too often see the traditional trio of cabbage, Brussels sprouts and leeks languishing in the ground long after harvest time, perhaps because the cook of the house can't abide them, or because far too many have been grown. Others prefer to grow a

47

small repertoire of the same varieties each summer. But it's worth moving out of your vegetable comfort zone and trying new variations that will lend a 'gourmet' edge to your growing. I tend to concentrate on crops that are more expensive or hard to obtain from the supermarket, so I grow red onions and shallots rather than boring old yellow onions, Pink Fir Apple potatoes instead of Desiree, and oak-leaf lettuce and Chinese greens rather than Iceberg.

One of the perils of growing a gourmet vegetable that's rarely commercially available is that you may have no chance to sample it first, so you run the risk of pouring a lot of time into a crop you later find you can't bear. I was tortured by a globe artichoke plant one summer: one of my allotment neighbours grew the most luxuriously healthy looking plant you can imagine, and every time I walked past it, the plump leaves were just hankering to be served with hollandaise sauce. Oddly, almost all the artichokes were left unharvested, perhaps because the family who worked the plot discovered they didn't like them. If you grow something that doesn't suit your palate, the least you can do is harvest the crop and give it to someone who will enjoy it.

Bridging the hungry gap

The late-spring period between April and early June is known by vegetable growers as the 'hungry gap', the period when stores of last season's vegetables are exhausted but the new crops are not yet ready. Depending on what crops you grow, you may find your personal 'hungry gap' varies year to year. Even if you know full well you won't starve if your allotment is bare for a couple of months, it's still worth thinking about how to spread your harvests throughout the year. It's all too easy to fall into the trap of planning a bumper crop of summer vegetables, only to come down with a thud in the winter months when there's nothing to eat from your plot. It's just as important to think about what you can grow during the autumn, winter and spring when fresh home-grown vegetables will seem like even more of a treat.

I have a few sure-fire favourites for ensuring a good year-round harvest: Swiss chard, for instance, will last for a year and a half before it flowers and becomes useless for cooking. If you protect it in a cold frame or with a covering of fleece, it will go on providing you with leaves and stems well past Christmas and into the spring. You can start growing some of the tougher salads such as Chinese leaves in a cold frame in early spring, which should help to secure an early harvest. See the month-by-month sowing and harvesting guides at the end of the book to find out what's possible. The key ingredient in extending the season of many crops is protection: any kind of covering that lets through the light and keeps off the frost will keep many vegetables cropping for several weeks after they would otherwise have collapsed into a mushy heap. This covering could be as low-tech as a white sheet secured with some wire hoops over a tomato plant or a row of lettuces, or as advanced as a Victorian-style cloche – a bell-shaped clear glass or plastic cover, that looks like a miniature greenhouse, to place over plants or newly sown seeds – which might set you back more than £100. Not every plant needs this kind of protection. At the end of this chapter, I'll tell you about salad burnet, the herb that will keep going strong in all but the most severe weather conditions.

A cunning plan

So by now, you should have a plot, an idea of what features you want for your plot and a rough list of what you want to grow. If you've got a plot, you've got to have a plan, whether it's a beautifully hand-drawn and colour-coded planting map, or a complex table of sowing dates and spacing measurements. The level of detail you go into, however, is completely up to you. I've seen every possible type of planning from Excel spreadsheets to notes pencilled on the back of a train ticket. Many of my plans are held, no doubt foolishly, in my head, but I do have a photographic memory for certain things, so I can look at a section of my allotment and tell you exactly what was growing on it for the previous few seasons.

However, I do draw a plan – sometimes several – every year (in case you hadn't guessed, I'll own up to the train ticket being mine), not least because it is interesting to compare it to the reality at the end of the season; inevitably, nothing turns out quite as planned. It's pasted into the back of my diary so I can check it when I need to, and consists of a not-to-scale line drawing of my plot, with the storage box, composters and beds marked. I scribble what will grow where, checking against a list of what I plan to grow, and noting roughly when each crop should be planted. I say roughly, because there's a great deal of approximation in any allotment plan. The danger of micro-managing the year's schedule is that inevitably you'll set targets that are nigh-on impossible to reach, and you won't be allowing for what I call 'plot serendipity' – when a neighbour donates you a surplus of leek seedlings, for example, or someone buys you a pile of manure for your birthday. By seeing in black and white how the layout will look, I've avoided mistakes like planting a tall, shade-creating crop such as Jerusalem artichokes next to vegetables such as tomatoes that need full sun. I try to leave space at the sides for extra notes that won't transfer to the graphical plan.

What to do if...

Once you have a plan in place, it's time to begin turning it into reality. It can be hard to know where to make inroads if you are faced with a seemingly impenetrable thicket of weeds. The guide below will lead you through making a start on your new plot, whatever state it's in when you take it over.

...your allotment is completely overgrown with weeds such as brambles, thistles and dock

First you'll need to don a pair of thick gloves and scour your land for the rubbish that often builds up when a plot is left abandoned for a few years. I've found everything from rotting wood and bits of greenhouse glass to old tools and compost bins on my plot. It's worth making this odious job a priority, as other plot holders, or even trespassers, may begin to treat your patch as a convenient place to dump their rubbish if it looks unkempt. Dispose safely of everything you find, preferably at the local waste collection centre if there aren't any rubbish bins on site. The same applies to any structures, such as sheds and greenhouses: clear out all waste and old chemicals, and remove anything illegal or hazardous.

Once all the rubbish is gone, take a close look at the land. You may be able to spot areas that have been tended more recently than others: perhaps a patch of plain grass in a plot otherwise dominated by weeds, or signs of cultivation such as beanpoles or neglected strawberry or blackcurrant plants amid the jungle. This is a good place to start, because the more recently ground has been worked, the easier it'll be to renovate. If it all looks equally overgrown, pick one area to work on, no larger than a third of the size of the whole plot. Once you've got that under control, you'll discover the confidence (and strength!) to crack on with the rest.

Mark out one or two beds to start with, using sticks joined by string. There are no hard and fast rules on bed sizes, but they should be small enough so that you can work on the centre of them without having to step on the soil; a maximum of 1.5m wide is prudent. Then use a spade to mark out the edges, or if you've decided to construct raised beds, build your bed sides up, making sure they are firmly secured in the ground for a stable foundation. You can either leave the paths as grass, or, even better, remove the turf and add a thick layer of bark chippings, which will be less slippery and won't allow grass roots to stray into your new beds. Another option is to create lazy beds, a cultivation technique used for centuries in Ireland and Scotland. Mark out the bed in the same way, then dig a trench around the margins and use the displaced earth to build up the earth in the middle, until the bed is as much as sixty centimetres higher than the surrounding soil level. While the initial labour of creating lazy beds belies their name, they are a good method of coping with poorly drained land, and it saves you buying materials to construct raised beds.

What you then do with the weed-infested soil is up to you. Some people prefer to use a soil rotovator (a mechanical device akin to a mini-plough) to break up the surface, but if you use this method you will need to dig over the ground again to remove weed roots. Others prefer to dig the soil with a fork and remove weeds by hand until the clods of earth are broken up and free enough from roots and debris for sowing and planting. There's more advice on weeds and how to control them in chapter nine. Whether or not you have chosen to install raised beds, you will need to add extra organic material to get the soil ready for planting. I'll look in more detail at what's involved in preparing the soil in chapter six, and for more suggestions on keeping your soil weed-free, see the section on mulches below.

…your allotment is neglected but not a jungle – annual weeds and a few perennials

Pick the areas or beds that are the least overgrown, and work on them first. The sight of a patch of well-tended soil that's ready for planting will lift your spirits and help to motivate you, so rather than doing a little bit everywhere, focus on a single area.

In your first year, before your compost heap starts churning out organic material, you'll need to find another way to enrich your soil. You can buy in mushroom compost or manure, but the free way is trench composting, which simply involves burying kitchen waste that you'd normally put into your compost bin at least a spade's depth below areas where you plan to sow hungry crops such as beans and pumpkins. (See chapter eight for more on composting.)

As to what to grow, don't think too big: grand schemes are all very well but until you have found your feet, restrict yourself to a limited number of your favourite crops. Plant potatoes in the most neglected areas, as they are reputed to help clear the land of weeds and break up soil. It's also worth investing in some soft fruit bushes and a rhubarb plant in your first year, which will pay off with a healthy harvest the following year. Adding permanent plantings like this will also add structure to the plot – it's best to group the soft fruit together so that you can cover a single area with netting to protect against pests such as birds and mice.

...your allotment has been cultivated within the last year

The first thing to do is give yourself a pat on the back: you have most chance at succeeding in your first year if you can rest – in part at least – on the laurels of your predecessor. The only drawback of taking on someone's pride and joy is that they may have had a very different idea about what the plot should look like. You may find rows and rows of broad beans or Brussels sprouts already in place when you can't stand them, or there may be raised beds when you want to grow in rows. But in your first year, it's wise to hold off making any huge structural changes until you have seen the lie of the land, quite literally. Concentrate on improving the soil and getting to grips with the growing conditions, and you will be ready to restructure the plot to your liking the following year.

Blanket on the ground: mulches

What do you do with the rest of the ground? Assuming that you don't want to spend the whole of your first year digging, it's wise to allow some of your plot to remain untended at this stage. That doesn't mean you leave the weeds to proliferate, though.

Instead, you can apply what's known as a mulch to the surface and leave it there for a period of six to eighteen months. A mulch is a thick layer of material that's spread on the soil in order to keep the water in and the light out. It holds the weeds in abeyance and improves the soil at the same time. Mulches can be made from many different weed-suppressant materials, ranging from black plastic sheeting to carpet, and involve very little work. That's how I gradually brought my five poles of land under control, and it was an extremely successful and labour-saving approach. I used old carpet scrounged from my local dump weighed down with a few old bricks I found, which did a great job of completely shutting out the light and, in the process, killing off all but the most virulent weeds. After a year or so, I lifted the carpet and dug over the land to remove the last of the roots, and hey presto, the soil was ready for planting. I should warn you, however, that there is some controversy in allotment circles over the use of carpet: some people worry that a carpet mulch doesn't let enough water through, and there are fears that chemicals present in the material could leach into the soil. Most organic gardeners now counsel against the use of carpet on these grounds, but there are plenty of alternatives, including weed-supressing fabric specifically designed for the job.

Mulches can be made from many other things you might have to hand or can buy in bulk cheaply: straw, hay, shredded paper, shredded bark, well-rotted manure, home-made compost, black plastic sheeting or even feathers and hair. Wads of newspaper also work well – there's no need to worry about the ink in newspaper getting into your soil as it has the organic gardening seal of approval and is made of natural materials these days, so will break down harmlessly as the mulch decays.

There is another free and easy alternative, and probably my favourite mulch: cardboard. Collect as many cardboard boxes as you can, break them down flat and remove staples and tape. Cut down and remove any really big weeds, and trample flat the remaining vegetation with your feet. Then you can begin making your cardboard layer cake. The ingredients can be whatever you can lay your hands on: start by sprinkling grass cuttings, manure, compost or organic fertiliser pellets on the surface of the land. Then add the cardboard, making sure the pieces overlap by at least ten centimetres to stop the weeds poking through, and water the top until it's completely wet (or do the job on a rainy day and let nature take its course). The final layer is added to hold the cardboard in place, and again, compost, manure or straw will all work a treat; it should be around ten centimetres thick or more. If your site is windy and exposed you may also need to add some weights, bricks or stones on top to stop the mulch blowing away. Wet the whole area again, then sit back and wait.

It may not be the most attractive form of weed control, but within months you'll find the cardboard is starting to rot down, and the worms will be doing their work by drawing the compost cuttings or manure into the soil. Within a year or so, depending on how thick the mulch was and what state the earth was in, the layer cake should be completely broken down and the weeds gone. If you're patient enough to wait months before doing any growing at all, you can renovate your whole plot using this method. If you are dealing with a pernicious weed problem, you may need to replace the mulch to truly clear the land, and dig up the really tough customers that surface above the cardboard, such as docks and thistles. You can even grow crops through the mulch: just part the cardboard and plant straight into the soil. This method works well for tuber crops such as potatoes and Jerusalem artichokes, and for planting tomato, bean, courgette and pumpkin seedlings raised in a greenhouse or cold frame. Or if you're too late for sowing seeds, just buy plug plants of your favourite vegetables (seedlings raised commercially and sold at the right size for transplanting into the ground) and make holes in the mulch for them.

A change is as good as a rest: crop rotation

The final piece in the allotment-planning jigsaw is crop rotation, something that can seem like a mystical art to anyone who hasn't been initiated. The principle behind it is simple, although the application's a little more complex. Like people, plants want different things out of life, or more accurately, the soil. For instance, brassicas – your cabbages, Brussels sprouts, kale, cauliflower, swedes and turnips – should not be grown in acidic soil, as this can encourage a rather nasty disease called club root. The solution is to add lime to the soil, but adding lime to places where you plan to grow potatoes the following year is a no-no, as you'll encourage another disease called scab in your potato crop. So you follow the brassicas with something else that won't mind the lime, such as peas or beans, perhaps. By growing families of crops together, and shifting these groups from bed to bed every year, you'll also prevent pests and diseases that favour particular crops from building up in the soil. For instance, I've had a serious problem with a fungal condition that attacks onions and the other members of the allium family, known as onion white rot. The fungus can survive in the soil for up to fifteen years, even without the presence of alliums, so each year I try to grow my onions in a slightly different area in a bid to beat the disease.

So where to begin? By grouping the majority of crops you're likely to grow on your allotment into like-minded tribes, and growing them together, you can keep your plants happy and healthy. And here's where the 'rotation' bit comes in: each year, the groups are grown in their own area, be that a raised bed, a number of rows, or simply a sector of the plot marked out either physically

Allotment diary

January 2005

Gardening as it is practised in my neck of the woods requires a little bit of forward planning. Crop rotation, regular watering, fertilising and weeding, sowing and transplanting, all must be done at their proper time (-ish). If you happen to be an inveterate list-maker like me, this results in the annual love–hate job of penning your yearly to-do list, marking on which weeks (or moon phases, if you're into that kind of thing, which I am not) each seed or plant will need attention.

with poles or fencing, or just in your own head. The following year, the groups switch locations so that no crop grows in the same spot for two seasons running. There are no hard and fast rules about what fits into which group, or even how many groups there should be: Monty Don and the legendary gardening writer Dr DG Hessayon are both three-group gardeners (although they disagree on which vegetables belong in which group), the experts at Garden Organic opt for four, while the Royal Horticultural Society has five. But as you've probably guessed by now, I like to make life easy for myself, so I stick to a three-pronged approach to crop rotation. There's a list of what fits where below.

Crop rotation is one of the few allotment activities that grows harder as the years go by. Assuming your allotment hasn't been cultivated for a few years, it matters not a jot where you plant your veg in the first year, although it is helpful to group plants that like similar conditions together. In the second year, areas that played host to group one crops should be planted up with the group two veg; anywhere that had group two plants last year should switch to group three. And group three areas will switch to group one, ideally with a heavy manuring (green or animal) in the interim (see chapter six for more on manures). There are drawbacks to such a simple three-group rotation system. Remember my earlier warning about following brassicas planted in limed soil with potatoes. If you add lime to any group three beds one year, you'll need to plant tomatoes or squash in that area the following year, not potatoes, to avoid the risk of scab.

My groups are:

Group one: *potato, tomato, let's call the whole thing off*

If you want to impress your friends and family, just tell them you're growing *solanaceae* and *cucurbitaceae*. Or, if you prefer to be a little more down to earth, it's potatoes, tomatoes, chillies, peppers and aubergines (all members of the *solanaceae* family of plants – they may look different but their flowers are the giveaway as they are very alike) and courgettes, pumpkins, other winter squash and cucumbers (the clan of *cucurbitaceae*). These are all hungry plants that should be grown in soil that has been enriched in some way, either with manure, a green manure or trench composting, or even all three (see chapter six for the practicalities on how to do this).

Group two: *bean feast*

Legumes are the peas and beans, be they broad, French or runner. This family fares best when planted on land which was fed nutrients for the previous crop of group one veg, say potatoes, rather than on a recently manured spot. Darned ingenious vegetables that they are, peas and beans grow 'nodules' on their roots: little bacteria-ridden lumps that can take the nitrogen from the air and store it. Long after the plant is dead, provided its roots have been left in the ground, the nodules will break down in the soil and release the nitrogen they've stored up, which will benefit the crop that should follow in the rotation – you guessed it, group three.

Group three: *beets, roots and leaves*

Group three is a broad church, taking in the alliums – garlic, onions, leeks and shallots – plus root vegetables such as carrots, parsnips, celeriac and beetroot, and the brassicas. It's worth noting that as well as the traditional western staples of cabbage, kale, Brussels sprouts and so on, the brassica family also includes radishes and rocket (or arugula as it's known in North America), as well as Chinese vegetables such as mizuna greens, oriental mustards and pak choi. All will benefit from the nitrogen being released into the soil by the remains of the previous crop of peas or beans: just remember to snip the plants off at ground level when clearing the legume plants, leaving the roots in place to break down of their own accord. Crop rotation is particularly vital for brassicas to try to avoid the scourge of club root, the number one cabbage killer. By shifting brassicas between different areas of your plot from year to year, the disease will be prevented from building up in any one patch on your plot.

The others: *permanent and semi-permanent residents*

There are also some crops that will have a permanent home on your plot, for example rhubarb, red, white and blackcurrants, and fruit trees. And others that will benefit from an occasional change of scene. Take your strawberry patch, an essential for any plot, in my opinion. It's worth moving this once every three years, replacing the old plants with newly grown ones, because their productivity tends to tail off after that time, and this also prevents the build-up of the viruses that strawberries can fall prey to.

Crop rotation caveats

Now, a lot of these groupings are loose, if not arbitrary, and life on the allotment is a lot more complicated than one-two-three. There's the little matter of where you place autumn-grown crops of onions and peas, not to mention where the lettuces go – some growers put them in with the legumes, others with the brassicas. Likewise, sweetcorn can fit in wherever you have a gap, although it is still worth trying to put it in a different place each year. Flexibility is key: keeping a complex crop rotation scheme running can feel like spinning plates – ultimately impossible to maintain without something crashing down around your head. So give yourself some leeway to try something different. Rules are there to be broken, and the allotment police won't come running if a few peas slip in among the roots. I've even been known to – *gasp* – plant the same crop in the same bed two years running. I have some large stakes at one end of my plot which I just can't face having to dig up and move, so I confess I have sown climbing French beans up them for several seasons now. So far, I – and they – haven't been struck down by any serious ailments. What I am trying to say is: be practical rather than pedantic about crop rotation, and you'll reap the rewards.

Sisters are doing it for themselves

There's one planting scheme that doesn't chime with most crop rotation systems, but nevertheless has an impeccable pedigree. It's known as three sisters planting, and is a way of growing squash, sweetcorn and beans together that's beneficial to all three crops. The technique was perfected by Native Americans, who valued these plants enormously for spiritual as well as physical reasons and wound many myths and legends around them. The teaming of squash, beans and sweetcorn also makes perfect sense in horticultural terms: the beans draw nitrogen from the air and transfer it to the soil; the corn plant provides a structure for the beans to ramble up; and the squash covers the surface of the soil, suppressing weeds, shading the soil from the heat of the sun and thus conserving moisture, while its spiky stems prevent animals from nibbling on all three crops.

The three sisters sowing technique is completely different from anything else I've tried, and I love it for that. The plants are grown in mounds of soil, with a couple of sweetcorn plants and two or three beans in each one, and a squash plant situated close to – but not in – every second or third mound (some people make separate mounds for the squash, which is fine too). All three plants like relatively rich soil, so try to enrich the earth with some manure or compost in the spring. Everyone has their own views on spacing and size of the mounds, but I try to make mine about a spade's depth tall and just as wide, with two or three times as much distance between each mound. The British climate being what it is, you may need to start growing your seeds inside and plant them out once the risk of frosts is over in late May or early June. The sweetcorn should ideally get a week or two's head start on the other crops; plant out the squash and beans when the sweetcorn is around fifteen centimetres tall. You may need to coax the beans to begin climbing up the sweetcorn, but they should soon be up and away. It's wise to provide the beans with some extra support in the form of wooden stakes as they'll probably grow faster than the sweetcorn. In particularly dry summers, it is worth applying a mulch to the mounds to preserve moisture, or using some of the other water-saving tricks you can read about in chapter nine. Once the sweetcorn has caught up you can retrain the bean stems towards the corn. It's fascinating to watch the trio of crops grow together and it's a fun way to teach children about vegetable growing, too.

Spotlight on...

SALAD BURNET

It's highly possible to cultivate a supply of salad leaves throughout the winter months, although you do have to work at it. Even the hardiest winter lettuce and Chinese greens benefit from some kind of protection, be it cloche or cold frame. But there is one salad – or herb, to be more accurate – that is well known for providing green leaves throughout the chilliest of winter weather: salad burnet, Latin name *Sanguisorba minor*.

Though its pretty, delicate, serrated, fernlike leaves taste of cucumber, salad burnet is, curiously, a member of the rose family, and a dye obtained from its roots was once prized as a means of tanning leather. The leaves, best picked young, are lovely scattered in a salad, served with fish such as salmon, used to flavour vinegars or mixed into cream cheese. It's a very underrated plant, and I wouldn't be surprised if it 'does a rocket' in the next few years, becoming the darling of the celebrity chefs and eventually ending up on the menu of every gastro pub from here to Aberdeen until we're all mightily sick of it. Admittedly, it's not to everyone's taste, but even if you don't like the flavour it's still worth growing for its decorative qualities.

In horticultural terms, it's an unfussy customer that likes full sun and well-drained soil, and as it's a perennial you don't even need to worry about sowing fresh seed each year. It would make a great edging plant around a herb bed on your plot: I wouldn't be without it as a stopgap once all the basil, coriander and parsley have died back. Although salad burnet may sag a bit in heavy frosts or snow it will soon bounce back, far faster than any other winter salad, despite its delicate appearance. It helps foliage production if you remove the flower heads, and it will seed all over the place if you don't. Conveniently, the red flowers can be used as a garnish, so they won't go to waste.

Seed sources: You should be able to get hold of it as a potted herb at good garden centres, or if you prefer to raise it from seed, you can source packets from Beans and Herbs, Chiltern Seeds or the Organic Gardening Catalogue.

Four
Tools, equipment and sheds

Everything passes, everything wears out, everything breaks.

French proverb

There is nothing more off-putting to the allotmenteer with a few seasons under their belt than seeing a first-time plot holder come waltzing in with their shiny new tools, fancy brand new compost bin and flowery designer wellies without a speck of mud on them. Whatever happened to reduce, reuse and recycle, or even make-do-and-mend?

There is a self-sufficient spirit to allotment holders that eschews solving problems by throwing money at them – not only because such an approach chimes with the green ethics associated with trying to grow your own food, but also because even the most secure allotment site can become the target of thieves or vandals. It's disheartening to find that a valued tool absent-mindedly left stuck in the earth overnight has developed legs, but it's even more frustrating to have tools stolen from a carefully locked shed.

Tools bring about strong emotions in some gardeners, and it can be devastating to lose a piece of kit that's become a trusted friend. Monty Don has a favourite spade that he won't let anyone else use. I know what he means. I had a spade given to me by my dad: the blade had grown thin and the wooden shaft was shiny and smooth from many years of use. It went missing from the plot one summer, but I haven't replaced it yet because I can't quite come to terms with the idea that it has really gone, and I miss it every time I go to do some digging.

You'll need to make a small investment in some tools if you want to cultivate an allotment. Just how much you spend – and the price for a trowel can start from as little as a couple of quid and reach nearly £100 – depends on your budget. Whenever I get a windfall I always have a new tool in my mind's eye; as I write, it's a pair of aluminium-framed, double-decker cold frames.

The internet has placed a huge variety of gardening equipment only a mouse click away and is a great way to compare prices. The downside to buying tools online is that you can't weigh them in your hands. Some tools just feel right, while others feel awkward. If you're anything other than average height and build it's worth getting tools that suit your size. Don't buy plastic handles if you can possibly avoid it: wood lasts longer and feels pleasant to the touch, and plastic is also harder on your hands. Ash is best, if you can afford it. If you're on a tight budget but still want quality tools, think laterally. Check with friends and family – you may find elderly relatives or lapsed gardeners with lovely old forks and spades tucked away in a cobweb-laden shed that they no longer use and would be more than happy to pass on to you. Or try your local charity shop or car boot sale, an online auction sites such as eBay, or the Freecycle website listed in the directory at the back of this book.

Here's a list of the few tools I couldn't live without:

- ☺ **Fork:** if you invest in nothing else, buy a digging fork. It will be your allotment workhorse, helping you to break up ground, ferret out weed roots and lift potatoes. It's worth keeping a couple so you can always lay your hands on one.
- ☺ **Trowel:** buy a decent trowel for every member of your family who's planning to help with the allotment, particularly children. They're great for transplanting seedlings, digging small holes and throwing at stray dogs about to lift their legs on your prize pumpkins. A hand fork – the same size as a trowel but with tines, like its larger relation – is also useful, particularly for weeding around seedlings.
- ☺ **Spade:** invaluable for heavy digging, cutting straight turf edges on your plot and turning your compost heap from one bin to another.
- ☺ **Secateurs:** another allotment staple, used for everything from pruning blackcurrant canes to lopping the heads off dahlias. Buy a decent pair that will last you a decade or more rather than cheap ones that disintegrate after a year. They're small enough to take back and forth with you to the plot so you won't need to worry about them being stolen. Buy a holster as well and you'll always be able to lay your hands on them. And if you end up swaggering around like John Wayne, just make sure you do it when none of your neighbours is around.

🍅 **Rake:** for your allotment, a flathead rake rather than one of the spindly rakes you see people using to collect leaves on lawns is what you need. It's perfect for creating the fine-soiled beds that you'll need for raising your plants from seed.

🍅 **Hoe:** these come in all kinds and the only way to find out which one suits you is to try a few out or ask your neighbours on the allotments. They're designed for weeding between plants and use either a pushing or pulling movement to slice off the stems at ground level. The key factor isn't the shape of the hoe, however, it's whether the blade is sharp.

🍅 **Gardening bag:** my rule of thumb is that I don't leave anything on the plot overnight that I'd be upset to lose. So I have a canvas bag expressly designed for the purpose of carrying small tools such as trowels, as well as my gardening gloves, seed packets and maybe a snack.

🍅 **Gloves:** I used to avoid wearing gloves, because I like to feel what's going on in the soil; it's also a lot easier to avoid accidentally squishing worms or insects if you can feel them. This does have its downsides in the form of occasional bee stings and scratches, and meant the state of my hands raised eyebrows when I plucked up the courage to go for a manicure. So now, provided the soil is not completely sodden, I use a pair of thick fleece gloves. They are sturdy enough to keep my hands clean and dry and they go straight in the wash after every allotment trip. And when I am doing really heavy work, like turning the compost heap, digging a compost trench or collecting nettles, I don fleece-lined leather gloves.

Where's the wheelbarrow? I don't have one. I can see why they'd be useful if you have a large plot, but I can cover mine in a few paces, and anything that needs to be toted about gets carried in a two-handled trug, which looks like a large laundry carrier, made of recycled plastic. The beauty of these carriers, which now come in various sizes and bright colours, is that they are flexible enough to be folded in half to pour liquid contents into a bucket, or stored flat in a shed. But I'm sure I'll invest in a wheelbarrow at some point, perhaps when I take the next logical step and double my growing area by taking on the abandoned plot next to mine. It is, after all, a piece of equipment whose design has been perfected over hundreds of years – since the Chinese general Chuko Liang came up with the idea in the third century.

Tool maintenance

Here's my dirty little secret: I am horrendous at maintaining my tools. I almost cried when I went to The Lost Gardens of Heligan, the Victorian gardens in Cornwall that were rescued from dereliction, and saw the neat rows of beautifully oiled and sharpened forks, hoes and spades, every one in their right place. Why can't I achieve such an orderly set-up?

It's partly laziness, as the time when I should be cleaning off and sharpening my forks and spades is precisely when I want to sit down and have a cup of tea. I am usually exhausted after several hours' work on the plot and unlikely to want to face the deeply unedifying job of removing every speck of dirt and mud. So the equipment usually goes back into my storage box or gardening bag still coated with mud. One ingenious time-saving solution to the

Allotment diary

November 2004

My gardening bag is fantastic: it's one of the best presents I have ever been bought. The trouble is that said bag, with its many ample pockets, has turned into a bit of a black hole – lots of items get put in, but nothing ever comes out. So today I emptied it out. No wonder it was so heavy; it contained a digital camera; a box of metal staples for attaching wire to posts; secateurs; a kneeler; a set of knee pads; two knives; gloves; a plastic bottle, two rolls of packing tape; a funnel; a wire spring; a one-litre bottle of seaweed fertiliser; two balls of string; three tiles; a soil pH tester; a packet of peas; a pair of scissors; a seed dispenser; four plastic labels; a key to turn on the allotment tap; a make-up brush; four Fairtrade muesli bars; seventeen CDs for use as bird scarers; and two wire cutters.

muddy tools problem is to keep a bucket of sand with a dash of vegetable oil added to it in the corner of your shed or storage box. Dip the blades into the mixture every time you're about to pack away your tools and you'll remove the mud and add a protective layer of oil in one easy step.

Old-school allotmenteers – the types who do their digging wearing a shirt and tie – will tell you that uncleaned tools won't last as long, will become blunt and could spread infection from plant to plant. And they're right. Unfortunately, there's more than a grain of truth in Confucius's adage that 'he that would perfect his work must first sharpen his tools'. Nevertheless, the world's not going to stop turning if your tool maintenance is sporadic. I try not to be

Allotment diary

February 2005

I've been given a bronze spade. Safe to say this is not going to be left down the allotment but stored with the greatest of care in my garage, possibly in a velvet-lined presentation case.

overcome with guilt every time I fail to clean my tools, and neither should you. Just accept that you can only do your best to find time to give your tools a cleaning and oiling every now and again.

If you do feel the stab of conscience, there are a few simple things you can do to get your tools back in shape. Wooden shafts or handles will be 'seasoned' by your hands as you use the tools and will benefit from being cleared of mud and then oiled once they've dried. Linseed oil is always recommended but I just use vegetable oil from my kitchen cupboard. I clean off the mud with a square of corrugated cardboard or a damp rag (if you want to look professional you can buy a wooden wedge designed for the purpose) and use a wire brush to get rid of any stubborn dirt or rust on the metal parts of the tool.

Even the highest quality tool is useless unless it's kept sharp. If you've ever tried to cut anything with a blunt pair of secateurs, you'll know what I mean. The traditional way of maintaining a sharp edge is to invest in a sharpening stone. You oil the stone and then push the tool's blade away from you as you rub it in a circular motion across the stone's surface, keeping it at a constant angle and applying only slight downward pressure; for bigger tools such as spades and hoes, it's easier to move the stone rather than the blade. Using a sharpening stone requires a bit of skill and practice, neither of which I possess in abundance. So I decided to buy a diamond sharpener tool, which is smaller and easier to use, particularly for getting an edge on curved blades such as secateurs. It uses water as a lubricant rather than oil, which is less messy, and the sharpening surface – being made of diamonds as the name suggests – is also more durable. I would recommend the Dia-Sharp sharpeners from DMT, which are really easy to use. Their sharpening surface is mounted on a plastic handle, which makes it easy to work with, and as with a sharpening stone you stroke the tool along the blade in an outwards circular motion. Do remember to sharpen both sides of the blade, except on tools with one-sided blades such as secateurs.

It's also important to keep other equipment such as propagators, pots, trays and plant labels in good condition. It's wise to carry out a shed audit once things have calmed down at the end of the growing season. Check over all your supplies, putting aside cracked or broken pots for recycling. Terracotta shards and broken plastic growing trays will come in handy when potting up large containers: place them in the bottom of the pot and the extra air spaces they create will aid drainage and save on compost too if it's a particularly deep container. Labels, pots, cloches and trays still coated in dirt should be scrubbed clean in a bucket of warm water with a dash of environmentally friendly washing-up liquid and dried off in the sun before being stored for the winter. That way you'll prevent the spread of diseases and save time in the busy growing season.

Living in the Bronze Age

Owning tools made of bronze and copper may seem like an unnecessary luxury for an allotmenteer. But I've fallen in love with mine. I first read about them in a gardening magazine, and was drawn to the shiny blades embossed with the vortex symbol of the maker's mark. They were inspired by the Austrian inventor Viktor Schauberger, who created a copper-plated plough. In field trials with rye, barley, winter wheat, maize, carrots and potatoes in the 1940s, earth turned with his plough produced higher yields and was plagued by fewer pests than that turned with an iron plough. But his ploughs were simply too expensive to be bought by the average farmer and his ideas never caught on. However, the Austrian company PKS has since revived the concept and is now turning out high-quality garden tools with blades made of bronze – an alloy of copper and tin that is very strong. PKS tools are available from Implementations in the UK (see the directory for details) and I've invested in a trowel and spade, both of which are a joy to use.

There's strong anecdotal evidence that the presence of copper helps to discourage slugs and snails. The jury's still out for me on

Allotment diary   *May 2005*

I sharpened my hoe and oiled my wooden fork and spade handles today. I felt infused with a smug glow of satisfaction until I remembered I had a pile of muddy plant pots festering on my potting table so large it was threatening to engulf me.

this one as I use a mix of steel and copper tools on my patch, but I have certainly noticed that the tools are easy to clean, apparently because bronze causes less friction than iron or steel, so the dirt simply slides off. Copper has always been recycled throughout history and around 40 per cent of the copper content in PKS's tools is recycled so, as the literature romantically puts it: 'your trowel may once have been part of a Roman centurion's breastplate'.

It's easy being green

While I am happy to spend money on a tool that will last me many years, I balk at some of the gardening paraphernalia – quaintly described as 'sundries' – that are sold in a lot of catalogues these days. It's highly possible to spend upwards of £10 on Victorian-style items such as a wooden block that allows you to construct plant pots made out of newspaper, or a 'tamper' to level the surface of the soil in seed trays, or dibbers for planting bulbs and seedlings. They may make good gifts for gardeners, but I'd never buy one for myself. You can make perfectly good newspaper pots using a small jam jar; I just tamp down soil with the back of my hand; and my dibber is the wooden shaft of a superannuated digging fork with the tip sharpened (an old wooden spoon or broom handle works well, too).

In fact, show me a common household object and I can probably dream up a way of converting it for use on the plot. I harvest the ubiquitous plastic drinks bottle for a host of different uses: as a sleeve around lettuces to stop the slugs and snails; popped on the top of canes to stop me accidentally poking my eye out; cut into a windmill shape and hung up as a bird scarer; buried top down in the soil with its bottom cut off, as a funnel to direct the water to a plant's roots; placed over the plant, topless, as a mini-cloche; and in its original state for storing home-made liquid fertiliser.

The same principle applies to anything else I'm about to throw in the bin. Holey socks? Put some manure inside, dangle in a bucket of water for a few weeks and make manure tea to fertilise your plants. Cardboard toilet roll and kitchen roll centres? Pots for seedlings. Old T-shirts? Sew up the arm and neck holes and hang up your pumpkins in them, in a cool place, until you're ready to eat them. When I asked members of Garden Organic for their suggestions, Esther Regenwetter came up with an inspired suggestion for a cheap way of protecting strawberry plants from marauding squirrels: picking up nearly new bird or hamster cages – the bottomless ones with handles at the top – from the metal section of her local dump.

You can buy pretty tins of twine that act as dispensers, but a tin or jam jar with a hole punched in the top and a ball of ordinary twine popped inside works just as well. And you can make a garden line for planting straight rows by tying the ends of a few metres of twine to two wooden spoons. An old foam-filled cushion bought at a jumble sale or charity shop will last you a season or two as a substitute for a kneeler or knee pads, and will probably be more comfy too.

Why buy seed trays when you can recycle the plastic trays that shop-bought meat and vegetables are sold in? Yogurt and margarine pots are great for starting seeds and can also be cut up vertically into strips to make plant labels; old pairs of tights work well as soft, strong ties for bigger plants such as Jerusalem artichokes; the plastic-covered wire tags that often come with bundles of wires on electrical devices can be used as ties for soft fruit canes; and old woollen blankets and cotton duvets make great covers for keeping your compost heap warm.

Even equipment that seems to be well past its prime can be rescued and put to use. I have a cheap back-up fork that I bought years ago: its tines are twisted from some abortive attempt to dig up a tree root but it comes in handy on the plot for jobs like holding the storage box lid open and pricking open bags of manure. In his book *Cowpasture: The Everyday Life of an English Allotment*, allotmenteer Roy Lacey recalls how an elderly plot holder he calls Chippy fixed a hole in the bottom of his galvanised watering can by pouring in a little thick paint and leaving it to dry for a fortnight – the can lasted another five years, as Chippy predicted it would.

The possibilities are endless, and half the fun is thinking up new ways of reusing stuff on the plot. It's a concrete way of putting the reduce, reuse and recycle credo into action in your everyday life, so consider yourself a green warrior.

Shed envy

The perception persists that the shed is the heart of every plot. Any TV drama featuring allotments will inevitably centre around it: just think of Arthur Fowler skulking around his Walford plot in *EastEnders* all those years ago. In fact there is now a whole 'sheddism' movement, promoted by everything from calendars featuring shed of the month to books dedicated to documenting men (and it is usually men) and their sheds. There's even a website called readersheds.co.uk where you can submit a photo of your prized shed and vote on other people's wooden creations – from those that look like mini Gothic churches to ones with thatched roofs.

But I don't own a shed. Not in my garden, nor on my allotment. There's nowhere to put one in my small garden, so all the tools have ended up in the garage, hung up against the wall, while plant pots, labels and seed trays are stacked in a tall grey filing cabinet, also in the garage. When I first took on my allotment plot, I wasn't sure how long I'd be staying and I didn't want to invest the time and money in putting up a shed. So I have a storage box that's about twice the size of a tea chest and has been so battered by the weather that its decrepit appearance now fits with the prevailing ramshackle aesthetic of the plots.

Every time I visit the plot I am bitterly reminded of the benefits of a dry haven from downpours, a secure space to store tools upright, and a place to potter. When the rain gets too heavy to work, I hunker down in front of the storage box, balancing on a raft of wooden stakes laid on the grass to keep me off the cold ground while the rain falls and I sip from a flask of tea. Once, just once, was the rain so heavy that I clambered inside the two-metre-wide, one-metre-high box in search of shelter. I was planting potatoes when an April cloudburst threatened to drench me, so I lifted the lid and climbed inside – not easy when your boots are slathered in mud and there are many sharp tools waiting to poke you in the behind. Since then I have become used to dressing for rain and watching the skies for a change in the weather. My home is close enough to the plot that I can usually make it there before a black cloud on the horizon becomes a storm over my head.

My shedlessness is far from ideal, and I am sure I will succumb to the charms of a shed when I take on my next, more permanent plot and can invest time in making it a comfortable retreat. But my experience is shared by many allotment holders. Many people don't want the bother and expense of erecting a shed and get along perfectly well without one. And on some allotment sites, particularly in London and other large cities, they are banned under planning rules that forbid any allotment structure taller than 1.2 metres, or even a metre in some areas.

Shed survey

If you are lucky enough to inherit a plot with a shed already on it, you will have to cope with someone else's legacy: many allotment sheds are rickety affairs, pieced together from old doors, fence panels and corrugated iron. That's all well and good, provided the end result is a solid structure that is not likely to collapse when it's windy and cause injury to you or anyone else. And inside you may uncover the cumulative detritus of many years of vegetable growing. That may include some useful tools, but could also mean a rodent infestation and a stash of dangerous chemicals.

It's best to start with a detailed survey of exactly what you've let yourself in for. Take a notepad and pen to the plot and examine the shed centimetre by centimetre, inside and out, not forgetting the roof. Try to answer these questions: Is it as secure as possible, with at least one decent padlock on the door? Are there any loose sections that could blow off in the wind and cause injury to someone? Are there any undesirable substances within the fabric of the structure, such as doors painted with old lead paint or an asbestos roof? Is the structure firmly anchored on a flat surface? Has the previous owner left behind a pile of junk inside that could include long since banned garden chemicals? Is it infested with mice? Is the floor solid and rot-free? Could it do with a lick of paint? Is the roof or door leaking?

Most of these problems, once identified, can be rectified with a bit of DIY work. But if your survey throws up a number of problems that are dangerous or render your shed useless for your purposes, the only solution may be to knock it down and start again. If that's the case, make sure you dispose of the scrap material safely: there are specific rules about dealing with asbestos, for instance. Don't try to do the demolition job on your own; rope in at least one helper, or consider holding a shed-razing party (make sure you dismantle the shed before you've had too many beers, though).

If you want to put up a new shed, or you take on a plot with no shed, make sure you check with the local council or other landowner first as they usually regulate the erection of new structures. Dig out your allotment agreement and read the small print, which should explain the process of applying for permission to erect a shed or other structure, including large static cold frames, polytunnels, chicken coops and greenhouses. It may stipulate maximum dimensions for both area and height, or ban the use of certain building materials.

Don't just put your new shed wherever the last one stood. Consider whether it would be better sited closer to the path, on a rough piece of ground that refuses to be cultivated, or in a sheltered spot in the shadow of a fence or hedge where it won't be battered by wind and rain. It's worth looking at how the sheds on the rest of your site are aligned: on mine, the majority face the same way, so that the door is positioned out of the prevailing wind.

Even if your structure complies with the rules, it's polite to mention your plans to your neighbouring plot holders, as new structures can cast a shadow on adjacent beds or act as a welcome windbreak. Polytunnels seem to cause particular concern on some sites. There was a lengthy debate at one annual meeting for my local allotments about whether one plot holder could erect a small polytunnel in place of a greenhouse. Some people were concerned about whether it would blight neighbouring plots, while others felt it would result in an excessive use of the site's water supply, given that the ground inside wouldn't get the benefit of any rainfall. Again, check before you invest in something that you could be forced to remove if you don't seek permission.

Bodge or buy?

If you decide you need a shed, should you buy one ready made, or construct your own? As David Crouch and Colin Ward write in their book *The Allotment: Its Landscape and Culture*: 'The way that people create structures and use the ground in the allotment represents something of their own culture – and, thereby, what that piece of land, and the activities on it, mean to them.' There is a grand tradition behind the home-made allotment shed, patched together from whatever materials can be scavenged. The shed has always been one place where allotmenteers have expressed their individuality, not least in the imaginative use of unlikely materials. The allotment landscape is defined by such structures: every day I see them from the train on my way to work, the ramshackle conglomeration of society's cast-offs nailed together to create pockets of individuality in an otherwise regulated landscape.

A shed's beauty truly is in the eye of the beholder, but I'm glad there's still room for a touch of eccentricity and architectural anarchy in our increasingly ordered world of decking and instant garden makeovers. (Perhaps, as *Organic Gardening* magazine columnist Mark Patterson suggests, sheds represent 'an aspect of gleeful untidiness in a Blairite society ever keener on regimentation'.)

And yet there is most definitely a place for the flat-pack shed, as sold by the ever more popular DIY chains, for those of us who don't have the time, tools or skills to design and build one from scratch. My storage box came as a self-assembly kit that I bought and put together without recourse to the dump or salvage yard. But if you want to make your own, there are dozens of websites that offer free shed designs for everything from a bog standard one measuring 1.8m by 1.2m to a grand model that resembles Doctor Who's Tardis.

Similarly, a cold frame – a wooden or aluminium-framed bottomless box with a hinged glass or clear plastic lid that is used to protect plants from extremes of weather – can be knocked together from old window frames. I've also used plastic shower doors that fold in half, positioned over plants in a tent shape, held in place with some stakes, and with a board or some fleece covering each end. Otherwise you can buy cold frames from £30 and up at garden centres and online.

All locked up

There are two different approaches to allotment security: either lock everything away securely, or take away any valuable equipment to store at home but leave the shed or box unlocked. The first approach is best if you keep anything at all on the plot that you'd be deeply upset to lose. But if, like me, you store most of your tools at home, and only leave bits and pieces that will be unappealing to thieves, such as buckets, compost bags and netting, on site, it may be better to leave your shed or storage box unlocked. That way, if thieves do come by, they won't find much to take, and they won't cause costly damage to your shed by trying to prize it open or breaking the windows.

Gardening books usually tell you to spend some of the slack time over the winter cleaning out your shed. While this is good advice on the whole (come spring there's nothing worse than trying to pull out a tool from a crowded corner and having a stack of plastic pots, a shower of compost and a mousetrap fall on your head), it's better not to be overzealous. The nooks and crannies in the walls and roofs of sheds and storage boxes can provide an excellent home for tortoiseshell butterflies, pond skaters, lacewings and other hibernating insects that you'll want to encourage on the plot, so take care not to dislodge them. And make sure you check inside before locking up sheds for any extended length of time, particularly over the winter, in case a bird, hedgehog or cat has become trapped inside.

Allotment attire

And finally, a word about what to wear on plot visits. First, take my advice: never pop down on your way out to a party or a business meeting, just to 'check on things', particularly if you're dressed smartly. I can't count the times I've glanced at my watch an hour later to find that not only am I running late, but my trousers are streaked with mud. It's simply impossible not to be drawn into some 'little job' that you're not dressed for.

It's better to wear your oldest clothes on plot visits, because they'll probably be ruined by the end of the season. I love the fact that I can go down to the plot looking like a bag lady in my woolly hat, a padded shirt and a pair of old cords and no one will bat an eyelid. I call it allotment chic: wearing what feels comfy. Of course your attire will evolve with the seasons. In winter, it's crucial to wear something warm and waterproof, particularly if you don't have a shed to shelter in when it rains. Layers are better than one chunky jumper, as nothing generates heat more than digging: even on the coldest winter day you may find yourself shedding your coat after half an hour of exertion.

My other must-haves for winter plot trips include a flask of tea as a pick-me-up, a wind-up radio for listening to *The Archers* or the football (depending on whether it's me or Rick at the dial), and a small snack. Another essential is a pair of strong waterproof shoes or boots for heavy work. These needn't be expensive: I wear an old pair of eight-hole Doctor Martens dating back from my student days, which I waterproof every winter; some people like to wear wellies but they don't suit everyone, as they tend to be uncomfortable for digging. In the summer, a hat and some suntan lotion are vital to save your skin from frying during allotment sessions. Even though I slap on the Factor 20, I always fall prey to what I call gardener's bottom, when the sun burns the band of skin between where your shorts begin and your shirt – rucked up your back as you bend to water or weed – ends. A bottle of water will keep you from dehydrating in the hot sun, but it is also worth timing your plot visits carefully. If you can go in the morning or evening, you'll find that not only are you less likely to be burned than in the heat of the midday sun, but the water you put on the plants won't evaporate from the soil's surface so quickly and anything you harvest will stay crisp longer. Just one final warning, though: if you decide to wear sandals, be extra careful how you wield your garden tools. I have heard several possibly apocryphal but definitely plausible tales of careless diggers accidentally spearing their foot with the metal tines of their fork. Ouch.

On a more serious note, it's worth taking along a first aid kit or keeping one in your shed or storage box, so you can deal with minor injuries such as cuts and scratches. If your allotment site is isolated and you visit it alone, consider taking along a mobile phone – switched off if you prefer – so that you have some means of calling help in the event of an accident, be it cuts from smashed greenhouse glass, allergic reactions to wasp stings or eye injuries from canes.

Spotlight on...

CARDOONS

In his book on vegetables, Italian chef Antonio Carluccio describes cardoons as looking as if they 'could have been stolen from a fairy tale'. Elsewhere I've seen them described as 'celery on steroids'. My cardoons are probably the plant I get the most comments about, both from curious passers-by and from visitors to my online diary, *Horticultural*. Usually these take the form of 'What *is* that, a giant thistle?' They're a curious

crop, made more so by the fact that, although they are edible, I've never got around to harvesting them. I grow them primarily for their stunning thistle-like neon blue flower heads, which bumble-bees will spend hours drunkenly circling, and for their huge, stately, silvery-green leaves. They can grow to two metres tall but are worth it in my book as an arresting backdrop to the rest of the plot; the flower heads can be dried and used in arrangements, or left for the birds, which love the seed heads. Garden writer and broadcaster Sarah Raven also swears by using the leaves as a foil to bright blooms in bold flower arrangements. The cardoon is a close relative of the globe artichoke, but while the edible part of the former is its flower head, on the cardoon this part of the plant is far too spiny to be eaten. It is the stem that is harvested (or in my case, not harvested) from the cardoon.

The reason I haven't harvested my cardoons is that I'm always away on holiday during September, the crucial period when the stems must be blanched to tenderise and sweeten them for eating. This is usually done by wrapping the whole bunch of stems in newspaper or straw and firmly tying the covering in place to exclude the light for around a month before harvest. In Italy, Carluccio explains, cardoons are often called 'gobbi', or hunchbacks, because the blanching is done by bending the plant over and covering it with earth.

The stems can be stewed, turned into soup, or fried. In France they are made into what Philippe Chandless, a reader of *Horticultural*, describes as 'an incredibly unctuous, creamy dish', which his grandmother Renée Gros used to make for up to forty people every Christmas. The stems are stripped of their fibres then cut up into bite-sized chunks and boiled with a soupspoon of flour in a large saucepan (the flour keeps the cardoons white). Once tender, they are covered with a white sauce made with cream rather than milk, sprinkled with Gruyère and baked in the oven.

It's unusual to find more than one variety of cardoon on offer. By the 1980s the seeds were extremely hard to get hold of, but they have seen a resurgence in recent years that has resulted in several seed companies' stocking at least one variety. The heritage seed company Thomas Etty Esq. offers two: the common cardoon or Plein Blanc Inerme, which dates back at least as far as 1750, and the Purvis or artichoke-leaved cardoon, from 1845. But cardoons have been around far longer than that. The Romans ate the young shoots as a salad.

Seed sources: Thomas Etty Esq., Organic Gardening Catalogue, Seeds of Italy.

Seeds and soil

Five
Seeds

> The bumblebee consults his blossoms and the
> gardener his catalogues.
>
> **Michael Pollan, *Second Nature:***
> ***A Gardener's Education*, 1991**

'Five thongs once established will give you enough to supply you all the year round'; 'glossy black, semi-long fruits with deep purple calyx'; 'large heads with creamy white hearts'. No, these aren't extracts from the *Erotic Review*, but snippets from a few of the seed catalogues I pore over every winter (referring to horseradishes, aubergines and cabbages respectively). Who said growing vegetables isn't sexy?

To the new allotmenteer, the lure of the seed catalogue may seem esoteric, but on a bitter winter weekend when the frost hasn't lifted from the back lawn all day, there is no better escape than daydreaming about what to sow next spring. I've always been fascinated by the brightly coloured pamphlets, full of the promise of bigger, stronger, sweeter, fresher, hardier, tastier fruit and vegetables than you've ever thought possible. The language of seed catalogues is that of the optimist; no mention here of late-June frosts wiping out your tender tomato plants, or slugs massacring your lettuces. It's been an obsession for me since I was a child, when I'd eagerly thumb through my dad's catalogue cast-offs, their pages plastered with gaudy photographs of flawless fruit and vegetables, imagining what packets I'd buy if I had my own garden. For reasons that now escape me, I always yearned to grow ornamental gourds, those odd looking but inedible squash that these days seem strangely pointless, when you can grow so many attractive – and more importantly, tasty – pumpkins and courgettes.

The sheer range of vegetables that make regular appearances on the British dinner plate has widened considerably since the early eighties: rocket and radicchio have overtaken rhubarb and runner beans in popularity. It's hard now to recall just how 'exotic' some of our vegetable staples seemed when I was young. One Halloween, my Brownie pack carved out our own jack-o'-lanterns from large swedes. It was a nod to the Irish origins of the tradition, but also I suspect a recognition of the relative difficulty of getting hold of pumpkins at your average greengrocer back then in Britain. Swede carving was a labour of Hercules that also put me off this fine root vegetable for several years, until I was converted by a rather delicious vegetarian gardener's pie, which features a mashed swede and potato topping.

In *Cowpasture* Roy Lacey remarks that a plot holder who grows globe artichokes, asparagus, salsify and garlic flies in the face of traditionalist vegetable growers. These vegetables did feature in the seed catalogues of the 1970s and 1980s, but still seemed outré to many allotmenteers. Today, they're allotment staples, particularly as some – salsify and globe artichokes, for instance – are hard to find other than at farmers' markets.

Variety is the spice of life

Think about beetroot for a moment and you'll realise that the only type you see in the supermarket is dark red, round and more often than not pickled in a jar or vacuum packed in plastic. But there are at least a dozen varieties still grown by allotmenteers and other gardeners: some are cylindrical for easy slicing (Forono and Cylindra), one is white (Albina Vereduna), another golden (Burpee's Golden), another has black, cracked skin (Rouge Crapaudine), and yet another has red and white concentric circles (Chioggia). There's a similar story with potatoes. Ask most people to name a type of potato and they'll say King Edward, Maris Piper or possibly Jersey Royal. But there are hundreds more you'll rarely – if ever – see for sale: what of the Pink Fir Apple, a delicious gourmet salad potato with pink skin that's too knobbly to look beautiful on the supermarket shelves? Or the delightfully eccentric Mr Little's Yetholm Gypsy, the only red, white and blue potato in existence?

Many of these more unusual varieties are heritage vegetables (also known as heirloom vegetables). These are varieties of plants that are pollinated by natural means (the wind, insects, birds and so on), as opposed to the modern so-called F1 hybrids that have come to dominate our seed catalogues. F1s are artificial crosses between two genetically different varieties, and which aren't much good for seed saving as the next generation of plants often fails to look like its parent plants. A plant's ability to produce seed for the next season's crop was, until recent decades, extremely important for any variety, because gardeners and farmers relied on their own seed stocks rather than buying seed in from merchants; indeed that's still the case for subsistence farmers in developing countries. Although there's some debate about the exact date, a heritage plant is a variety of fruit or vegetable that was introduced before 1951 and is no longer grown commercially because it doesn't conform to the requirements of industrial-scale agriculture and the legislation governing the sale of seeds. Either it crops over a long period rather than in one easy harvest (actually a boon to the allotmenteer), or it is too delicate or perishable to survive long-distance transport, or it is too variable in size and shape. In the parlance of the Plant Varieties and Seeds Act 1964, this translates as not 'distinct, uniform and stable' and means it cannot feature on the national list of seed varieties that can be sold commercially.

To be eligible for the national list, each seed variety must undergo tests at government-approved centres to ensure that they fulfil these three requirements: distinctness – in other words, they should be different from every other variety on the list; uniformity – that a group of plants grown from the seed will all reach the same size and be ripe for harvesting at the same time; and stability – that each subsequent generation of seeds will remain 'true', keeping exactly the same characteristics as the original seed stock. The tests cost the seed merchant thousands of pounds, and even if a variety passes, annual fees must be paid to keep it on the national list. The cost is the same regardless of how many packets are sold, so it just isn't economically viable for many seed merchants to keep selling as wide a range of varieties as they once did. Instead, they concentrate on the varieties they sell in the largest quantities and, inevitably, these are the seeds preferred by commercial growers.

Such a reduction in seed biodiversity is worrying. When a new pest or disease comes along, a uniform crop will, unsurprisingly, uniformly fall prey to it. The Irish potato famine of the 1840s, when Lumper was the only type of potato grown, is a tragic example of the dangers of relying on a single variety for any one crop. A fungal blight destroyed almost the entire potato stock; had several varieties been cultivated, there would have been more chance of finding a blight-resistant potato that would have continued to feed people. As new pests and diseases emerge and the effects of climate change increase, it is likely that gardeners will need to be able to call again on the rich diversity of heritage types to help breed new varieties or rediscover old ones that can withstand drought, resist disease or survive in poor soil.

Part of the delight of heritage varieties has always been the stories that lie behind the names. Sometimes their history is easy to decipher: there are several peas, for instance, with patriotic names such as Commander and Admiral that emerged in the wake of the First World War, while others honour their place of origin, such as the Martock broad bean, which has been grown in the Somerset village of Martock since the 1300s. One of the most evocative names I've come across belongs to a French bean, Cherokee Trail of Tears, a staple in the diet of Cherokee Native Americans. The story goes that when they were driven off their land in what became North America by western settlers, the Cherokees carried the beans with them on a forced march of over a thousand miles during the winter of 1838–9, hoping to sow them when they reached their destination. That journey became known as the Trail of Tears because so many Cherokees died of hunger, exhaustion and disease. These days the bean is prized for its purple pods, which can be eaten when young or left to ripen for the small black beans inside; it's still many people's favourite.

So why are heritage seeds important? If they can't be sold, aren't they the has-beens of the vegetable world? Well, for one thing, the market gardener's priority – uniformity – is utterly at odds with what the consumer is probably after, namely flavour. It doesn't matter a jot to me if my tomatoes ripen over a period of weeks, have delicate skins or wouldn't win a beauty contest, as long as they taste delicious. And I like a vegetable with a bit of a backstory, not something cooked up in a laboratory: something with a firm footing in horticultural history, like the Cherokee Trail of Tears bean.

So how can you get your hands on heritage vegetables if they can't be legally sold? Fortunately, you don't need to track down a dodgy seed dealer who'll slip you a wrap of Essex Wonder tomato seeds in a darkened alleyway. There are people who are doing their best to preserve heritage varieties while still working within the law. The Heritage Seed Library, which is part of Garden Organic, has been nurturing hundreds of heritage varieties since the 1970s. By becoming a member of the HSL, you can choose up to six packets of heritage seed varieties every year, and get access to its huge network of seed swappers. Members pay to join the club, but pay nothing for the seeds. Because the heritage seeds are being given away rather than sold, this neatly bypasses the legislative ban on selling seeds not on the national list. In North

America, where there are also rules about which seed varieties can be sold, the Seed Savers Exchange fulfils a similar purpose. Other small-scale seed producers who are passionate about heritage veg get around the ban in a similar way, by encouraging you to join their club and then charging you for postage and administration rather than the seeds themselves.

Where to source your seeds

In October and November the arrival of the post often brings the groan of 'not another seed catalogue' from Rick. But there's a good reason for trying to get your hands on as many different companies' seed lists as you can. Each catalogue has its own style, specialities and idiosyncrasies, so I subscribe to around half a dozen, and usually order my seeds from three or four, picking and choosing the best, most interesting varieties. I spend around £35 a year on seeds. I always buy some dead certs that are reliable croppers on my particular soil, which is slightly sandy but also prone to waterlogging due to its position at the bottom of a slope; these include Gardener's Delight tomatoes, Nantes carrots, a colourful Swiss chard mix called Bright Lights, and traditional bright orange Rouge Vif d'Étampes pumpkins. And I also always throw in a few (OK, more than a few) curiosities or gambles: seeds are cheap enough that I am prepared to blow the price of a supermarket mango on some exotic variety that may or may not make a go of it on my plot. (One recent success was Physalis Cape gooseberry.) Plus I save some of my own seed, but more of that later. Seeds are easy to care for until it's time to sow. Just store them in a cool, dry environment – a shoebox in an unheated spare room is ideal. Here's a summary of my favourite catalogues, and a sampling of what they offer; see the directory at the back of the book for relevant websites.

🍅 **The Organic Gardening Catalogue:** this one's the official catalogue of the organic association, Garden Organic, in a joint venture with Chase Organics. It's one of my favourites, not least because its excellent website is great for buying online. It has a particularly good range of seed potatoes, green manure seeds and tomatoes, and nearly thirty types of squash, including one called Lady Godiva, which is grown for its seeds rather than its flesh: they have no shell and can be roasted and eaten. If you're a Garden Organic member there's a 10 per cent discount too.

🍅 **The Real Seed Catalogue (formerly Vida Verde):** an unpretentious catalogue from a family firm that holds a rich mix of interesting heritage seeds that have been selected for earliness, great flavour and high yield. Proprietors Ben and Kate promise 'real seeds for real gardeners wanting to grow proper vegetables', with unusually honest descriptions to match. The 'mystery mix' summer and winter squash packets are ideal if you want to try out different squash but don't want to end up with dozens of plants or lots of wasted seeds. This catalogue also wins the prize for the oddest name, Collective Farm Woman, a Ukrainian melon that's said to ripen as far north as Moscow. You can have a look online to see pictures of its stock.

🍅 **Thomas Etty Esq.:** the theme here is old varieties grown in Victorian gardens, with illustrations and descriptions to match. Extracts and pictures from nineteenth-century gardening books add to the quaint feel, which you'll either love or hate. There's a wonderful range of seeds on offer, with some intriguing types you'll have trouble finding elsewhere; I'm thinking of trying a large red-and-yellow-striped tomato called Pineapple, because it's supposed to resemble that fruit when cut in half. It also contains useful information about how long most seeds will stay viable, which is handy if you only want to plant a small quantity of anything.

🍅 **Heritage Seed Library:** not so much a catalogue as a club, members can choose a shortlist of twelve varieties from the annual HSL catalogue, of which six will be delivered. Just as important is the seed swap section, which lists members with spare seed they're prepared to pass on to you.

🍅 **Kings Seeds:** although this company sells a great deal of flower seeds, the focus on vegetables is apparent from their pride of place at the start of the catalogue. It boasts an extensive choice of oriental greens and a pleasing range of what in the gardening world is known rather charmingly as 'sundries' – plant labels, fertilisers, propagators and other pieces of kit for allotmenteers. Kings also claims to have produced the perfect purple Brussels sprout: Rubine. The company is also behind the marvellously comprehensive Suffolk Herbs catalogue.

🍅 **Tamar Organics:** a 'no frills' catalogue on plain recycled paper helps keep the prices down for this Devon-based firm that has an excellent range of good value seeds, both organic and non-organic, as well as a website for online purchases. The lack of pictures leaves more room for a wide range of varieties, including organic seed potatoes, seeds for sprouting and an extensive range of herbs.

- 🍅 **Thompson & Morgan:** this is a seed catalogue as I remember them from my childhood, packed with bright pictures of vegetables overlaid with phrases like 'Grow a giant!' and 'Heavy cropper'. It's particularly good on carrots, with more than twenty types, including four specially selected for their health benefits when eaten raw. I particularly like their range of mini patio vegetables, which are great if you have limited space or mobility and want to grow your crops in containers.
- 🍅 **Meadowmania:** this catalogue focuses on wildflower and grass seeds and mixes, but it has a good range of organic herb seeds and a small list of competitively priced vegetables that will appeal if you want to keep things simple.

Offsets and sets: when seeds won't do

Sometimes it's hard to shake off the feeling that seed companies are being wilfully confusing to the newbie. Take horseradish, a delicious herb that's hard to buy in its raw form in the shops and makes a tasty sauce for serving with roast beef. When I first saw horseradish described in a catalogue, I noticed it was being sold in packs of five 'thongs'. I've since learned that, as well as being a term for skimpy underwear (and the US equivalent of the British flip-flop), a thong is another word for a section of root used to grow a new plant. Why can't gardeners simply call a spade a spade, or a root a root for that matter? Given the quantity of gardeners' jargon that the catalogues are strewn with – offsets, sets, crowns and slips, to name a few – it's no wonder people get confused (see the glossary for definitions).

Many of these terms refer to different methods of propagation. For example, some vegetables – such as rhubarb and asparagus – are best not grown from seed but bought as crowns (the central core of the plant), while others, like globe artichokes, reproduce best from offsets (the shoots that grow off the side of a plant and develop their own roots). Jerusalem artichokes, meanwhile, are grown from tubers rather like potatoes, while sweet potatoes are coaxed from root cuttings called slips. Onions can be grown either from seed or from specially prepared 'sets' – mini-onions which will grow leaves and swell into a handsome harvest given the right conditions. Shallots are similar, except rather than getting bigger, shallot sets simply multiply, so you end up with a cluster of bulbs of roughly the same size as the sets you began with come harvest time. I always opt for onion and shallot sets rather than seeds as a time saver: no one's going to report you to the allotment police for taking this welcome shortcut.

Allotment diary   *April 2005*

I must be the only person I know who gets excited when a bag of what look like faeces arrives in the post. Fortunately this parcel represents not the beginning of a childish hate campaign, but the arrival of a central plank of my organic autumn/winter food supply, in the form of an order of Jerusalem artichoke tubers – a variety called Fuseau. The instructions order me to plant the tubers NOW (not altogether practical when opened late on a Thursday night).

Sets and tubers are a little more tricky to store than seeds. Take them out of their packaging as soon as they arrive in the post to allow them to breathe. Don't, as I've done in the past, leave the package on a shelf until whole new civilisations of mould have set up residence in the warm sticky interior of the bubblewrap. Instead, put them in a paper bag or cardboard box and find a cool, dark, dry and frost-free place to store them until it's planting time. A well-insulated shed or garage is perfect; failing that, the coolest room in your house will do. The benefit of the latter is you're more likely to remember to check on them regularly. Your seed company should try to time the delivery to roughly the right month for planting, as the less time between delivery and planting, the better.

Potato chits

Chitting potatoes is one of those allotment practices that, to the uninitiated, is about as unfathomable as a Donald Rumsfeld press conference. To chit is to sprout, so chitting simply means that you're giving your potatoes a head start by allowing them to sprout growth before you plant them in the ground; in other words, exactly what happens if you leave spuds in the kitchen cupboard too long.

Every experienced allotmenteer will provide you with Byzantine instructions on how to chit potatoes, involving precise timings and temperatures, number of daylight hours, positioning of the tubers in a particular way, and the location of the moon in relation to Venus (OK, I may have made that last one up). But it's an inexact science. And chitting's dirty secret is that it doesn't really matter how, or even if you do it – your spuds will still grow all the same! I am a chitter, but more for reasons of psychology than necessity: putting my potatoes in a row in early spring makes me feel as if I am getting the gardening year started, even if it's still freezing outside.

So can you take those shop-bought, sprouty potatoes and put them in the ground? Well, you could, but they're often sprayed with chemicals to inhibit sprouting, so it's best to buy what are called 'seed potatoes' from a seed company or garden centre. These potatoes are specially bred to be sprouted and are also guaranteed to be free of disease, which is important for what can be a delicate crop. Perhaps the most startling thing to the chitting neophyte is the discovery that spuds have a top and a bottom, which is a fact to conjure with next time you're tucking into a jacket potato. The top or 'rose end' is the one with the most eyes or buds, and this needs to be placed uppermost as you position your potatoes in a cardboard box or egg box. Leave the potatoes in a light, warm (about 18°C) room, out of direct sunlight until sprouts begin to appear, and as the time for planting out approaches, move them somewhere cooler to toughen them up for outside temperatures. Some gardeners will tell you to start chitting in the dark, only bringing the tubers out into the light when they have begun to sprout. In my experience, this doesn't make any difference, and if you order your seed potatoes early you may find that sprouts will appear while the seed potatoes are being stored in the dark ahead of chitting anyway. My seed potatoes sit on a box in my study, which happens to be the coolest room in the house and a place where I can observe their progress when I am supposed to be writing: it's more interesting than watching paint dry, at least. To concentrate growth on the strongest stems, I rub off all but the two sturdiest shoots – some people just leave one – before planting. If this all sounds like too much hard work, just leave the seed potatoes in a cool dark place until you're ready to plant them out. Easy!

Some seed companies will also offer you what are known as 'potato microplants' for a number of the rarer, heritage types. Rather than the traditional tubers, around May or June you'll receive mini potato plants that have been propagated in a laboratory. They need to be planted out straight away and should provide a good crop in their first year, albeit not quite as bountiful as you would harvest from a seed potato plant. If you live in warmer climes, it's highly possible to grow another less familiar tuber on your allotment: sweet potatoes (they're on my 'must try' list, right below Chinese artichokes). You can buy slips (rooted cuttings of sweet potatoes) from several British seed suppliers, including via the Organic Gardening Catalogue (which sells a variety with the uninspiring name T65), but other allotmenteers tell me that growing them naturally is a bit of a labour of love, as the plant needs higher temperatures than most of us can achieve. Planting through black polythene sheets is said to help. Perhaps one of those things to try one year as an experiment, or if you live north of the Watford Gap, hold off until climate change makes it more viable!

Seed saving

Some people still save their own seed, not just for economic reasons, but also as a gesture towards self-sufficiency, a way of nurturing the genetic diversity of heritage varieties and learning something new about the crops they grow. It's unrealistic to imagine that you'll never have to look at another seed catalogue again, and as I've already explained, you wouldn't want to abandon this rich source of inspiration. But once you've begun to grasp the basics of growing your own vegetables, it's worth investigating seed saving as a next step towards a fuller understanding of the crops you cultivate.

Seed saving can be as easy or laborious as you make it, although there is always going to be a certain amount of fiddly work and time commitment. For me, it usually involves little more than allowing a couple of dozen French bean pods to ripen and dry out on the plant. Once they're completely dry, I pop them out of the pods and into a glass jar with an airtight lid ready to be sown the following year. More tricky customers, such as brassicas and beets, are probably best left to allotmenteers who can make daily plot visits and have enough time and space to work on preparing seed. French beans are self-pollinated, meaning that fertilisation happens when pollen moves between the sexual organs on a single flower, or between different flowers on the same plant. There is little chance of one variety crossing with another, so they will remain true to type. In other words, the next generation of plants will have exactly the same characteristics as their parents, be that variegated leaves, stripy fruits or resistance to a particular disease. Tomatoes, lettuce and peas are also self-pollinators, so they are probably the best plants to start with if you're new to the practice of seed saving.

There's a trick to getting seeds from soft fruits such as tomatoes. Mix the seed from the fully ripe, gently mashed fruits with some water and put the resulting goo in a jar. Stick on the lid, place the jar in a warmish place (your kitchen will be fine – just don't mistake it for a jar of tomato purée) and wait. Given a few days, the mixture will ferment, which helps to clean the seed. Don't worry about any mould that develops on the surface. Then open the lid – be warned, it will smell hideous – add some fresh water, and swill it about. Drain off the water and any seeds that haven't sunk to the bottom. The remaining seeds are the ones you want to keep, so put them on a plate for a day or two until they are completely dry and papery to the touch, then transfer them to an envelope for storage.

Allotment diary

April 2005

If you happen to be a reader of the *Guardian*'s letters pages, you'll probably know about the recent exchanges over uses for 35mm film canisters.

For me, they're a great way of storing surplus or self-collected seed: airtight, dry and secure. The only trouble is, these days they're in short supply as I usually ditch my bulky SLR in favour of my digital camera.

Other vegetables that are pollinated by wind or insects, such as courgettes, pumpkins, peppers and leeks, present more of a challenge – unless you're happy to gamble on an unpredictable outcome. It's all down to the risk of cross-pollination, whereby a plant can breed with another cultivar (cultivated variety) in the same family. In other words, your jack-o'-lantern type of pumpkin

An at-a-glance guide to seed saving

The first column rates the ease of seed saving for each crop:

1 means easy: suitable for beginners;

2 means intermediate: try once you've got the hang of seed saving;

3 means hard: best left to the experienced seed saver with plenty of time and space on their hands.

The second column indicates how the plant, left to its own devices, will pollinate, the third column shows how regularly you can expect it to pollinate, and the final column shows to what extent those vegetables that are pollinated by wind or insects will need to be isolated from other plants of different varieties within the same family.

	Rating	**Pollination**	**Annual/ Biennial**	**Isolation**
Aubergines	2	Self	Annual	Some
Beans, French	1	Self	Annual	Some
Beetroot and Swiss chard	3	Wind	Biennial	Yes
Cabbage	3	Insects	Biennial	Yes
Carrots	2	Insects	Biennial	Yes
Leeks	2	Insects	Biennial	Yes
Lettuce	1	Self	Annual	Some
Onions	2	Insects	Biennial	Yes
Peas	1	Self	Annual	Some
Peppers	1	Self	Annual	Some
Radishes	2	Insects	Biennial	Yes
Squash and cucumbers	1	Insects	Annual	Yes
Sweetcorn	3	Wind	Annual	Yes
Tomatoes	1	Self	Annual	Some

plant may have been fertilised with pollen from a cucumber plant on the other side of the allotment site, rather than pollen from an identical pumpkin next to it. They're both of the *cucurbitaceae* family, and will cross-pollinate, so the next generation you raise from the seeds could take on a mix of the parents' characteristics. On occasion, I've saved some pumpkin seeds just to see what the hybrids produced from a cross-polinated plant look like. Some were barely edible, others were exact matches of the parent pumpkin, while a few had qualities such as incredibly tough skin or unusual colouring. It's an interesting if unpredictable way to save seeds.

If you want your saved squash seed to stay 'true', however, you'll need to prevent pollen from another variety reaching the female flowers. That's not especially hard, but does require frequent attendance at the plot, which may be too much of a tie for some. Like an anxious midwife, you need to tie up the petals of both male and female flowers with a rubber band or some tape to prevent insects – which could be dusted in pollen from another squash – from entering. Choose flower buds that are just on the cusp of opening and are beginning to switch from green to yellow. You can tell male from female flowers because the latter have a swelling at the base of the flower that is an ovary or immature fruit that will only develop if pollination occurs. Then the next day, when it will be at the right stage for pollination, you simply hand-pollinate the female flowers with a male flower by rubbing the two together, before closing the female flower up again. The squash should then be allowed to grow and ripen as usual, but make sure you mark it out from the rest of the crop.

Spotlight on...

A BEAN CALLED CASEKNIFE

This climbing bean came to me by chance, I think as part of a 'welcome gift' when I joined the Heritage Seed Library, an organisation dedicated to preserving old vegetable varieties. I still have the printed scrap of paper that was attached to the brown seed packet. It reads: 'This very old haricot variety dates back to at least 1820. It is a strong climber and good producer of stringless, flat pale green pods, shaped like a little knife blade.' I grew this bean, and it was a good performer, providing both fresh pods for steaming and, once the casing had dried, a tasty bean for stews and soups.

But I became interested in tracking down more of the history of this bean when I saw it mentioned on the website of the Williamsburg Foundation in the USA. It stated that Caseknife was first mentioned in a newspaper advertisement in 1793, and that seventy years later, in 1863, writer Fearing Burr called it 'common to almost every garden'. I was fascinated by the idea that a vegetable variety could have grown so popular in seventy years, and then some time in the course of the next two hundred, fall to obscurity, only to be saved from total oblivion by heritage vegetable enthusiasts. And I have to agree with the Heritage Seed Library seed guardian Mrs JS Wilson, who is quoted on my scrap of paper as saying: 'An "old man" of a bean, rather set in his ways but likes to give quality and a huge crop of beans when it's ready.'

Seed sources: Heritage Seed Library.

If all you're managing to do is struggle to keep the thistles at bay on your plot, and all this hand-pollination malarkey sounds like way too much of a commitment, take heart. Even the most accomplished seed saver will still get a thrill from buying and swapping seeds, and by buying from small companies who promote seed saving, or by joining the Heritage Seed Library, you'll be helping to keep alive parts of our gardening history and secure our future biodiversity. See the directory and bibliography for more sources of help and information on seed saving.

Six
Soil

As far as rites of passage go, it must rank up there
with my first kiss or being given my first razor. I'd even
go as far as saying that it's more life-changing than
reaching the age of eighteen, or getting my driving
licence. Yes, as a slow-life-craving twenty-six-year-old, I
eventually gave in to buying manure.

Al Milway, *Anything But Sprouts* blog

What is soil? Not a question that had troubled me particularly
before I got my own allotment: it was merely the stuff that plants
and trees grow – or fail to grow – in. But once I had an allotment,
suddenly the earth – what it was, what it was for and what it could
do – meant the world to me, if you'll pardon the pun. The trouble
is, most of us treat soil like dirt, as the *HDRA Encyclopedia of
Organic Gardening* puts it. We no more think about what soil is
made of than we think about what wood is made of.

In good soil, pockets of air and water make up half the volume.
The other half is comprised of a mixture of living organisms,
organic material and particles of silt, sand and clay. Living
organisms doesn't just mean worms: spend a few minutes turning

over a patch and you'll probably find slugs, millipedes, centipedes, ground beetles and spiders. These help to break down into smaller particles the organic matter that is added to the soil as plants rot. Organisms you can't see also make a huge contribution: bacteria, nematodes and fungi, to name but three. These micro-organisms carry out an array of different vital tasks to keep the soil healthy, including breaking down minute particles of organic material, and releasing nitrogen into the soil.

It's important that you get to know your soil. I remember crouching over a newly dug patch, rubbing the soil through my hands as if I was panning for gold. Somehow I knew that the dark crumbly stuff I'd happened upon was good, that I was lucky enough to live in an area where the soil, like the porridge in 'Goldilocks and the Three Bears', was just right: neither too heavy nor light. 'It's beautiful, friable loam!' I blurted out, not sure where the words had come from. I'm sure the phrase was one I'd learned from my father during some childhood gardening lesson, but I hadn't uttered it for years. Friable simply means crumbly. And if your allotment contains loam, you have, quite literally, hit pay dirt. Loam is a type of soil that contains roughly equal shares of silt, sand and clay. It's easiest to grow things in because it will drain well, so plants do not become waterlogged, but will still retain enough water for plants to live on. Other types of soil occur where different particles dominate; depending on the local geology, you might get sand, chalk or peat soils, for instance.

If you're not sure which category your soil fits into, just grab a moist handful and work it between your fingers until it's smooth. Then shape it into a ribbon, if you can. If it's gritty and won't hold together at all when moistened, it's sandy soil; if it feels and acts like plasticine, it's clay soil. As any geologist will tell you, classifying different types of soil is a lot more complex than this, but for our purposes such a crude analysis will reveal enough to help decide how to make the best of your particular soil make-up.

Another handy, although rather more sweat-inducing, test you can carry out will reveal how free-draining the soil is. Dig a hole at least a spade's depth and width – a bit deeper if you can – and chuck in a bucket of water. Then wait and observe. (If your spending rather a long time apparently staring into a hole in the ground raises a few eyebrows, you may wish to explain to neighbouring plot workers that you are, in fact, carrying out an analysis of soil type and water retention.) If the water drains away within a few minutes, hey presto, you have fast-draining soil. If it takes forty-five minutes or more, it's slow-draining; more than an hour and it's a bog – well, not quite, but you'll certainly need to work on improving the soil structure. The table overleaf explains six basic types of soil you may come across on your plot and explains how to identify them.

The acid test

The reality is that most of us won't be blessed with perfect growing conditions. Although my soil is good, because it's on the sandy side of loam it also tends towards the acidic, which can be a problem. It's important to determine your plot's pH – whether it is alkaline, acidic or neutral – because this will help you to assess which plants will grow well and which will struggle. To do this you

Basic Soil Types

LOAM
Characteristics:
Holds together when moist but doesn't feel like plasticine

Pros: Easy to work, doesn't dry out in summer, holds nutrients and water well, suitable for a wide range of plants

Cons: None

Action: Count yourself lucky for having the perfect soil! Of course even the best soil can be further improved by adding compost from your heap and regular mulching

CLAY
Characteristics:
Feels heavy and slimy when wet, hard and cracked when dry; slow-draining

Pros: Naturally fertile, provided you add humus to it

Cons: Digging is heavy work and soil can become waterlogged

Action: Add oodles of organic material in mulches, manure or compost – whatever you can lay your hands on

PEAT
Characteristics:
Dark, rich soil that feels spongy and won't hold together when worked

Pros: Easy to work, warms up quickly for spring sowings

Cons: Soil is acidic and holds few nutrients, limiting what can be grown; can be slow-draining

Action: Apply lime or mushroom compost to reduce acidity, and restore nutrients with organic fertilisers

CHALK
Characteristics:
A handful of soil contains lumps of white chalk and flint

Pros: Quick-draining, easy to work
Cons: Alkaline, so some plants may not be suited to it; flints can
make sowing difficult
Action: Dig in plenty of organic matter to improve water retention

SILT
Characteristics:
Feels silky rather than slimy to the touch

Pros: Retains moisture and nutrients well
Cons: Can become compacted and may form a hard crust on the
surface or be heavy to work
Action: Mulch to keep the soil surface moist

SAND
Characteristics:
Gritty, won't hold its shape when handled

Pros: Light, free-draining and very easy to dig; warms up quickly in
the spring
Cons: Nutrients are easily washed away, along with calcium, which
can make sandy soils acidic
Action: Add mushroom compost to correct pH levels, and other
organic material to improve water retention

need to buy a basic pH testing kit, available for a few pounds. You probably last conducted an acid test in the science classroom, lowering a strip of litmus paper into a test-tube full of an unknown liquid and watching as the paper changed colour to anything from deep red for strongly acidic to turquoise for alkaline. However, unless your allotment is situated next to an industrial site, your soil test is unlikely to find such extremes. If the test indicates a pH level of 1–7, your soil is acidic; neutral soil has a level of around 7, and alkaline soil 7–14. The vast majority of crops you'll want to grow on an allotment will prefer a pH of between 6.5 and 7 – though potatoes like things a little more acidic. Fortunately for me, turning acidic soil neutral is far easier than trying to change the pH of alkaline soil. You simply sprinkle slow-release ground limestone or dolomitic limestone on the surface of the soil and wait for the calcium to reduce the acidity. If your plot is alkaline, there is no easy fix, although as is true of every soil type, it will benefit from the addition of organic material.

Making humus: an organic experience

One wrinkle to be aware of is that the soil on your allotment may not be the same as the soil elsewhere in the area, and it may even vary from one end of the plot to the other. The state of the earth on your patch represents the legacy of perhaps several generations of growers, who may have been adding organic material by the barrowload – or depleting its fertility by pouring on quick-fix commercial fertilisers and little else. When added to soil, organic material is turned into what's known as humus by micro-organisms. This dark, sweet-smelling substance does wonders for your soil structure, helping to break up compacted spots, improving water retention and aeration, and encouraging the growth of beneficial fungi and bacteria. It makes life happier for your crops, encouraging strong roots and providing the nutrients they need to thrive. Generally the darker your soil, the more humus it contains. Conversely a plot that has been starved of organic material over many years will tend to have paler soil and may have sunk to a lower level than the paths around it.

Whether or not your plot has been denied it in the past, regular additions of organic material are absolutely vital to the health of your soil. Unlike liquid fertilisers, which simply provide an injection of the nutrients plants require to grow, soil improvers, as organic additions are known, will also improve soil structure and drainage and help to create humus. But what kinds of organic material can you use? We are, of course, talking manure (about which, more later), but we're also talking wormcasts, woodchips, leaf mould, shredded bark and composts made of domestic and municipal green waste. These are increasingly being sold by garden centres, but can also be bought in bulk by mail order and delivered to your door. Each must be treated differently, so make sure you follow the instructions on the bag: some can be used as a mulch, others are better dug into the soil. Buying in such products can become expensive, though, and you'll find one bag covers a lot less ground than you'd think. In your first year, you may have no other choice, but it's worth thinking about how you can create your own free alternatives for future years. These include:

🍅 **Leaf mould:** you can make this yourself simply by bagging up fallen leaves and leaving them to decompose for a year or so. Either dig into the soil or leave on the surface as a mulch.

🍅 **Worm compost:** if you have a worm composting kit, or wormery (for more on which, see chapter eight), you can add worm compost to your soil as a mulch or dig it in.

🍅 **Home-made compost:** of course you can make your own free soil improver in the form of home-made compost – a business so crucial to the life of your allotment that I've devoted a whole chapter to it. Again, add this around the base of crops or dig into the soil as a preparation for planting.

Allotment diary

April 2005

If you're trying to turn a big pile of leaves into leaf mould and, like me, you're impatient, you can speed the process along by spreading the leaves on the ground and running your lawnmower over them a few times. It'll make a bit of a mess but it's great fun. Once the leaves are shredded, you can sweep them up or collect them in your lawnmower's grass bag. Then put them into a bag with holes in it or a cage made of chicken wire, and let the elements do the rest.

Manure

Then there's manure. Alongside the compost heap, it's traditional to have a big pile steaming away on your plot. But not everyone favours this approach. If you're vegan, for instance, you'll want to stick to soil improvers that aren't by-products of animal farming.

And even if you're not, organic gardening authorities counsel against using manure from conventional, intensive farms where animals have been treated with antibiotics and hormones; unfortunately most organic farms are unwilling to part with their own manure, which they usually reserve for improving their own ground. Manure can also harbour thousands of weed seeds that will sprout merrily on your plot and create a lot more weeding work.

So where do you find suitable sources of manure? One answer is to set up your own manure factory: keep a few hens, and their faeces and bedding will do wonders when added to your compost heap, being particularly potent stuff, high in nitrogen and phosphates. If that's out of the question, search out non-intensive sources such as local riding stables, city farms and smallholdings, whose manure should present less of a contamination worry, although Garden Organic does recommend avoiding manure from animals that have been recently wormed.

Assuming you've laid your hands – preferably gloved – on a source of manure, the next conundrum is what to do with it. Most gardening books bang on about the wonders of well-rotted manure, but it's worth spending a moment to consider what 'well-rotted' actually means and how it's obtained. Fresh manure, which is usually a mix of varying proportions of fresh animal faeces and bedding, either straw or sawdust, should not be dug straight into the plot or applied as a mulch to the soil surface. Why? Because its high levels of ammonia will 'burn' plants, and the fresh bedding will take an inordinate amount of time to break down and be incorporated into the soil.

Here's where the rotting part comes in. If you're dealing with a relatively small amount of manure – a couple of bags, say, or a modest but regular supply from your own animals – it can simply be added to your compost heap or bin along with your garden and kitchen waste. This will help to kickstart decomposition, speeding production of a stock of some of the best home-made compost around. If, however, we're talking a trailer load, you'll need to create your very own manure pile. Choose a part of your plot that will provide easy wheelbarrow access, then set up your pile. Water it well and cover it completely with a tarpaulin or plastic sheeting (weighted down against high winds) to prevent the rain leaching away the nutrients. Then wait. Have the occasional poke about under the tarp to check that the process of decomposition has begun, and, within six months to a year, depending on how big the pile is, you should find the contents have broken down to a crumbly, dark substance that is suitable either for digging into the ground or for use as a mulch. If you'd prefer not to wait, you can buy specially prepared manure from garden centres, which is a more expensive option, but the bonus is that it will be weed free and ready to add straight to your soil.

Green manures

Now, I realise this might sound too good to be true, but there is a way to improve soil fertility and condition without recourse to animal by-products: you can use green manure instead. So whether you're a vegan, can't find a source of manure or just hate the potent aroma of a steaming pile of animal poo, here's the lowdown. There are certain super plants – sometimes known as living mulches or cover crops – that, when grown in the right way, will actually make your soil better, rather than draining it of goodness. The table overleaf shows what to use where and when – some are best grown in summer, others in winter. The most useful green manures are the plants that act as nitrogen fixers – bacteria live on their roots that take nitrogen from the air and convert it into a form that plants can use as an essential soil nutrient. The nitrogen is stored in the plants until you dig them into the soil and they decompose, gradually releasing the nitrogen into the soil where it can be taken up by subsequent plants. This helps to enrich the soil and provide ideal growing conditions for nutrient-hungry crops such as squash. Field beans are among my favourite nitrogen fixing green manures: they're tough as nails, won't be fazed by winter wet or cold and are easy to dig in, although they don't grow densely enough to lock out the weeds in the same way as the grass-like Hungarian grazing rye, for example.

There are some green manures that don't fix nitrogen – they tend to grow more vigorously and are less fussy about soil conditions, so don't discount them from your plans. Even if it doesn't provide an edible crop, any green manure that you can grow to cover bare earth for a minimum of effort is well worth it. They will at least prevent nutrients from leaching out of the soil; the roots will hold the soil together while those with deep roots will break up compacted soil, and in the summer, they will prevent soil washing away in storms, and protect the surface from wind and sun.

The crucial final step is incorporating the green manure at the end of the cycle. With bigger plants, try to chop them up with a sharp spade and then dig them into the first few centimetres of soil.

Types of green manures

Nitrogen fixers

Common name	Latin name	When to sow	Dig in after	Requirements
Alfalfa	Medicago sativa	Late spring	3 mths–2 yrs	Good drainage, neutral pH
Alsike clover	Trifolium hybridum	Spring–summer	2–24 mths	Tolerates most soils
Bitter lupin	Lupinus angustifolius	Early spring–early summer	2–3 mths	Prefers light, acid soils
Crimson clover	Trifolium incarnatum	Spring–summer	2–6 mths	Won't thrive in heavy soil
Essex red clover	Trifolium pratense	Spring–summer	3 mths–2 yrs	Prefers good soil
Fenugreek	Trigonella foenum-graecum	Early spring–summer	2–3 mths	Well-drained soils
Field beans	Vicia faba	Autumn	Over winter	Won't thrive in light soil
Trefoil	Medicago lupulina	Spring–summer	3–12 mths	Dislikes acid soils
Winter tares	Vicia sativa	Spring–late summer	2–6 mths	Prefers heavy soils; avoid acid soils

Non-nitrogen fixers

Common name	Latin name	When to sow	Dig in after	Requirements
Buckwheat	Fagopyrum esculentum	Spring–late summer	2–3 mths	Prefers poor soil
Grazing rye	Secale cereale	Autumn–early winter	Over winter	Tolerates most soils
Mustard	Sinapis alba	Spring–early autumn	1–2 mths	Tolerates most soils
Phacelia	Phacelia tanacetifolia	Spring–early autumn	1–6 mths	Tolerates most soils

You'll need to do this at least three months before you plan to sow or plant crops on the patch, to give the plant material time to break down and so the nitrogen stored in the roots of the legumes can be released into the soil.

The only warning I'd proffer is that getting your timing wrong on the incorporation of green manures can store up trouble later. Some, such as field beans, won't survive a rough turning of the soil, even if part of the plant remains above ground, while others, like grazing rye, will regrow if you leave it too long or don't dig it in deep enough.

See the table opposite to work out which green manure is suitable for your needs.

Comfrey confidential

If there's one plant you absolutely must have on your allotment, particularly if you're an organic grower, it's comfrey, a relative of borage and the forget-me-not. Comfrey is a wonder plant. It's been used as a herbal healing remedy (hence its other common name, knitbone), but, more significantly for us its leaves hold high quantities of the nutrients other plants need to thrive, namely potassium, nitrogen and phosphorus. They are also quick to rot, so can be used as your own personal fertiliser factory, releasing plant food back into the soil for the benefit of other crops and cutting down on your need to buy soil improvers.

This should give you a clue as to why comfrey has almost mythical standing in organic gardening circles. But to elaborate, I should explain a little about Lawrence D Hills, the Henry Doubleday Research Association (HDRA), and Bocking 14. If this sounds like some kind of edgy cult, relax, it's a lot less scary than that. Hills founded the HDRA (now known as Garden Organic), and named it after Henry Doubleday, a nineteenth-century horticulturalist who pioneered the use of fast-growing Russian comfrey in Britain and conducted extensive research into its many qualities. Hills championed comfrey's powers as a soil improver and fertiliser and in the 1950s developed several comfrey hybrids at the headquarters of the HDRA, which was then located in the Essex town of Bocking. Of these hybrids, Bocking 14 proved to be particularly useful as it is sterile and so its flowers won't set seed and colonise your whole plot. Bocking 4 is especially good for feeding chickens.

Two words of warning, however, about comfrey. First, the reason why comfrey leaves are so full of nutrients is that the plants have very long roots (reputedly up to a metre) that reach deep into the soil. Needless to say, this perennial is hard to eradicate once in situ, so think carefully about where you want to plant it rather than doing what I did and dumping it in the nearest available spot. It's best sited in a damp corner away from other crops as it may compete too vigorously with other plants for available water and nutrients. It seems to be impervious to pests and diseases and, though it will die back over winter, it needs no special protection and will bounce back in the spring. Once it's established you can cut it back to ground level several times in a season; to keep it in tip-top condition, you can replace some of the nitrogen that the comfrey is removing from the soil by planting a ring of nitrogen-fixing green manure around each plant, or mulching it regularly throughout the summer with grass cuttings. Warning number two: comfrey is covered in tiny prickles that can cause an uncomfortable reaction in some people, so do wear gloves when harvesting, and situate it away from paths where it may brush against bare legs.

There are at least ten different uses for comfrey in an allotment:

🍅 **Bee magnet:** if you let comfrey flower, you'll spend the whole summer listening to the relaxing sound of dozens of bees drunkenly rooting around in the bell-like purple-pink flowers. Provided you've chosen Bocking 14, the flowers shouldn't set seed.

🍅 **Chicken feed:** poultry love comfrey. If you can spare some freshly cut leaves, feed them to your hens as part of their diet. The Bocking 4 cultivar is particularly recommended for chickens, and the wilted leaves can also be fed to rabbits, goats, geese and pigs. Some smallholders also swear by them as a pick-me-up for sick animals.

🍅 **Comfrey concentrate:** this version's even smellier, and should appeal to the scientist in you. As Michael Rand puts it in his book *Close to the Veg: A Book of Allotment Tales*: 'Try stuffing a raw mackerel down the back of a radiator. Then shut all your windows. Wait a fortnight.' Get the idea? However it's a little more efficient than that: cut back your comfrey and stuff the leaves tightly into a large plastic bottle with the base cut off and the cap removed. Upend the bottle over a plastic collecting pot: a fortnight later, black ooze should be emerging from the bottle as the leaves rot. Peg on nose, pour the black stuff into a tightly sealed container and then dilute it as you would orange squash when watering the plot.

- 🍅 **Comfrey leaf mould:** comfrey leaves mixed half and half with other leaves can be stuffed into a plastic sack with a few holes cut in it and left in a damp corner to break down. After as little as six months, the whole lot should have become a sweet-smelling leaf mould that will be great for using in plant pots, although it will probably be too rich in nutrients to use for sowing seeds.

- 🍅 **Comfrey tea:** this is tea for your plants, not you, but the process is similar. All you need to do is put a few handfuls of comfrey leaves in a bucket or dustbin (nettles or borage will work as substitutes), add several litres of water, put a lid on it and let it steep in the liquid for about a month. The comfrey will turn to black goo and you can pour out the (now distinctly whiffy) water to apply to your plants. You can leave the goo and simply add more leaves and water to start again. I'd advise not watering with comfrey tea while anyone you care about is downwind of you.

- 🍅 **Compost heap activator:** for the reasons I've explained above, comfrey is a great addition to your heap. Just cut it down and add a layer every now and again: the extra nitrogen will help to kickstart the decomposition process.

- 🍅 **Foliar spray:** some organic gardeners believe that comfrey tea, when sprayed on the leaves of plants, strengthens resistance against diseases such as mildew. If you want to give this one a try, prepare the tea as described above, mix with a drop of environmentally friendly washing-up liquid and spray onto the leaves of your crop (the detergent helps the spray to stick to the leaves).

- **Potato planting:** some plot holders swear by burying a handful of wilted comfrey leaves with every tuber as a way of preventing the unsightly disease, scab.

- **Surface mulch:** one of the quickest ways of dispatching your newly cut comfrey leaves is to pile them a good ten centimetres deep around the base of crops, making what's known as a sheet mulch. This will help to suppress weeds, keep the soil moist and supply the crop with nutrients as the comfrey breaks down. I particularly favour this method for tomatoes.

- **Trench composting:** include some handfuls of comfrey leaves when trench composting (burying 'raw' kitchen waste straight into the soil to feed hungry crops such as beans).

Allotment diary

November 2005

I can't say that having an allotment is stress free, but the worries it provokes are utterly different from those that plague people's work and home life. Rather than 'Will I lose my job in the latest corporate downsizing?', or 'Does my wife still love me?', it's 'Will those pumpkin seedlings survive the cold weather tonight?', or 'Did I prune those blackcurrants properly?'

The five-minute walk from my house to my plot – up the road, past the corner shop with the gaggle of teenagers hanging about, across the patch of waste ground where Tripod the three-legged cat sits, down the alleyway and through the gate – is usually long enough for any nagging worries to slip away, and if not they'll certainly disappear as I pull carrots or dig potatoes while watching the sky for rain or a beautiful sunset.

Fertilisers

There's a powerful argument in the organic gardening movement which holds that, provided you are composting, making home-made liquid feeds from comfrey or nettles and adding other soil improvers to your plot, adding extra fertilisers such as bonemeal, pelleted chicken manure or seaweed feed isn't necessary. It's certainly another expense that you could do without. And adding too many nutrients to the soil at the wrong time can lead to plants growing too fast and the resulting lush growth falling prey to pests and diseases. The adage 'feed the soil not the plant' comes into play.

But if you don't have a compost heap up and running and can't face adding manure or making comfrey tea, a bought-in seaweed feed – either in liquid form that you can dilute for watering directly onto the soil, or pellets that you can dig in or sprinkle on the soil surface – is ideal. It will contain all the nutrients your plants need, including nitrogen, phosphates, potassium and magnesium. (If you're lucky enough to live by the sea, you can make your own compost feed by adding seaweed to the compost heap.)

To dig or not to dig?

Get a group of plot holders together and one thing you can guarantee they'll disagree about is digging. Some will swear that it's essential to turn over the whole plot during the winter, without fail. Others will say that digging is a no-no, except on compacted ground. Beginners will wonder who's right. As with most debates, both sides have valid arguments, and who you side with will depend on you, your plot and your approach to it.

The thinking behind the no-dig system, which is popular but by no means compulsory among organic gardeners, is that digging damages soil structure and brings weed seeds to the surface. Rather than regularly disturbing the complex ecosystem that is the soil, no-dig growers apply mulches of organic material to the surface. This is drawn down into the soil by worms and other soil organisms and helps to improve the structure. It's a method often combined with raised beds, which we looked at in chapter three. It will take longer to improve a poor plot using a no-dig approach, but it is a lot less labour intensive, and so could make the difference between success and failure for you if you want to avoid heavy labour or are short of time.

The digging camp argue that their approach helps to break up hard clods of earth, incorporate organic material and improve drainage. Many allotmenteers also develop a taste for the physical exertion of turning over a patch of soil and relish seeing a crusty, unloved patch of earth being transformed into an evenly dug crumbly tilth (which is a soil with the consistency of crumble topping, or instant coffee grains, rather than concrete rubble) by the work of their own hands. One small caveat though: many growers, myself included, are often tempted to dig when conditions aren't suitable, for example when the soil is too wet and clings to the spade, your feet and just about everything else, or when it's too dry and hard to work. Wait until the soil is dry enough to pull the spade from the ground without huge clods of soil still attached to it, but damp enough to be easily penetrated.

While I am firmly in the organic gardening camp, I do tend to sit on the fence on this particular argument. I like to dig over some parts of my plot, while other areas are dedicated to raised beds which are rarely touched with a spade. I like the flexibility of being able to switch between the two methods. Talk to other allotment holders, try both approaches and see which one works for you.

Improving drainage

A final note on a subject close to my heart – how to deal with badly drained or waterlogged soil. As we've already seen, adding humus is vital to improving soil structure and water retention and digging to break up compacted earth can help, but there are other more drastic measures you can take. Digging a trench of a spade's depth and width around your entire plot will help to direct water away from your crops, particularly during particularly wet months. However these trenches will need re-digging every year, and can be a hazard for the unsuspecting visitor if you allow them to become overgrown with grass: it's all too easy to step in one and twist your ankle. A better and more long-term option would be to turn over as much of your plot as possible to raised beds, which should lift your crops above the level of the water. If your plot is made up of clay soil, buy in compost to fill the beds and you'll instantly improve the situation for your plants. And if you scrupulously avoid walking on the beds, the soil should stay free-draining.

Spotlight on...

PURPLE SPROUTING BROCCOLI

You can keep your asparagus; for me PSB is the king of the seasonal gourmet veg. Harvest time is March and April, when the rest of your plot may be looking distinctly unproductive, so the deep purple spears are particularly welcome as a way of livening up your veg offering when you've run out of pumpkins and are still waiting for your lettuces to be ready.

There are early and late varieties on the market, so you can ensure that your PSB harvest stretches out as long as possible. It takes a long time to grow PSB from seed to crop, so you'll need patience: the seeds are usually sown in trays or a seed bed in July, then transplanted to a final growing position when still small. The only trick you need to know when harvesting PSB is that the central stem should be picked as soon as you can, as this will spark growth in the side shoots, which will provide the mainstay of your crop.

Picked and rushed to your kitchen, PSB needs very little cooking: both sprouts and leaves are delicious steamed or added to a stir-fry. Tasty as it is alone, its flavour is sturdy enough to be combined with strong flavours such as anchovies cooked in butter, a sweet chilli sauce or a drizzling of lemon juice and zest. If you're looking for further inspiration, Hugh Fearnley-Whittingstall is such a fan of PSB that he offers ten recipes for it in his book *The River Cottage Year.*

Seed sources: The Real Seed Company, Organic Gardening Catalogue, Johnsons Seeds.

Seven
Sowing and planting

Sowe Carrets in your Gardens, and humbly praise God for them, as for a singular and great blessing.

Richard Gardiner, *Profitable Instructions for the Manuring, Sowing and Planting of Kitchen Gardens,* 1599

The earliest seed I remember sowing was moss curled parsley, which my mum chopped up for a sauce to serve with white fish and new potatoes. I can't remember why I chose that particular herb: perhaps there were some spare seeds in the shed, or maybe I was keen to provide my mum with a ready source of ingredients for my favourite dish. I must have been around seven years old. I sprinkled the seed in a meandering row along the flower bed below the kitchen window, a patch of earth that was lit up every year by those vivid yellow and red tulips so popular in the seventies, stamens wobbling under the weight of dusky pollen and a colour so bright that, when you held the red ones up to your face, they cast a crimson shadow across your cheek. I remember going back to check my seeds the following day, naively assuming that a few hours in some damp soil would be time enough to allow them to sprout. I had to wait a couple of weeks – a long time for a child – but they did grow, providing my first harvest a few weeks after that. I was astonished that such a simple recipe of soil, seeds, sunlight and water could produce leaves with such a fresh, unique flavour.

Things haven't changed much: I still find the process of seed germination miraculous. One week, the soil is flat and barren, the next, it's covered in fresh green shoots. And I still sow parsley every year, the flat-leaved Mediterranean type as well as the curled. I also marvel at the relative ease with which such a diverse range of fruit and vegetables can be grown on the same rectangle of soil, from the deep crisp purple of a cabbage to the soft sweetness of a June strawberry. And even now I will sow seeds on a whim with a particular meal in mind, and impatiently examine the soil a day later to check if anything has happened.

I've usually given up all hope of any germination by the time the seedlings pop up. This gets me into all kinds of trouble. One season I put in a packet of leek seeds and was so convinced that they had utterly failed to germinate that I planted some tomatoes on the site of the rows. It was only a few days later while weeding that I realised that what I thought were grass shoots were the all too quickly abandoned seeds.

With no greenhouse to my name, I have to make do with whatever space I can find to service my sowing addiction. From around the beginning of January to the end of May, the windowsills in my house are festooned with pots and trays of every conceivable size, all playing host to the different seeds I am hoping to grow that year. Not everything needs to be cosseted indoors or under glass:

some crops can be grown in situ on the plot, while others can adapt to either start in life. It varies from seed to seed, so my first top tip on sowing is mundane yet routinely ignored: read the back of the packet. While I can understand the temptation to chuck away the manual for your new DVD player or laptop, the instructions on a seed packet are usually only a few lines long, and could make all the difference between success and failure.

Grabbing a random handful of packets from my seed box, I can see the potential for confusion: no two seed companies display the relevant information in quite the same way. But there are a few key facts to look out for:

- **Best-before date:** most seeds won't last more than a few years at best so make sure you use up or give away any seeds before the expiry date.
- **Sow direct or under glass:** plants that hate being transplanted are best sown in the spot where they are to grow; others need to be nurtured in warm conditions that only a greenhouse or windowsill can provide, then transplanted to their final cropping position once it's warm enough.
- **Depth:** some packets will tell you how deep to plant the seed, which can be very useful as this varies according to the type and size. As a general rule, seeds should be covered with a layer of soil no deeper than their own diameter or they won't germinate; in other words, the smaller the seed, the finer the soil cover. But if in doubt, take a ruler down to the plot to measure the depth of your sowings and make sure they don't exceed the packet's instructions.

- 🍅 **When to sow, transplant and harvest:** all crucial information, but don't follow it too slavishly: I've sown things months late and still had a bumper crop.
- 🌱 **Spacing:** this can be the most confusing of all. The packet should tell you how far apart each plant should be along a row, and also how far apart each row should be. But sometimes the distance between each plant will be described only as, say, '30cm x 15cm': is that rows thirty centimetres apart and spacing within rows at fifteen centimetres? Do check. Nonetheless, spacing is another one of those somewhat arbitrary rules that are there to be broken, so don't let yourself become obsessed by measuring things out to the millimetre.

Before you read any further, let me say this: much as I evangelise growing from seed, it's by no means a must for the budding allotmenteer. There should be no shame in buying seedlings by mail order or from a nursery: you'll still end up with a crop that you have lavished attention on, and having an allotment shouldn't be an exercise in guilt. Seed sowing is one of the most time-consuming jobs, so if you don't have time for it, ditch it, or mix and match, raising some of your own plants and buying in others.

Plug plants are ideal if you lack suitable windowsills for seed trays or if you don't want the bother of preparation, sowing and pricking out. If you decide to follow this route, you can skip merrily down to the section on transplanting, safe in the knowledge that you won't have to worry about all that waiting and watering.

The practicalities

As you may have realised by now, every allotment gardener has their own idiosyncratic method of growing, and sowing seeds is no exception. Some allotmenteers will swear by making their own pots out of old newspaper, while others will insist that seed trays are the one true way. You can only find out what works best for you through trial and error, but here are a few pointers to help you along the way.

As I've already said, some seeds need to start life 'under glass', in other words, on your windowsill, in a greenhouse or at the very least in a cloche or cold frame. If you want to grow Mediterranean veg such as tomatoes, peppers, aubergines, chillies and sweetcorn on your allotment, you'll need to find a warm, south-facing windowsill to start them off, preferably covering their pots or tray with clear plastic bags to create a warm environment. If you have the funds, invest in a heated propagator, which will keep your seeds at a balmy 19°C or 20°C, the optimal temperature for germination success for these lovers of warmer weather. Once the seedlings have emerged, provided the room is relatively warm, you can switch the heat off, although if they are situated on a windowsill that gets chilly at night, you may wish to leave it on to prevent the young plants being shocked by a sudden temperature drop.

Some plants, like salad crops and brassicas, benefit from being started off in a controlled environment even if they don't need the extra heat. They can get going without the threat of slug or snail damage and you can wait until they're strong enough to withstand pest attacks of all but the most serious kind before transplanting the seedlings. Other crops will have no objection whatsoever to being planted straight into the soil on your plot, provided the conditions are right; in fact it's even preferable for many root crops that don't like to be disturbed while growing, such as carrots, beetroot and parsnips.

Sowing mix: passionate about peat-free

Sowing seeds inside can be a deeply satisfying enterprise. It is a way of spending the gloomiest February or March day that will have you dreaming of the sun on your back a few months hence, knowing that the work you are doing now will pay dividends in the summer. There's nothing better than switching on the radio, getting my seeds out and pottering around, sowing up a storm. I'm not too fussy about the compost I use in seed sowing. As long as it is peat free, moisture retentive, and contains lots of air pockets for the seeds to develop, there's not much else required: the seedlings won't be in there long enough to need much in the way of nutrients. I tend to use a mix of two handfuls of bought-in potting compost to every one handful of sharp sand and one handful of vermiculite (a lightweight, flaky mineral that absorbs water well). When sowing fine seeds such as lettuce it's worth sieving the mixture to remove any big lumps that might restrict the young plants' push upwards towards the light.

One ingredient that will never show up in my seed trays though is peat. Britain's peat bogs are teetering on the edge of total oblivion: 94 per cent of the UK's original lowland peat bog habitat has gone, largely to the trade in peat for gardeners, who use it in potting mixes and soil improvers. Around 60 per cent of the peat you'll find at your local garden centre comes from peatland habitats in Britain. Why should you care about bogs? Because they're unique habitats that are rich in wildlife, from carnivorous plants to rare birds. The frustrating thing is, despite the fact that peat-based compost still dominates the market, there are plenty of peat-free alternatives made from composted bark, municipal green waste, and coir (coconut husk fibre). You may find they take some getting accustomed to if you've been used to peat-based mixes, but given that the government's target is to reduce peat in compost by 90 per cent by 2010, it's about time we allotment holders got with the programme.

Sowing hardware

There are a number of choices when it comes to sowing hardware. The most basic and cheapest of all is a seed tray – a shallow rectangular plastic container with drainage holes in the base, which can be salvaged from supermarket fruit packaging; small seeds are scattered randomly on the surface of the compost while larger ones are sown in grid patterns. However, using a seed tray means you will at some point need to transplant (prick out) the tiny seedlings into individual containers, so you may want to avoid this by starting instead with either module trays, which have moulded rows of separate slots for each seed, or individual pots, which are easily made out of folded newspaper or recycled yogurt pots with a drainage hole punched in the bottom with a screwdriver. You can also buy clever little dried soil discs covered in netting called Jiffy 7s that expand to form capsules and make for hassle-free transplanting. One increasingly popular sowing shortcut is to plant seeds thinly in a length of plastic guttering bought from a DIY store, ideally keeping them in a greenhouse or under some kind of cover over the spring. When the seedlings are big enough to be transplanted, you simply prepare a shallow furrow, or drill, on your plot and slide the row of plants and soil into the slot with minimal disturbance to the roots. Peas seem to take to this method particularly well.

If you want to avoid plastic altogether, there are plenty of alternatives. Young root systems and stems are very vulnerable to damage, so there's certainly something to be said for pots that can be planted straight into open ground with minimal disturbance to the seedlings. Some allotmenteers swear by using the cardboard centres of toilet rolls for certain seeds that need lots of space for their roots, such as sweetcorn and beans; home-made pots constructed from newspaper or cardboard also work well. If you prefer to avoid a DIY job, pots made of coir are one answer. They're sold in a variety of sizes and thicknesses, and the looser-weave pots can be put straight in the ground when your seedlings are ready to transplant. One final tip that comes slightly out of left field is eggshells as pots. Yes, eggshells, not egg boxes (although they'll work too). According to the classic American self-sufficiency book *The Mother Earth News Almanac*, provided you crack your egg carefully at one end and wash it out thoroughly, an eggshell makes a perfect container for seedlings: when it's transplanting time, the shell can be gently broken to encourage the roots to poke through once ensconced in the soil. And the minerals released from the shells as they break down are good for plants, so everyone's a winner.

Allotment diary   *March 2006*

And so it begins: my annual mission to grow tomatoes outdoors, without the protection of a greenhouse, on my allotment. It's an exercise fraught with danger and tinged with the hope of achieving delicious ripe tomatoes. On Sunday evening, far too late for any non-obsessed person to start such an enterprise, I decided to start sowing tomato seeds. Even though lots of tomato-seed packets suggest sowing in February or March, if you are sowing to grow outside it's best to hold off until the end of March. Otherwise you're left with leggy seedlings desperate to be planted out when it's still too chilly for them to thrive.

How to sow

Once you have combined your potting compost, sand and/or vermiculite, it's worth moistening the resulting mixture before you begin loading up your chosen seed containers: this will make it easier to work with as you fill the pots or trays, and will also mean you don't need to risk disturbing the seeds by flooding the soil when they are already in place. I tend to put the compost into a bucket or bowl, add some warm water and stir it around with my hands like a cake mix to ensure that the soil is thoroughly damp but not soaking wet. It's better to use warm rather than cold water, not only because it's kinder on your hands, but also because the seeds will get less of a shock if they are placed in a warm environment, which should aid germination. If you forget to add water before sowing, put some warm water in a dish and sit the pots in it so they can soak it up from below. Fill about three-quarters of the pots with compost and tamp it down a little – an old-style 35mm film canister is ideal for this job as it can be used circular end down for individual pots or rolled across the surface of the soil in seed trays.

Then sow your seed, as thinly as you can. Two or three seeds per pot or module will do. I don't think there's ever been an occasion when I've thought 'I wish I'd sown more seeds'. If the seed is particularly small and fiddly, bulk it out by adding a few teaspoons of sand to the seed, then sprinkle the mixture on the compost. Then you can add a thin layer of vermiculite or compost. It's best to err on the side of caution: as I mentioned before, it is important to follow the instructions on the seed packets when trying to assess how deep seeds should be sown. If you sow seeds too deeply, they may exhaust all their energy before they break through the surface. Some seeds prefer to be left exposed: again, scrutinise that packet!

Label each new sowing carefully: don't assume that you'll remember what's what, particularly once you've shifted your trays from your potting bench onto the windowsill. I've made this mistake many a time and expended much time trying to work out whether a particular tray of seedlings were Brussels sprouts or kale. (Don't have a potting bench? Nor do I – I just use a couple of old tea trays on some old newspaper on either the dining table or a table in the garage.) Make a note of the variety and the date sown, so you can accurately judge how long they take to germinate – particularly useful if you are as impatient as I am and eagerly waiting for the first green shoots. The gap between sowing and germination varies from seed to seed. I've seen radishes germinate in as little as three days, but more tricky customers such as celeriac and parsley could take up to a month. And not all the seeds from the same batch will sprout at the same moment: some could take a fortnight to appear when their fellows are already reaching for the sky.

If you are using a seed tray, once the seedlings have grown a strong stem and developed at least a couple of real leaves (as opposed to the cotyledons, the first pair of leaves that emerge after germination and which usually look nothing like the subsequent leaves), they'll need transplanting into individual pots. This process is known as pricking out. Gently dislodge the soil around the base of each seedling with your finger or an old kitchen fork until the roots lift free as you raise the plant by one of its leaves. Never touch the stem: a seedling will probably survive a damaged leaf, but if the stem is broken it will inevitably die.

Pricking out is fiddly, time-consuming work, which is why it's almost always better to sow two or three seeds in individual pots or modules, if you can. Then you can pick the strongest performer in each one and thin out the remaining two. Thinning out simply means gently uprooting and discarding a proportion – usually a half or two thirds – of the seedlings you've germinated to give the remaining ones room to develop. This was always a bit of a mystery to me as a new gardener. Why kill off so much of the new life you have just successfully created? The fact is, most of us sow seed far too thickly. It's easily done, particularly with tiny seeds that slip through your fingers at an alarming rate. And although it seems like a waste, it's much more inefficient to grow two plants that are fighting for resources and space than one that has the ideal circumstances for strong growth. So steel yourself, and thin those seedlings. Then you'll only need to move the remaining seedling once, from the pot or module into its final cropping position on the plot, usually once weather conditions are right, and the plant is mature enough.

Allotment diary

March 2005

One of my favourite parts of gardening is planting seeds and watching them grow: spotting the first green shoots breaking out of the compost and expanding to meet the sunlight.

The other potential problem when raising plants from seed is the fact that sometimes your young charges will collapse for seemingly no reason. Aside from a lack of water, a condition called damping off is the most likely cause. Damping off is caused by fungi that thrive in the damp environment that prevails in seed trays; it's particularly prevalent in heated propagators, where conditions can become fetid if you forget to open the air vents on top of the clear plastic covers regularly. If just one or two seedlings keel over, you might get away with scooping them out along with the surrounding compost and leaving the rest to grow on. If the whole lot is affected, it's best to start all over again. To avoid this problem in the first place, you should resist overwatering – keep the compost damp but not wet by watering little and often – and maintain good hygiene, in other words wash containers in between sowings and use fresh compost for each new batch of seeds. A great tip to prevent damping off I gleaned from a fellow plot holder is to water with camomile tea – once it's cooled, of course. The tea possesses anti-fungal compounds that will help to stave off the problem before it kills your seedlings. Which, if you hate this herbal brew as much as I do, is just about all it's good for.

Making a seed bed

Sowing seed directly into the ground will save some, but not all of the labour involved in sowing in trays or pots. First you'll need to create a seed bed. Think of this area as The Ritz of your allotment, the high-end accommodation offering the best start in life for its star residents, your seeds. They'll need a bit of pampering if they are to develop – and most importantly crop – well.

One of the many mistakes I made as a newly minted allotmenteer was falling prey to impatience and trying to sow seeds when the soil just wasn't ready. As I learned to my cost, it really is a waste of time capitalising on a warm spell in early spring to sow some sweetcorn when it will rot unless the soil temperature is at or above 17°C. Seeds just won't germinate if it's too cold or wet for them, although the exact temperature needed varies from plant to plant: broad beans and cabbages can cope perfectly well with 5°C while tomatoes need at least 15°C. A soil thermometer will help you check when the temperature is right, but if in doubt, wait.

If you don't want to invest in yet another piece of allotment kit, there is another way. In medieval times, gardeners would test whether the soil had reached the required temperature by sitting bare-bottomed on the ground. If it was bearable (excuse the pun) to stay seated, the time was right. To avoid embarrassment, you can use the back of your hand instead. You can easily tell if the soil is too wet for sowing by checking your boots. If the dirt is clinging to them in heavy clods, it's too sodden for sowing; if the earth falls off easily, the time might just be right. And there are ways to beat the weather. The laying of black plastic sheeting on the soil surface a few weeks before you plan to sow will not win your plot any beauty contests, but it will help to warm and dry the soil surface and allow you to get going a little earlier. Covering the ground with some horticultural fleece, a cloche or cold frame will serve the same purpose and these can also be used to keep the soil temperature up once the seeds are sown.

The second must-have for a seed bed is a relatively flat, weed-free, fine and crumbly soil surface. I include the word 'relatively' largely out of guilt, because I have been known to bung in a row of seeds in less than perfect conditions. This usually happens because I've left it late to sow a particular vegetable and don't have time to turn the soil into a *Gardeners' World*-style 'fine tilth'. All I can say is, do your best. It's actually pretty hard to prevent every single seed from germinating through poor soil preparation (although I have achieved this rare distinction in the past), so don't despair if you don't have time to make your seed bed absolutely perfect.

But assuming you have a bit of time on your hands, try to work the soil with a fork or hoe until the soil's fine and crumbly, with lumps no bigger than your thumbnail. A rake is great for smoothing over the surface, and if you end up raking away the largest clods and putting them somewhere else on the plot, that's fine. As when making jam or chutney, you know you're getting there when the soil forms a dip when you run your finger in a line through it. If it does, hey presto, you have created a v-shaped indentation, or drill, just right for sowing your seeds in. But I suggest waiting two or three weeks between preparation and sowing. This will fool all the weed seeds on the patch of earth into germinating. Then you can clear them away, allowing your chosen seeds to germinate competition-free.

You may notice on a trip around your local allotments that there are two ways of thinking about how to sow seeds. The old school approach is straight, uniform rows across the width of the plot. The alternative approach – often teamed with raised beds – is a less formal system of sowing, where an area – which could be as small as a handkerchief or as large as a few square metres – is sown in blocks, either using regimented spacing in a grid pattern, or with the seeds scattered completely at random.

If you decide to sow in rows, there is no need to feel restricted to straight lines – there are any number of ways of arranging your seeds. If you do like things regimented, you can ensure ramrod-straight rows by using a garden line – a length of string tied to a stick at either end, which you can place in the ground and use to trace your seed drill. If, like me, you prefer things a little more random, forget the straight line and sow as you please: try a pattern of curvy lines or even a circle. Whether you plant in a straight or curved line, the seeds should be sown at the same spacing as indicated on the packet. If the seeds are so fine that they stray out of your line and onto the surrounding earth, you can always tidy up by thinning straggling seedlings once they've surfaced. And never feel compelled to sow a complete row of a single crop: better to sow shorter rows of the same crop over a number of weeks to produce a longer harvest period, or sow short stretches of several different vegetables at once.

When sowing in blocks in a raised bed, the spacing can be closer than that recommended on the seed packet, but you'll have to experiment to find out what works for you: just how close together your vegetables will happily grow depends on the soil, the weather and what you decide to grow. Do bear in mind that if you err on the side of planting closer than the packet recommends, you can always remove plants if things become too crowded: it's a lot more hassle to sow extra seeds amid a crop that's already growing.

With bigger seeds such as squash, you can 'station sow': put two seeds in every spot where you want to end up with a plant, ensuring that at least one of the two will germinate; if both do, just remove the weaker plant. Alternatively, you can sow your squash in pots in May indoors or in a greenhouse, and transplant them to their final growing position once the risk of frost has passed in June. Either way, courgettes and pumpkins always need more space than you think. Consider leaving a metre or more between sowings. Any less than that and the plants may become stressed because they are battling each other for water and nutrients, and may stop fruiting.

It's a matter of personal choice which sowing style you go for, and one that's as subjective as whether you prefer coffee or tea, however many advocates of each method may try to convince you otherwise. Each has its benefits: the row system can be easier to weed and water, while block planting combined with raised beds will maximise growing space, help to crowd out weeds and avoid damage to the soil structure by using clearly defined paths between beds, meaning you won't be compacting the soil used for growing by walking on it. I have tended to use a mix and match approach, block sowing some crops and sticking with rows for others. There's one crop that you absolutely must sow in a block, and that's sweetcorn. The cobs will only develop if the flowers are well pollinated, and the best way for that to happen is by planting in a cluster – ideally a square.

Allotment diary

January 2006

Traditionally onion seeds are sown on Boxing Day (26 December for any non-UK readers). I've always been convinced this is just a way out of spending any more time in fraught family situations ('Sorry love, must go and sow my onion seeds now, couldn't possibly play Twister with Aunty Mary and the kids again'). I was a day late with my onions, which went in on 27 December.

Seed storage

If you've overenthusiastically ordered far too many seeds for the size of your plot, the issue of how, and indeed whether, to store them in between seasons will become an important one. Seeds have a varying life span. According to the experts from Kew Gardens who are working on the Millennium Seed Bank Project, certain hard-coated seeds have been successfully germinated when hundreds of years old, while Dan Jason, founder of the Seed and Plant Sanctuary for Canada, claims to have grown tobacco plants from one-thousand-year-old carbon dated seeds found sealed in a native American burial site in Ontario.

But I wouldn't leave your seed stash that long if I were you. Most plants you'll be growing on your allotment will have seeds that remain viable for at least a few seasons, but it's always best to use seed that's as fresh as possible. Pumpkin and other squash seeds are reputed to last around six years or more, while parsnip seeds will fail to germinate if left for more than a year. If, like me, you become a serial over-orderer of seeds, then think about giving the surplus away to your allotment neighbours, or sow more than you need so that you can pass on the extra seedlings to someone who doesn't have the time or space for growing their own plants.

If you have any half-full seed packets left after that – or if you have saved your own seeds (see chapter five for how to do that) – it's best to find a place for them where they'll stay in tip-top condition. While it may be tempting to put spare seed packets in your allotment shed or storage box, I'd advise strongly against it unless you can be absolutely sure that conditions are completely dry and frost-free. Seeds do best in an entirely dry but cool environment: an unheated (but not damp) room is best. The kitchen's another no-no as it's too humid and warm.

I store my seeds in a lidded cardboard box in a cool room, where they can be easily accessed for each week's sowings, rather than shoved away in a drawer where they are easily forgotten. A concertina file with sections for each letter of the alphabet works well, or you could file them by which month they will be planted, or by family – all the brassicas (cabbages, Brussels sprouts, cauliflower,

149

etc.) together, and so on. Some people prefer to store seeds in airtight jars, and this method is probably best if you're serious about keeping a lot of seed.

Of course, carefully storing your seeds away in a labelled box isn't always possible, or even desirable. Many old-school gardeners swear by putting melon and squash seeds into their coat pocket for several weeks before sowing. The idea is that the detritus inevitably found in the pocket of every gardening jacket – sand, dried leaves, grit and so on – will score the seeds' hard coating and speed germination once they are put in the ground. There are other ways of encouraging seeds to sprout. Seeds with hard coatings such as beetroot can be soaked in water for twelve to twenty-four hours prior to sowing to soften them up and encourage the green shoot to burst through into the light. Sometimes fate intervenes, however. There is always the possibility that a packet of peas will burst in your gardening bag and several months later you'll notice that some of them have germinated when your water bottle leaked on them. I treat such mishaps merely as opportunities for an unexpectedly late pea harvest.

Planting out

How do you tell when a tender plant, such as a tomato or squash, that started its life indoors or in a greenhouse is ready for the cruel world of the open plot? First of all, the plant must be big enough to survive outside. It must have grown its first two sets of adult leaves, as opposed to the cotyledons or seed leaves that first appear when a seed germinates, and it should have a firm stem and enough of a root system to survive the trauma of being moved outside – if the roots are visible from the hole at the bottom of the pot, that's a good sign. Soil and air temperature must also be right, but then, anything that you've grown under glass will get a shock when it moves into the open air and bright sunlight. To soften the blow, every plant first needs to be given a chance to acclimatise to their new conditions. This is a process known as 'hardening off' and if it's not done, you'll probably find your carefully raised specimens will keel over from the shock of the chill, draughts or blazing sunshine – take your pick. Even plants that started life in a cold frame will need this, although not for as long a period.

Hardening off can begin with putting trays of seedlings outside in a sheltered spot or inside a cold frame for a couple of hours on a sunny day. Bring them back inside, but gradually introduce more and more exposure to the elements. The process can take two to six weeks, depending on the plant and the weather. You'll be able to see the plant changing, as the soft growth put on during its time inside becomes harder and the stem becomes more sturdy. Unfortunately there's no magic indicator that says a plant is fully hardened off, but provided you have gradually increased its exposure to the elements over a period of weeks, you should find they cope well with their new home. Once you think your seedlings are fully hardened off, get them ready for their final trip to the plot by giving them a good dousing at least half an hour before they are moved. Planting out, or transplanting as it is also known, is the most stressful procedure for a young plant and ensuring that they are not thirsty will help to ease the transition. It also helps to do your planting out on an overcast, cool day, when the plant will find the move less traumatic.

When it comes to moving a plant from pot to plot, the main rule is to try to limit disturbance to the delicate root system that you've been sweating over. Make sure you dig a hole that's larger than the root ball (the root system and the soil that's clinging around it), with plenty of room to spare. Once you've inserted the plant, backfill the hole with more soil, gently pressing down around the base of the stem to firm it in. Try to make sure the soil level is roughly the same as it was in the pot: if in doubt, err on the side of burying the stem deeper. Indeed, some seedlings will benefit from such treatment. I got into the habit of planting tomato, courgette and pumpkin seedlings to just below the first leaf, after observing that they will throw out extra roots from any section of their stem provided it is covered in soil. Not only does this help to support the growing plant, but it also encourages an extensive root system that enables the plant to deal with the sometimes erratic watering that can occur when you can't get down to the plot every day during hot summer spells. I was delighted to discover recently that I wasn't the first to think of this: Native Americans in hot, dry parts of the USA plant their seedlings so that only the top few leaves are visible.

Again, there are various things that could catch you out: check back to the seed packet (you did keep the seed packet, right?) for instructions on when and how to plant out, as it could contain vital information that might vary from vegetable to vegetable. Take leeks. The roots of each seedling need to be trimmed by a third before they are placed in individual holes, each about fifteen centimetres deep, so there's not more than five centimetres of leaves visible above the soil; you need to trim off any excess. You can make the hole with a dibber (a pointed stick used for making holes in the earth), trowel handle or wooden spoon. Having transplanted the seedling, pour water into the hole but don't fill it with soil. This will give the leek breathing space to develop a long thick white stem.

Tender plants such as winter squash, courgettes and tomatoes should not be planted outside until all risk of ground frost has passed. Depending on where in Britain you live, this can be anywhere from mid-May to the end of June. And beware of being caught out by a random warm spell. If you want to plant out anyway, make sure your plants have some protection at night from fleece, a cloche or cold frame; otherwise you'll have to watch the weather reports like a hawk and be ready to make a mercy dash to the plot.

Everyone seems to want to add something to the bottom of the hole when transplanting. For seed potatoes, it's comfrey, or torn-up newspaper, or compost. For brassicas, it's chopped-up rhubarb leaves to act against cabbage root fly. With courgettes and cucumbers, it's a carrot. Yes, you read that right – a carrot stuck into the ground next to a new courgette plant is reputed to attract nematodes (parasites) that would otherwise attack the plant. You'll learn through trial and error what works for you, and neighbouring plot holders may offer up (possibly conflicting) advice, too.

Planting direct

Seeds, on the whole, are tricky customers. Sometimes, when sown carefully in pots on the windowsill, they don't germinate. Sometimes, they die when transplanted from seed tray to plot, because their roots are accidentally damaged, or because of an unexpected cold snap. Other times, when sown direct on the plot, they germinate, then the seedlings get wiped out by a slug in week one. The potential pitfalls are considerable.

So it is with a lighter heart that I turn to the diverse group of crops which, on the whole, make life easier for the allotmenteer, because they don't involve seeds and can be planted direct into the soil.

This group includes potatoes and Jerusalem artichokes, which, in the case of the former, come in the former of specially-prepared mini-tubers known as seed potatoes. The planting direct group also includes rhubarb and asparagus, which can be bought as dormant plants, known as crowns; globe artichokes, which can be purchased as mini-plants known as offshoots; onions, garlic and shallots, which can be bought as sets (specially-prepared mini-bulbs which, in the case of onions, swell to their full size, or in the case of shallots and garlic, multiply to create bunches of bulbs), and soft fruit, which can be bought and planted out in the winter as canes – barerooted stems that will grow away nicely once planted in a good spot.

Each has their own foibles, but on the whole, they are easier to work with than seeds and less vulnerable to sudden collapse. The general rule is this: buy them as close to the desirable planting time as possible, and plant them as soon as you can after purchase, weather conditions allowing. Every plant will be happier in the soil than stuck in a pot, bag or net. This is particularly true of soft fruit canes: raspberries, blackcurrants, gooseberries and blackberries. These are usually bought as dormant plants in the autumn and winter; see the monthly tasks list at the end of the book for guidance on when to plant what.

When it comes to planting potatoes, there's a lot of rot talked about how you must do this or that, otherwise they simply won't grow. Anyone who has accidentally left a spud or two behind in the soil only for it to sprout next season, or seen a potato plant poking out of a compost heap, will know that this is a myth. In reality they're dead easy and just about as close as you can get to a must-have crop: fun to harvest and universally welcome in the kitchen, particularly if you try one of the more unusual varieties.

The old-fashioned way of planting potatoes is to dig one long trench to put the tubers in, but I find it easier to make individual holes of about a hand's depth for each potato; a bulb planter – a cylindrical tool that is pressed into the earth and then withdrawn to remove a 'plug' of soil, leaving the perfect-sized hold for a bulb or potato tuber – works well for this task. Put the tuber in the bottom of the hole and try to remember to make sure any sprouts – which form the plant's stems, not its roots – face skyward. Don't cover it with soil until every potato is in the ground, as it's easy to tell where you're up to that way, particularly if you're interrupted by an unexpected rain shower or a chatty neighbour. Finally, make a little hillock over each one, to protect the emerging stem from frosts and also to remind you where the tubers are.

With onion and shallot sets, the key is to plant them shallow – leave the very top poking out of the ground. Birds seem to love playing with them, and if you return to the plot to find them strewn all over the place, replant a little deeper so they are completely covered; this won't do any harm, but they will take a little longer to emerge. Don't just force them into the ground, but use a dibber (or dibber substitute) to make the hole, otherwise you risk damaging the onion's nascent root system and slowing its growth.

Overwintering

Overwintering is one way you can get ahead of the pack each spring. In gardening terms, overwintering in its widest sense simply means a method of caring for a plant during the winter that will ensure it will survive – for instance by bringing tender garden plants such as fuschias into a greenhouse or conservatory to protect them from frost. In allotment terms, overwintering means planting specially-prepared seeds or sets in the late summer or autumn which will start growing, survive the winter and supply you with an early harvest – far sooner than would be possible for crops started in springtime. Peas, garlic, broad beans, lettuce and onions are some of the most popular crops for overwintering, but do make sure you buy seeds or sets that stipulate they are specifically produced for overwintering – look out for the varieties marked as 'overwintered' or 'overwintering' (the terms are interchangeable) or 'autumn sown' on the packet.

Trying to grow overwintered crops can be a hit and miss affair. Too much rain or a boggy soil and your onions may rot away to nothing: a really bitter winter could kill every one of your young plants off. So any protection you can offer your overwintering crops from extremes of temperature and hungry birds, the better: a layer of horticultural fleece held up with hoops or wire or canes or

Spotlight on...

BEETROOT CHIOGGIA

This is my favourite beetroot variety, not least because it has the ability to completely surprise unsuspecting dinner guests with its startling appearance. The skin is dark pink, but cut it in half and you'll reveal concentric rings of white and blood red that look rather like a bull's-eye boiled sweet. Beautiful isn't an adjective often used in relation to beetroot but this variety really deserves the description.

Think of beetroot recipes, and you probably think of the Russian soup borscht. But as its name suggests, Chioggia hails from Italy. This isn't so surprising, given that beetroot was originally cultivated from a wild plant found growing in coastal Mediterranean regions. Chioggia seed is frequently sold as 'barbabietola di Chioggia': 'barbabietola' just means beetroot in Italian, and the 'Chioggia' bit comes from this beetroot's place of origin, an Italian coastal town some twenty-five kilometres south of Venice. As is often the case with old vegetable varieties, the Chioggia beetroot doesn't have a precise birthday, but it has been around since at least 1840, although it's likely that it was first grown much earlier than that – perhaps even as early as the sixteenth century.

Chioggia is easy to grow like all beetroots, but it has a delicate flavour that's a little less earthy than other types. I find it ideal for roasting whole, which is less messy and time-consuming than boiling, and when it's turned into soup the resulting dish has a pretty pink hue. It's best picked when it is between golf and tennis ball sized.

Seed sources: Organic Gardening Catalogue, Seeds of Italy, Tamar Organics, Thomas Etty Esq.

an extra layer of compost around the young plants will help, as will a free-draining soil. Of course, if you have cold frames, cloches, a greenhouse or polytunnel where the overwintered vegetables can shelter, you're far more likely to reap a bumper crop.

However you do it, growing a handful of overwintered crops will extend your growing period by several weeks, and give you a warm glow of satisfaction at managing to grow a crop while the rest of the plot lies dormant.

Eight
Composting

> My whole life has been spent waiting for an epiphany,
> a manifestation of God's presence, the kind of
> transcendent, magical experience that lets you see
> your place in the big picture. And that is what I had
> with my first heap.

> **Bette Midler, 'Los Angeles "Compost Queen"',**
> **Los Angeles Times, May 1996**

An allotment without a compost heap is like a car without an engine: going nowhere. The heap is both a free, easy way to enrich the soil and improve its structure, and a repository for the huge amount of plant waste generated by your plot. And yet I've noticed that a surprising number of plots don't feature one. Why? Perhaps the plot holder is in denial about what happens to their waste once it's been bagged, binned, and carted away; or perhaps they see composting as a waste of time when fertilisers can provide everything a growing crop needs; or maybe they have tried to make compost but gave up after a few months, having only managed to produce a slimy mess.

As Michael Pollan writes in his book *Second Nature: A Gardener's Education*, there is a 'halo of righteousness' that hovers over compost and those who make it. But don't be discouraged if you're not a compost convert yet. Composting is happening all around you – that pile of leaves in the corner of the garden, the apples from the neighbour's fruit tree rotting on your lawn, the banana skin slung away on a picnic. As the Garden Organic guide to composting on their website (listed in the Directory at the back) explains: 'Composting just happens – it is nature's way of keeping our planet clean.' Using a bin or heap just speeds up the process and allows you to harvest the resulting compost for your plot.

The word compost comes from the Latin 'compositus', literally 'put together', and the key to successful composting is this putting together of a variety of organic materials. Over the course of six months or so, the organic material gets broken down, with the help of millions of bacteria, plus worms and insects such as woodlice, into 'black gold', a rich, dark, crumbly compost (think Christmas cake crumbs) that's often referred to by gardeners as humus. It would almost be an act of alchemy were it not so simple.

Taking up composting requires us to not only take responsibility for the waste we produce, but also to process some of it on our own doorsteps. It's estimated that at least 60 per cent of what we throw away could be added to a home composting system. Given that British households generate 31 million tonnes of waste a year, that's a significant reduction in our impact on the country's landfill sites. The government's public information website on recycling, RecycleNow, calculates that if you're eating your allotted five portions of fruit and vegetables a day, you'll be creating enough kitchen waste to fill a two metre fridge-freezer every month. As Hollywood actress Bette Midler points out in the quote printed at the start of this chapter, understanding the cycle of growth, death and decomposition can help us understand our place in the world – which, looked at one way, is at the centre of a big pile of waste.

I can't imagine living without a compost heap now, and find it hard to jettison green waste when I am away from home: I have been known to secrete used tea bags in my pocket to take back for my own ever-hungry compost pile. The compost bins and heaps are almost as central to domestic harmony in my household as the oven and the washing machine.

In one end goes all the plant waste from my garden and allotment, from grass cuttings to dahlia stalks as thick as your wrist; old potting compost; dead houseplants and cut flowers; kitchen waste in the form of vegetable peelings and eggshells; manure from the local stables; and shredded bank statements, receipts and other waste paper and cardboard. Around a year later, out the other end comes crumbly compost which I add to my allotment beds as a mulch and a soil improver, boosting the soil's water retention, fertility, and overall condition.

So let's get this straight: you're turning something you don't want and would otherwise throw away into a free material that vastly improves your allotment or garden, allowing you to grow even more delicious fruit and vegetables and save money on fertilisers. And while it's rotting down, your compost bin or heap provides a home for beneficial creatures such as worms, ground beetles and woodlice, and vastly reduces the amount of your rubbish that ends up marooned on a landfill. Brilliant!

How I became a rotter

My own composting journey began when I was a reporter on a local newspaper. The local council was trying to promote its compost bin scheme, where a plastic bin could be bought from a nearby garden centre at a discount price when you presented a voucher from the council. So I decided to try one out and write a feature on it for the paper (complete with a picture of me grinning cheesily next to my brand new composter). The green plastic bin was plonked on the bare soil in a shady strip near my back door and I started harvesting my potato peelings and apple cores to add to it.

I read numerous books and leaflets on how to make sure my compost turned out right and tried my best to follow the instructions on what could and couldn't be added. At first, it seemed like magic because however much green stuff I added, the level of compost never seemed to rise. Eventually though, the bin began to reach capacity, and I realised that I needed two bins: one to leave to rot, and another to start afresh.

I had a few false starts: adding a summer's worth of grass left me with a binful striped with sticky layers of solid goo. But about a year later some of the contents had turned into the crumbly dark brown stuff you see in the books, albeit a bit lumpier than I'd have liked and with the occasional brightly coloured fruit sticker jarring the eye (those things never decompose). I added it to the heavy clay soil in my garden and, when I saw how it helped to make the soil lighter and more manageable, I was converted to the composting cause.

It wasn't until I moved house and got my allotment that I realised the full value of having a heap. I brought my plastic bin along, and inherited an identical one from the previous plot holder that was half-full of extremely well-rotted compost. I also inherited a heap so ancient that its wooden stakes were like papier mâché. Once Rick had built a compost box on the plot, the old heap was gradually dismantled. One year I grew a bumper crop of pumpkins right on top of it, and the next year the rotten wood was stacked up as a haven for beneficial insects as well as frogs and lizards and the compost was spread around to create one of the most fertile areas of the plot. As I write, Swiss chard, Little Gem lettuces, radishes and leeks are all enjoying the rich soil.

Bin versus box: which composter is right for you?

There are two basic categories of composting structures: let's call them the heaps and the Daleks. You'll probably have seen the Dalek types being offered at a discount rate by your local council, or on sale in garden centres. They're usually bottomless plastic containers slightly larger than a domestic rubbish bin, with a lid and a 'hatch' at the base for retrieving the compost once it's ready. They work well if you're not trying to compost a huge amount of plant material, and they can produce compost fairly quickly. These bins now come in all shapes and sizes, with exotic names such as the Volcano System, the Komp 800 and the Compost Tumbler.

The other option – the heap – can be just that: organic waste material piled up in a corner of your plot, waiting to decompose. But it's tidier and more efficient if the compost is held in by some kind of square wooden structure fitted with a front that can be removed when you're turning or taking away the compost. You can spend upwards of £70 on wooden composting boxes shaped like beehives or made of woven hazel panels, but most allotmenteers' structures are jerry-built affairs, often consisting of little more than a trio of wooden pallets nailed or strung together, or an old plastic dustbin with holes cut in it. If you go for the pallet design, try to make your compost as snug as possible by tucking cardboard or newspaper in the holes between the slats: that way the heap will warm up, stay moist and decompose more quickly.

After a season or so on my allotment I got my hands on some decent wood that was destined to be burned on a building site, and Rick constructed a double-bay composting system. Actually, that makes it sounds a lot more fancy and hi-tech than it is. It's really no more than two wooden-slatted, lidless boxes, held together with planks nailed at regular intervals to four vertical posts, and lined with cardboard sheeting for insulation. This works extremely well as while one heap is being added to, the other is allowed to rot down. Once it's ready, the compost is dug out and added to the plot, while the other heap is turned into the newly empty bay. Three bays work even better if you have the room and the spare wood.

Another advantage of the heap over the Dalek is that you can easily turn your heap with a fork to check on its progress; turning the heap can also help to speed the rotting process by mixing the browns and greens and introducing air. If you don't like the thought of rooting around in rotting waste, take heart: research from the Centre for Alternative Energy found that a 'high-fibre' approach to composting, where you add large quantities of wastepaper and card to provide extra carbon, removes the need for turning altogether. Although I don't have a £200 garden shredder,

I do have a £20 office shredder, which produces a fluffy, air-filled carbon treat for the heap every week.

The positioning of your composter is probably more important than what it's made out of. As Ken Thompson comments in *An Ear to the Ground*, everybody puts their composter in the coldest, dankest, shadiest corner, when actually it's ideally suited to a sheltered position where the sun can warm the heap and keep the bacteria working at top speed – that's why you'll notice that your compost decomposes faster during the summer than in the winter. If you get conditions in your composter right, the temperature can reach 40–70°C, which is officially known as 'hot composting' and is a great way of killing off any weed seeds that have made their way in. You're most likely to create a hot heap if you're able to build it in one go, rather than adding the materials to it over the course of several months. But don't worry if you can't manage to 'hot compost'. Things will still rot if they're 'cold composted', they just may take a little longer. You should also consider minimising the distance between the heap and the allotment beds you wish to improve, which will save a lot of backbreaking trips back and forth.

Unless you're able to visit your plot once a day, it's advisable to invest in a kitchen caddy. This is not, unfortunately, someone who stands beside you at the stove passing over cooking utensils as if you were a culinary Tiger Woods, but a plastic or ceramic container for storing your kitchen waste until you're ready to take it to your composter. My first one was a handled, lidded plastic box from a well-known Swedish retailer. Composting technology has moved on in the last few years, and lots of kitchen caddies now have in-built carbon filters to absorb any odours from your bin, and kitchen caddy liners to save you the job of washing out the container every time you empty it. Although a ceramic caddy will look more attractive on your kitchen counter, it's also heavier and more fragile, which is worth bearing in mind if you intend to take it on trips to the plot.

What can and can't be composted

Whole books could – and have – been written on this subject. Every experienced composter has their own 'sure-fire' method. Sometimes the recipe describing what can be added to your composter and in what quantities is so detailed that it resembles a complex cookbook, which can be off-putting. But provided you follow some basic rules, you will still end up with compost, even if it doesn't look quite as scrumptious as the stuff you see on *Gardeners' World*.

Here's my list of what you should and shouldn't add to your heap. The four key requirements for decomposition are carbon, nitrogen, water and air. 'Brown' materials supply the carbon, 'greens' supply the nitrogen, and the other two essentials should come from rainfall and exposure to the air, although these can be encouraged by adding extra water in hot weather, and by using a lid or cover (mine's just some cardboard sheeting weighed down with bricks) in wet winter weather and taking it off in the summer. When you're adding material to the heap, think trifle: add the different ingredients in layers no more than 5cm thick. Alternate greens and browns, and add plenty of material with air pockets, such as shredded paper and cardboard.

The browns: carbon-rich materials

🍅 Waste paper, shredded bank statements, bits of cardboard
and used kitchen roll and tissues are all good, especially if
they're scrunched up, which will help air to penetrate to the
centre of the heap.

🍅 Leaves, prunings, sticks and twigs will take longer to decompose, so if you can break them up or shred them, all the
better. Or try putting them in a 'wildlife pile' instead.

The greens: nitrogen-rich materials

🍅 Coffee grounds, eggshells, tea bags, vegetable peelings and
fruit that's over the hill is excellent for your compost: bung
it in!

🍅 Plant waste from your allotment or garden in the form of
carrot tops, beetroot leaves, holey lettuces and substandard
cabbages will help.

🍅 Human hair and pet hair, although it will take some time to
break down, can also be added to your compost.

🍅 Grass clippings need to be added gradually, rather than in
large quantities in one go. When you mow, add a quarter to
the compost heap and use the rest as a mulch: just sprinkle
it around the bases of your soft fruit bushes, onions or other
crops and it will help to suppress weeds and reduce the
amount of watering you need to do.

🍅 There's debate about what weeds you should and shouldn't
add. I avoid adding weeds with tough roots that are very
slow to decompose and could survive the composting
process, such as thistles, dandelions and docks, and any

weeds with flower heads that could add unwanted seeds to the compost. There's no need to throw them away though, as you can put them in a black plastic sack or bucket of water until they've turned to mush and then add them to your heap.

🍅 Manure, feathers and seaweed are all great additions to your heap.

🍅 Comfrey and nettles are both very high in nitrogen and make great compost activators. And who's going to mind if you do a bit of nettle-trimming in your neighbourhood's alleyways?

The no-nos

🍅 Although many books recommend it, I am reluctant to add the contents of my vacuum cleaner bag to my composter, because I know what kind of stuff my vacuum picks up, and some of it definitely isn't compost-friendly – not least the amount of non-natural fibres and chemicals present in carpets and soft furnishings.

🍅 Meat, dairy products and cooked food are best avoided by the home composter, because they attract vermin and flies.

🍅 Dog and cat faeces can't be added because they can contain dangerous organisms that won't be killed by the decomposition process. The same applies to human faeces (having said that, there is the 'humanure' movement dedicated to this rather specialised form of composting; Joseph Jenkins' *Humanure Handbook: A Guide to Composting Human Manure* explains how it all works).

🍅 Glossy magazines are best avoided because of the chemicals used in the printing process, and you should try not to put charcoal from your barbecue on your heap. If you do, it will be there long after you are food for worms. Also, it may have been treated with chemicals that you'd rather not find in your compost.

Allotment diary

January 2005

I am getting my hair cut this morning. The question I am struggling with is: do I ask my hairdresser for a bag of my hair? Apparently it's a good source of nitrogen. But will she think I am a complete weirdo? Hang on a minute, I am a complete weirdo!

What I really want for my compost heap is some manure. I am hoping that one of the horses that is occasionally ridden down my road will decide to leave me a gift. There's only the embarrassment of scooping it up into a bag as my neighbours look on in horror.

Most composting guides recommend shredding larger vegetables and bits of garden waste – melon skins, grapefruit skins, stems thicker than your finger and so on. But if life's too short to stuff a mushroom, it's definitely too short to spend time slicing rotten fruit and vegetables and cutting up pumpkin leaves, and nor do I fancy spending £200 on a shredder, so I simply add my garden and allotment waste as it is. So shoot me, Alan Titchmarsh. It probably takes a few months longer to make the finished product, but unless you have a particular need to get some well-rotted compost very quickly, it seems like an unnecessary extra step to me. The bulky bits will break down, given time. And I've found that adding a mix of different ingredients in small quantities is the key to speedy compost production.

The most common complaint I hear from first-time composters is that the bin is a slimy, smelly chunk of half-rotted grass cuttings. In fact a lot of compost bins I poke around in (note to self: must stop rooting around in people's gardens during summer barbecues) seem to consist of a solid cube of semi-decomposed grass. I avoid this problem altogether by only putting very small quantities of grass cuttings on the compost heap and either spreading the rest of the cuttings back onto the grass or using them as a mulch around my raspberries and blackcurrants. I do add torn-up newspaper and shredded bank statements and bills – after all, what identity thief is going to bother rooting around among the rotting cabbages for strips of paper containing my bank details?

Once the compost is ready, any remaining really bulky bits such as twigs can be removed by hand or with a soil sieve (all that shaking from side to side is great exercise for the waist, by the way) and put back on the heap to continue breaking down. Store any really tough stuff such as sunflower stems and so forth on an 'insect shelter': a pile of wood, broken bamboo canes and long, tough stems that provides a perfect home for hibernating hedgehogs, slow worms and overwintering lacewings and ladybirds, all of which help to control pests such as aphids. This tougher material will also gradually rot away, given time, as you'll know if you've ever found an old shed disintegrating slowly in the corner of a neglected garden. You can spend quite a lot of cash buying handcrafted 'insect boxes' specially designed for the job, but although they may be more picturesque, I am sure my pile is just as effective.

How to give your compost go-faster stripes

You can buy what are marketed as 'compost activators' in the shops to speed up the process. Generally they contain high levels of nitrogen, as well as lime, which help to counter acid conditions that bacteria won't thrive in. If your heap is set up correctly it should trundle along quite nicely without it, so they're not worth the expense. If you want to 'activate' your compost cheaply, sprinkle on a light dusting of ground limestone every time you add a new layer of material and include some human urine to boost nitrogen levels.

Yes, you did read that last sentence correctly. Your pee is a high-nitrogen treat for your heap, virtually sterile and not in short supply. What better way of saving water on toilet flushes and helping your compost break down? However, unless your allotment is extremely well concealed from your neighbours, you may wish to consider collecting your 'activator' in a (preferably opaque) plastic bottle in private to take down to the plot rather than adding it directly. If all this sounds, well, just too weird, grow nitrogen-rich comfrey and cut it for the heap, or harvest nettles and add them – the end result will be exactly the same.

Of course, there are potentially quicker ways of doing things. In Val Bourne's book *Seeds of Wisdom: A Handful of Seasonal Tips from Britain's Head Gardeners*, David Standing, the manager of the eighteenth-century naturalist Gilbert White's garden in Selborne, Hampshire, describes how one of the garden volunteers simply chops up and digs in plant material as he goes, saving himself a trip to the compost heap and earning him the title 'dig-it-in-Jim'.

Finding other ways of shortcutting the compost heap can make life easier and help to provide crops such as pumpkins and beans with the nutrients they crave. Every autumn I decide where the following year's courgettes and winter squash are going to go, and trench compost the area. I got this idea for quick, dirty composting from visiting the Garden Organic gardens in Ryton. There, the gardeners dig a trench or hole where every row of beans or courgette plant is to be sited, about one spade deep, and add in uncomposted kitchen waste generated by their restaurant such as potato peelings, rotten fruit and so on. They cover the waste with soil to stop vermin getting to it, and continue adding and covering until the trench is full. It also helps to line the trench with corrugated cardboard, which will help to retain moisture and is particularly useful for free-draining soils. It's a good idea to put a couple of markers in place so that you don't end up, as I did, crawling around your plot looking for trench-shaped indentations that might reveal where you've buried the compost. Give the trenches a couple of months before planting the crop so that the contents have a chance to rot down.

Top five compost questions and what to do about them

1. **Rodents move in:** I'm not scared of rodents – I think they're rather cute actually – but I did shriek with surprise when I lifted up my plastic bin to harvest some compost and a vole jumped out. It had made a home in some of the shredded

paper and you can see why: here was an attractive bolt hole – warm, dry, and with a few nibbles of food. Assuming you're not keen on offering respite care for homeless rodents, you should avoid adding any cooked food, meat or dairy products to your composter, and be sure to regularly turn the heap or lift up the plastic bin as any four-footed intruders won't like being disturbed and will find somewhere else to nest. If all else fails, there are some rodent-proof bins on the market.

2. **Crumbly compost? It's a solid block of green slime!:** Did you read the bit above about grass cuttings? No? OK, well here's the deal: grass cuttings can be great for your heap but don't add them all at once, as you're forcing your compost to over-dose on greens. Turn it regularly to allow air to get to the bacteria that break down organic material, and add plenty of carbon-rich 'brown' material such as newspaper, toilet rolls and dead leaves in between applications of grass. Newspaper ink is made from natural materials and is approved for organic garden use as it will decompose without introducing anything untoward into your soil.

3. **Things are getting rather smelly:** Contrary to popular expec-tation, well-rotted compost doesn't smell, or if it does, it's a sweet, earthy odour that shouldn't have you reaching for the sick bucket. If your kitchen caddy is the source of the odour, try emptying it more regularly, or investing in one with a carbon filter that'll help to absorb the smell. If the stench is emanating from the heap or bin itself, it's probably because you're adding too much green material and not enough

brown. This is a particular problem in the autumn when you're clearing your plot of heaps of plants such as pumpkins and runner beans. Get to work ripping up some wastepaper and layer it in with the green stuff, and if you can, get a fork into the compost and give it a good turn. This should help to restart the decomposition process and the smell should fade.

4. **The compost is infested with little brown flies:** Fruit flies, as the name suggests, will be attracted to the bits of kitchen waste you add to your compost. They could be getting to the fruit when it's waiting to be composted in your kitchen, or when it's left exposed to the air on top of the compost pile. Books will tell you that by covering kitchen waste in newspaper, soil or a thin layer of grass cuttings every time you add some to the heap, you can avoid fruit flies. In my experience this isn't completely true: some flies will find their way to the fruit whatever you try, although everything you can do to prevent the flies reaching the fruit to lay their eggs will help cut down on their numbers. The upside is that fruit flies are harmless to humans, albeit rather irritating.

5. **Ugh, my compost's full of little red worms – and slugs:** You may think this is a problem, but it's actually a good sign of a healthy heap. The presence of these brandling or red wiggler worms means that everything is progressing well: these composting specialists will be working along with the bacteria and insects to break down the material into humus. Try to get over your aversion, because these worms are your compost-making machines. The other thing that these worms tell you is that your compost isn't ready yet, as they tend to disperse

once their work is done and the compost is nearing completion. And the slugs? Well, of all the places slugs could be found on your allotment, the compost heap is probably the least annoying. There they can munch away on vegetable waste, rather than eating your prize lettuces. They also tend to congregate around the rims and lids of plastic bins, so if you're squeamish, wear gloves when checking your compost.

Opening up a Can-O-Worms

Most compost addicts will consider moving onto the hard stuff after a few years of regular compost creation – the wormery. This is a plastic bin designed to provide the perfect home for worms to eat your kitchen waste. Essentially you're creating a "worm factory", where each worm is a composting machine that processes your kitchen waste and turns it into wormcasts (excreted soil) and liquid feed, both of which are great for your allotment's soil. Most wormeries are made up of a stack of trays: the worms munch their way up through the vegetable waste in the bottom tray while you add fresh waste to the top layer: eventually the worms will abandon the bottom tray once they've finished eating all the waste, so you can harvest the resulting wormcasts, then reposition that tray to the top of the pile and start adding waste to it. Most also have a reservoir with a tap at the bottom which you can use to drain off the liquid feed.

Wormeries are not ideal for the allotment unless you visit very regularly and have a sheltered position in a shed or storage box to house it, as freezing temperatures will kill off your little composting army. But if you have room for one at home in your garage or shed, where you are on hand to tend to it daily, a wormery can be a valuable addition, providing you with a source of natural fertiliser in the form of the worms' by-products. It's also a great way of teaching children about what happens to their waste – they'll be endlessly fascinated by watching the progress of their very own worm farm.

Despite reading up on all the worm composting literature, I've not got around to buying one yet, partly because of the expense and partly because the shortcuts I make when composting would result in some very unhappy (in other words, dead) worms. You really do have to shred the waste so the worms have a chance to chew, and you must keep a close eye on the worms' diet and environment so that they are working at top performance. Much like us, worms need a varied diet, warmth, moisture and oxygen; they dislike too much acidity, so lots of citrus fruit is a no-no, and you can't add any non-vegetable waste such as fish or meat.

You shouldn't just gather any old worms though, as the worm you'll generally find in the soil on your allotment, *Lumbricus terrestris*, is a different beast to the red wiggler or brandling worm, *Eisenia foetida*, that is best suited to wormery life. You should get a supply of the right kind of worm when you buy the wormery.

If you want to know more, including how to make your own wormery, the seminal works on worms are Mary Appelhof's book *Worms Eat My Garbage* and Amy Stewart's *The Earth Moved: On the Remarkable Achievements of Earthworms*; check the bibliography for more details.

Spotlight on...

PUMPKIN ROUGE VIF D'ÉTAMPES

This was the first pumpkin variety I ever grew and it is still my favourite. *Rouge Vif d'Étampes* hails from France (*Étampes* is a commune of Paris) and is always referred to as being the variety that inspired the fairy godmother's magical transformation of pumpkin into coach in the Cinderella story; some seed catalogues even market it as the Cinderella pumpkin. *Rouge Vif d'Étampes* has probably been around in France since the 1830s, but its seeds were first sold in the USA by W Atlee Burpee in 1883. Two years later, the French classic *Le Jardin Potager* (The Vegetable Garden) by MM Vilmorin-Andrieux reported that this was the variety of squash most commonly seen at the central market in Paris.

Its deep orangey-red skin ('*rouge vif*' means bright red) and flattened globe shape make it the quintessential pumpkin for me; ideal both for Halloween carving and for culinary uses, it usually weighs in at between four and ten kilograms, with two or three fruits on each plant. Its flavour is not the absolute finest you'll find in the winter squash family (for me, that honour goes to a squash from Guatemala called Pink Banana), but the flesh is ideal for tasty soups and hearty stews, and is also particularly good for making a no-holds barred, calorie time bomb pumpkin pie, accompanied by lashings of cream, as it's served in the deep south of the USA.

Seed sources: Seeds by Size, Organic Gardening Catalogue, Thomas Etty Esq.

Tending and reaping

Nine
Weeds and watering

> We have three problems. How to cope with too
> much wet, how to cope with too much dry and – this
> is the really interesting one – how to cope with both
> within the same year as a matter of course.

Monty Don, _My Roots: A Decade in the Garden_, 2005

When I think about my little patch of earth, cornered between
tennis courts and football pitches, the farmer's field and the
housing estate, I don't picture the lettuces under the cold frame or
the raspberry canes bursting into leaf. I think about the couch grass
that's inching its evil roots into the soil next to the Swiss chard, the
patch of docks on the pathway that have designs on a
neighbouring bed, and the dandelion seeds gently drifting onto the
bare soil like special forces parachuting over enemy lines.

Weeds are usually the one thing that destroys the confidence
and enthusiasm of the new allotmenteer. Sometimes they force
newcomers to give up altogether. Writing in _The Guardian_
newspaper, Sally Weale explained how the weeds that spread 'at
the rate and with the destructiveness of Ebola' brought her to
breaking point with her plot. This is a common allotment horror

story. If you take over a plot that's been well tended, you may be lulled into a false sense of security and find the weeds sneak up on you gradually before putting you in a horticultural half nelson. If your plot is a jungle to begin with, you may feel like giving up before the first season has ended.

I nearly did. I inherited my plot around May. I read in the allotment information sent out by the local council, which all comes on bright green stationery, that I could call in the allotment's ground staff to clear the plot for me using a rotovator (a kind of junior plough) for the princely sum of around £2. Some sites offer this service, while others may have a pool of Rotovators and other tools that you can hire and use. At the time, I thought: what a great idea! With the land cleared, I'll get a head start for the coming season. But the Rotovator didn't remove the roots of the perennial weeds like thistles and docks. Oh no. It just broke them into thousands of tiny pieces, like mini-landmines waiting to explode into growth. Inevitably I didn't have time to follow swiftly behind, clearing the roots and making beds. I steered clear for a few weeks, only to find that when I blithely wandered down to the plot to sow some seeds, the bare soil was gone, replaced by a million stalks, even more virulent than before.

I managed to carve out a small bed at one end of the plot, where I planted climbing French beans and some strawberries, and put in some blackcurrant bushes my dad had donated. It was a sorry sight: the beans hurtled up their poles but looked like an island of order in a sea of confusion. Why worry, you may ask. So what if things get a bit messy, you can always clear the ground later. It's not like the weed police are going to come and give you a caution, is it? Well yes, actually. With the allotment community to think about, your weed problem is everyone's weed problem. One of the clauses present in many allotment agreements – that piece of paper most people probably sign without bothering to read the small print, as I did – impels you to keep your plot 'in a good state of cultivation and fertility and in good condition'. That includes not allowing weed seeds to proliferate and spread to other plots. Failure to do so can result in what's referred to in hushed tones as the 'untidy-plot letter' – a warning from the allotment managers (usually the local council) that unless you clean up your act, you could be evicted from your plot. I've received two of these since I took on my allotment, and each one had me writhing with embarrassment.

The first untidy-plot letter turned up a few months in, just when I was at my lowest ebb, having put in an awful lot of hard labour without very much in the way of vegetables to show for it. I decided to carry on, probably more out of pig-headedness than any expectation that I could turn things around. I managed to chop down the seed heads that were getting increasingly dirty looks from my neighbours, who were rightly concerned about windblown weeds scattering onto their plots. With a demanding full-time job, I just didn't have the time or resources to turn a piece of rough ground into a productive vegetable patch in one season, and I was foolish to think I could. Once that fact dawned on me the autumn after I took the allotment, I set about finding ways to stem the onslaught of the weeds while I got small sections of the plot into some sort of usable state. Slowly, painstakingly, over the course of five years, I have managed to get the whole of the plot into production, barring one corner next to my storage box that remains stubbornly untameable. But weeds remain my number one worry.

Know your enemy

I decided that, as Sun Tzu says in *The Art of War*, the best way to defeat your enemy is to know them. So a few years back I invested in a weed identification book with drawings of each weed variety as full-grown plants and as seedlings. Weed guide in hand, I crawled around my plot separating the fat hen from the fennel – no, scratch that, I soon learned that fennel seedlings can spread like weeds too, so make that the carrots from the couch grass.

Brace yourself; here's the list of weeds I've recorded growing on my plot: common chickweed, fat hen, dandelion, hedge bindweed, groundsel, hairy bitter-cress, creeping buttercup, knotgrass, redshank, plantain, small nettle, smooth sow-thistle, broad-leaved dock, couch grass and creeping thistle. And probably a few more besides that remain unidentified. I've managed to eradicate some of the perennial weeds almost entirely – the creeping thistle and docks only make occasional appearances like the ghost of Christmas past. But there are some annual weeds I salute like old adversaries when they sprout each spring.

Not only did this tactic of identifying the enemy prevent me pulling up the seedlings of my precious crops, it also gave me a profile of my soil, because some weeds only thrive in certain conditions. For instance, the creeping buttercup, which is one of the most common weeds on my plot, likes damp, slightly acidic soils. No surprise then that my soil is damp and slightly acidic. The worst mistake I made as an allotment beginner was to see a small, lush-looking plant that I'd swear hadn't been there when I visited the plot the previous weekend, and jump to the conclusion that it was some exciting new crop rather than recognising it as a weed. If you can't face identifying every strange plant on your plot, here's my number one rule of weed spotting: any seedling on your plot that looks particularly healthy or fast growing is a weed; anything spindly, weak and slug-munched is probably a vegetable. Get rid of the former before it becomes a flowering dock plant, dandelion or bindweed.

When I grouch about the relentless onslaught of weeds encroaching upon my vegetables, friends will regularly quote Ralph Waldo Emerson's famous maxim that a weed is a plant whose virtues have never been discovered. Clearly neither they – nor Emerson – ever had an allotment. As garden writer Michael Pollan has explained in *Second Nature: A Gardener's Education*, weeds are not just plants in the wrong place. They are plants that have managed to adapt to the presence of humans by taking advantage of ground disturbed by humans, be that roadside verges, railway sidings or your allotment. They are 'nature's ambulance chasers, carpetbaggers, and confidence men', as Pollan puts it. Weeds can bully a bed of vegetables into submission with their sheer physical presence, by blocking out light and strangling young stems, and they also take up valuable nutrients that your crops need.

Many allotmenteers say bindweed is their bête noire. Not me. I might be about to commit allotment blasphemy here, but I don't have a big problem with bindweed. Or rather, I have a big problem with bindweed, but it has dawned on me that, rather like James Bond movies on television at Christmas, it'll always be with me and I must simply tolerate it. Even if you don't recognise the name, you'll have spotted bindweed with its pretty white or pink trumpet-shaped flowers, perhaps rambling through a hedge on the side of the road. Provided you're vigilant, it's easy to keep under control through regular exhumations of the white roots that spread undetected underground until they surface where you least expect it. The tiniest scrap of root will always be left behind, and the plant will soon start to regrow. But eradicating it is universally agreed to be impossible, so why go to the bother of spraying with weedkiller?

Finding out more about weeds can also add a different dimension to your allotment habits. Ralph Waldo Emerson was half right – weeds do have some virtues but they *have* been discovered. People throughout history have found medicinal, horticultural or culinary uses for most weeds you can name. The invasive perennial weed horsetail, an odd-looking plant with leaves that resemble pine needles, is ancient: it's been around for thirty million years. It used to be known as pewterwort because its high silica content made it very useful for scouring pots and cleaning pewter. Your plot may look a state, but my, your pewter will sparkle. You don't have any pewter? Well, perhaps you should invest in some, then you can just tell your nosey neighbours you're growing the stuff for a reason. And couch grass? Just say you've decided to become a herbalist. The seventeenth-century herbalist Nicholas Culpeper believed this weed to be 'worth five acres of carrots twice told over'.

For me, the most annoying and possibly most prolific of the annual weeds – those that spring up in early summer and die back in the autumn, but not before they have dropped their payload of evil seeds – is the delightfully named fat hen, less well known by its Latin name, *Chenopodium album*. You'll have seen this plant thriving on waste ground, or perhaps tucked into a crack between wall and pavement: it's a nondescript plant with dull silvery-green leaves and clusters of green, bobbly flowers. I don't garner much comfort from the fact that this weed was sometimes grown for food – indeed it's now a popular ingredient in gourmet restaurants. (It's worth knowing if you keep chickens, however, that fat hen seeds, as the name suggests, make a very good chicken feed.) Every time I sow a row of vegetable seeds, the earth disturbed in the process will throw up a few fat hen seeds along with other interlopers, which inevitably germinate far more prolifically than the intended crop. Another of my weed regulars, the hairy bittercress, has even evolved a way of shooting its seeds from the pods to a distance of nearly a metre, hence its other common name, poppers.

Plants you've deliberately cultivated can become as troublesome as weeds if you're not careful: chicory roots, overgrown Swiss chard stems the girth of my arm, and potatoes that have gone AWOL and resprouted in the following year's lettuce bed have all played havoc with my crop rotation schemes. And you may encounter what are known in polite gardening circles as 'volunteer plants', where flowers have dropped their seed around the neighbouring soil. The name springs from the fact that the plants volunteer to grow, rather than being sown by you for a purpose. You can use these to your advantage: one year my most prolific tomato plants were the ones that had grown from the seeds of tomatoes accidentally dropped and crushed into the soil. And when my row of chive flowers dumped their seed far and wide, I discovered that cuttings of the tiny seedlings were delicious sprinkled on top of a salad or sandwiched between hummus and lettuce in a pita.

Aside from being able to identify individual weeds from your crops, it's also important that you know the difference between annual and perennial weeds. The annuals – fat hen, chickweed, speedwell and hairy bittercress, for instance – will spring up each spring from seeds scattered from the previous year's flower heads, then die off in the winter after flowering and seeding themselves to complete the cycle. Perennials, on the other hand, will survive the winter by storing nutrients in their roots. While they may die back above the surface of the soil, they'll be alive below ground, and as soon as the weather warms up they will multiply across the plot using spreading roots – creeping thistle, horsetail, couch grass, dandelion and dock are among the usual suspects in this group.

Once you've sussed their utterly different modus operandi, it's obvious why your approach to weed destruction needs to be different too. Let's take the annual weeds first. Your main period of work when it comes to weeding annuals will be spring and early summer, before the young plants have had a chance to flower and set seed.

Weeding tools and techniques

Not for nothing do gardeners repeat the old adage 'one year's seeding, seven years' weeding'. In other words, neglect annual weeds at your peril, because they can and will multiply if allowed to scatter their seed. The only way around this is to cultivate a dogged 'little and often' approach, hoeing down a weed every time you see it. For slightly more expansive weeding sessions around larger crops, it's best to set to work when the soil is quite dry. The aim here is to slice the weed stems as you move between rows of crops, for which a longer-handled hoe is both more practical and less backbreaking. Move the hoe backwards and forwards just below the surface of the soil, taking care not to damage the crops. The sharper the blade on your hoe, the easier the job will be. Regular hoeing gradually reduces the number of annuals that come up from hundreds to dozens. If you have a bare patch of earth that you've just cleared after harvesting or weeding in spring or early summer, don't let it stay empty for long. It's worth having something – anything – planted, as you're more likely to bother weeding if you think there's a crop at the end of it, and also the growing plants will provide the weeds with some competition.

But what about perennial weeds, which will simply regrow if hoed? With these, it's the roots below the surface that you need to eradicate, and it's a job you can do at any time of year. When I spot a particularly heinous thistle, there's nothing more satisfying than throttling it and pulling it clean out of the ground. You may be itching to start this job as soon as you've rented your plot, but wait until after a good downpour. When I first started gardening I remember wondering why weeding was such hard work, until one of my neighbours gently pointed out that two weeks into a hot dry spell is probably the most difficult time to be trying to winkle dandelion roots out of the ground. If the soil's anything other than gooey you'll probably leave something behind, and six weeks on you'll be back where you started when the root regrows and the plant pokes through the surface again. I use a hand trowel for close work around crops when the soil is damp, prising out the dandelions from around the base of easily damaged plants and seedlings. This can be a Zen-like activity that's ideally suited to a preoccupied mind incapable of more skilful jobs. As the inimitable garden writer Christopher Lloyd put it in *The Well-Tempered Garden*, weeding is a task that leaves a grower's mind 'free to develop the plot for their next novel or to perfect the brilliant repartee with which they should have countered a relative's latest example of unreasonableness'. But if you're dealing with an overgrown plot that hasn't been weeded for weeks, months or even years, you'll need unending patience as well as a digging fork and a pair of thick gloves to root out those vicious perennial bullies like brambles and thickets that tend to colonise neglected plots.

Allotment diary

October 2004

I spent a few hours at the weekend in an overgrown area of the allotment, battling with thistle roots that looked unpleasantly like fat white maggots. The feeling I got from rooting them out of the ground was akin to pulling out a loose baby tooth as a child – painful, but somehow deeply satisfying. It's hard to explain to non-gardeners why weeding can be such a relaxing and stress-relieving activity. Perhaps it's the feeling of bringing order from chaos. Or maybe it's just the bracing effect of an hour in the fresh air and a break from the office.

Even if the ground is deliciously moist, there is a powerful argument against doing too much aggressive weeding over the winter, particularly if you haven't got around to planting green manure plants on any bare patches or beds. Say, for example, you've got a patch of ground recently cleared of potatoes that you plan to grow some lettuces on next year, but from late autumn onwards, it's empty. Gradually a few perennial weeds appear: some clumps of grass, a bit of clover. You could clear every single weed from the patch to keep it looking pristine. But they are helping to hold the soil structure together during heavy rain and preventing nutrients from being leached away from the soil. And the clover is doing another important job because the tiny nodules on its roots provide a home for bacteria that are nitrogen fixers – micro-organisms that take nitrogen from the air and convert it into a form that plants can use. If you let the clover grow and then either dig it into the soil or put it on the compost heap once it's growing time again, it will benefit your soil. I do try to get rid of perennial weeds with creeping roots as soon as I can, such as couch grass, docks and creeping thistles. Even so, they won't put on a huge amount of growth over winter and can be left until early spring. Anyway, that's my argument for not spending hours weeding in winter, and I am sticking to it.

Mulching – the technique of laying something on the surface of the soil to suppress weed growth and enhance the health of the earth – is invaluable for keeping weeds under control. As described in chapter three, it's the best way of coping with a new plot that's simply too large to deal with all at once, but it's also very handy for keeping smaller patches of allotment earth weed-free.

For instance, I've been plagued with weeds growing under my blackcurrant bushes: dandelions, greater plantains and even escapees doing a runner from the strawberry patch. They weren't doing a lot of harm to the currants, but their seeds would probably have spread to other parts of the plot where they were definitely not wanted. So rather than risk a back injury by scrabbling about under the bushes trying to dig or hoe the weeds, I made a mulch of old newspaper (two editions of the *Guardian* did the trick), to the recipe described in the earlier chapter, and left it. A couple of months later and I lifted what was left of the paper to find that all the weeds had been obliterated. It's worth bearing in mind that slugs and snails can find the damp hidey holes created by some mulches rather attractive, so if you use it around delicate or slug-prone plants, you'll need to conduct regular patrols to remove them. As I've already explained, carpet is a heavy-duty mulch among many other mulch options, but it's perhaps best avoided in favour of cardboard or another mulch for reasons discussed in chapter three.

Water wisdom

The other major benefit of mulches is that they help to cut back on the need for watering – that other time-consuming activity you'll find yourself doing on every trip to the plot, in summer at least. Mulches slow down evaporation of water from the soil, as you'll know if you've ever lifted up a wad of grass clippings to find that the earth is damp underneath, even if the surrounding soil is dry.

Some allotment sites – mine included – have year-round hose-pipe bans. Good. Hosepipes are an enemy of good organic gardening, in my opinion. As you'll have already gathered, I am not one to make life hard for myself, but access to a hosepipe encourages lazy watering; just spraying the stuff around doesn't always reach the plants that need it. You can try a little experiment to see how ineffective this is by spraying a patch of ground with your hose for, say, a minute. Then take your trowel and have a dig down. I'll wager the water won't have penetrated more than a few centimetres, depending on the consistency of your soil, and certainly not deep enough to reach the plants' roots. Also, when you have to trudge back and forth dozens of times between the standpipe and your plot, it'll really concentrate your mind as to how to save water. I have four watering cans at hand so that all visitors can muck in (especially those who envisaged a pleasant afternoon sipping a cool lemonade and admiring the vegetables from their deckchair).

Allotment diary   July 2005

Wet weather in July isn't something I am routinely in the mood for shouting from the rooftops about, but the downpours this weekend signalled I didn't need to spend time sweating around the allotment, cans in hand, to quench the thirst of my crops.

Don't make the assumption that every vegetable benefits from a regular dousing. Not so, it seems. I'd been diligently watering my onions for a couple of seasons when someone broke the news to me that they don't benefit at all from extra water. Since then I haven't bothered and haven't seen a dropping off in the size or quality of the bulbs. Likewise I discovered that there are certain points in the growth cycle when watering will make a big difference, but others when it won't. For instance, all seedlings transferred to their cropping location should be placed in well-watered soil and kept moist until they are settled in. And most crops, including peas, beans, sweetcorn, courgettes and potatoes, will get a big boost from a dousing while they are flowering. However, root vegetables such as beetroots, carrots, radishes, parsnips and turnips may end up producing more leaf than flesh if you give them lots of extra water.

You can collect water by sticking a bucket or old dustbin out in the open in the winter, but a more efficient way is to install a water butt that picks up the run-off from your greenhouse or shed, if you're lucky enough to have one. You can use 'grey water' – what goes down the plughole when you've done the washing-up or had a bath – too, if you can face carrying it to the plot. But it makes a lot more sense to find ways of helping the soil hang onto the moisture it already contains, and to focus on getting the water you do add right to the roots, where it's needed. Mulches will help a great deal, but there are other ways.

Improving the condition of your soil will help to cut down the need for watering. The more organic material you can add to the soil in the form of compost from your heap, the more water it will be able to hold. The first year I took on a plot, it was waterlogged all winter. These days, with the addition of lots of compost and some extra drainage, it's simply sodden. Now that's progress.

One trick I learned from my allotment neighbours was creating a dinner-plate sized indentation in the soil around each plant to prevent the water from running off (usually towards the weeds encroaching from the pathway). This idea can be further refined by directing the water right down to the roots. Just slice the end off a plastic bottle and bury it upside down next to the plant – preferably when you plant out the seedling to avoid disturbing it later – with the lip of the bottle level and just a centimetre or two above the soil surface. You can either leave the lid off, or keep it on but loosen it, depending on how fast you want the water to emerge. When you water, pour straight into the bottle and it will gradually spread through the soil rather than puddling on the surface.

It also helps to make sure plants have a well-developed root system to take advantage of every drop of water they can reach. One ruse I discovered by trial and error. I noticed that the tomato seedlings I grew threw out new roots from the base of the stem. So when I transplant them onto the plot, I always make sure the lowest leaf is just above the level of the soil, so that they can develop a strong root system. With pumpkins or any other squash that tends to creep around, you can pin down the growing stems at intervals to allow more roots to grow, which will help to keep them from getting thirsty. Wind will also evaporate a lot of water from the surface of the soil. The best edible windbreaks I've found are raspberry canes or, if you want something really tall, Jerusalem artichokes and cardoons. You can grow vegetables that benefit from a bit of cooler shade, such as lettuces, in their shadow.

Spotlight on...

BRANDYWINE TOMATOES

Beefsteaks, those outsize giants of the tomato world, are, at their worst, bland and watery. But the heritage variety Brandywine will blow your beefsteak preconceptions out of the water. An advertisement for Brandywine in a 1889 edition of *The Ohio Farmer* describes it as the 'largest, smoothest and handsomest of all', and most tomato experts agree that its flavour is one of the finest

around. The variety dates back to the 1880s, that much we know, but its origins are somewhat confused. Some seed companies claim that it was developed by the Amish community in the USA and named after Brandywine Creek in Chester County, Pennsylvania, but I'll leave that to the heritage vegetable historians to debate and concentrate instead on the star qualities of this monster, whose fruit can weigh as much as half a kilogram apiece, sometimes even one kilogram. Curiously, it's what's known as a potato leaf variety, and the leaves really do look like its relative in the *solanaceae* family.

Brandywine's superior flavour has made it one of the pre-eminent tomato varieties on the heritage seed circuit, but you're unlikely to see the fruits on sale, because their thin skins – a boon for the home grower – make it hard to transport to market without damage. The flesh is particularly good in sandwiches, as a single slice will fill the bread edge to edge, and it makes delicious passata and tomato soup.

Given the size of the fruits, which have pretty pinky-red skins and splashes of green on the tops, Brandywine plants need very solid support from stakes to prevent the plants from toppling over. Once four trusses – the tomato's flowering stem – have begun to set fruit, pinch out the growth at the top of the plant to prevent it putting more energy into new growth and allow it to concentrate on fruiting.

Seed sources: Organic Gardening Catalogue, Thomas Etty Esq., Tamar Organics, Thompson and Morgan.

Ten

Pests and diseases

Do what we can, summer will have its flies.

Ralph Waldo Emerson, 'Prudence',
from Essays: First series, 1841

One October I was on my hands and knees, grubbing about in a small bed of Swiss chard, Little Gem and Lollo Rosso lettuces, picking out some weeds by hand and harvesting leaves here and there for that night's salad bowl. Then I spotted a brown slug, a good ten centimetres long, just beginning to nibble its way through a lettuce leaf. Once my initial repulsion had faded and I began to take a closer look, I realised there was a strange beauty to this creature: its cappuccino-coloured body was edged with neon orange and purple frills and its head was laced with delicate lilac veins and sported two pairs of antennae that recoiled at the slightest touch.

However, somewhere in my head was running the thought that if I left the slug alone, by morning that spot would be littered with lettuce skeletons. I picked him up with a trowel and placed him at my knees, still undecided as to what to do next (note how I'd started referring to the slug as 'him'). The slug retracted his antennae and became stiff and still, as if in grim expectation of his fate. Should I put him in the hedge to eat something wild? Would he come crawling back? Yes, he would.

I dispatched the slug in the quickest, most humane way I could think of, snipping him in half with the blunt pair of kitchen scissors I had used to cut the lettuce. Better that than a protracted death slathered in salt or drowning slowly in a pool of beer. The coiled guts spilled onto the soil and I left them there, hoping a bird from the nearby hedgerow would at least benefit from the kill. Nevertheless, it would have been better, for my tender soul at least, if I'd kept the slug off the lettuce bed in the first place.

Much as with weeds, an exact definition of a pest is hard to come by. For example, some allotmenteers curse the cats that treat the fine soil of their seed bed as a litter tray, or the stray dog (or child) that tramples newly planted seedlings. In the 1980s BBC series *The Victorian Kitchen Garden*, the wonderfully knowledgeable head gardener Harry Dodson gleaned from various gardening books of the past a list of Victorian pest remedies. One of these advised, under the heading 'Boys': 'Smear garden wall top with red ochre and grease. Indelible mixture. Observe passing trouser seats.'

Some organic gardeners take the concept of biodiversity so seriously that they shrink from the concept of 'pests'. They believe they can share their plot with all God's creatures, so either they eschew any kind of pest control, or they leave some sacrificial plants for the caterpillars to feast on because they love to see the fluttering of the cabbage white butterfly later in the summer. The bottom line is that it's better to fortify your plants against attack rather than taking reactionary measures once the beasties have struck. Like us, plants are at their most vulnerable when stressed through lack of water or nutrients, or because of the wrong soil conditions or temperatures. If your plants are healthy they have a much better chance of fighting off whatever nature throws at them.

Slugs and snails and puppy dogs' tails

Nonetheless, even healthy plants fall prey to slugs, which seem to do the most damage to the widest range of fruit and vegetables. Everyone appears to agree on their universal peskiness, but why are they so troublesome? In an online guide to slug control that he posted on the Cardiff University website, slug expert Dr Bill Symondson called Britain the 'slug capital of the world', and with good reason. Our temperate climate is ideal for the upwardly mobile slug and there are at least thirty different types in the UK, although not all of them will be responsible for the damage to your allotment plants.

A whole industry has grown up around keeping slugs away from prized crops. A quick scan of any garden centre worth its salt will throw up – well – salt, plus at least a dozen slug control devices, from the traditional blue pellet and 'slug pubs' – dishes buried in the ground that lure slugs to a foamy death in a pool of cheap beer (they're actually just attracted to the yeast – a spoon full of instant yeast powder in warm water works just as well) to copper tapes and aerosol cans containing yucca extract, both of which are reputed to repel slugs.

There's intense disagreement about just how wildlife-unfriendly traditional slug pellets are. The slugs are attracted to the lumps of cereal and are killed by the poison – usually metaldehyde – that they contain. The manufacturers claim that, when used responsibly, pellets pose no threat to wildlife, the environment or pets, whereas wildlife charities blame them for killing off hedgehogs and garden birds that eat the dead slugs. The official advice from Garden Organic is that slug pellets should not be used in an organic garden because they contain toxic chemicals. And given the number of alternatives now available, they simply should not be necessary as part of your battle against the slugs.

The slug pub has its drawbacks, too, however. Lots of useful insects are likely to fall to a yeasty death if you place the 'pub' at ground level, including the very useful ground beetle, which just happens to eat slug eggs. The organic gardening expert, Bob Flowerdew, suggests offering such beneficial insects an escape route via a twig or two to act as a ramp out, or you can make sure the lip of the dish is a centimetre above the ground. The trouble with the slug pub approach is that you'll need an awful lot of them to make a significant dent in your slug population on even the smallest allotment. Buttered leaves or scooped out grapefruit halves scattered around vulnerable crops are particularly attractive to slugs, who then gather to feast on them and can be picked off.

Another approach is to put barriers around vulnerable plants to stop the slugs reaching them in the first place. Copper tape, rings and mats repel slugs with a tiny electrical charge contained within the metal, or there's a wildlife-friendly gel that can be squirted around plants and is reputed to stop the slugs in their tracks. There are also cheap or free options such as encircling tender crops with crushed eggshells, sharp gravel, wood ash or soot, all of which should be too uninviting for the slugs to cross, although these will need careful monitoring in wet conditions to ensure they don't wash away or become ineffective, and must be regularly reapplied. A sprinkling of bran is another method to test out, as slugs love eating the stuff but it makes them swell up and die. Growers report differing levels of success with the various barrier methods, so it's a question of trying them out to see what works for you. But for a really radical solution to your slug problem, it pays to see things in a different light. As allotmenteer Graham put it in Chris Opperman's book *Allotment Folk*: 'You don't have an excess of slugs, you have a duck deficiency.' Ducks love hoovering up slugs, so their benefits are obvious; it just depends if these outweigh the extra responsibility that keeping poultry will involve.

On the beat

I can't really picture spending my weekends buttering cabbage leaves. One of the best methods I've found of staving off slug damage is weekly or daily slug patrols. The patrol is as crude as it sounds and entails heading out at dusk or dawn with a torch and a pair of gloves, to get down on hands and knees and pick the slugs and snails off as they dine. They can be dispatched by whichever method you find the least distasteful: dunked in salted water or snipped with secateurs and the remains left for the birds or hedgehogs to vacuum up without fear of harm. Some allotmenteers refuse to kill slugs, preferring to re-home them somewhere else. This does seem excessively maudlin to a slug patroller like me, but if you must insist on it, the compost heap is a good re-homing pen, provided you keep it topped up with munchable plant waste, otherwise they could be back in your salad bed before you can say slime.

My other favourite weapon is the nematode, a microscopic parasite worm that naturally occurs in the soil. This smart approach to the slug problem has only been available to the allotmenteer for a few years, but is already proving hugely popular with organic gardeners. You order a sachet of powder containing the nematode *Phasmarhabditis hermaphrodita* – I don't think it's been given a more pronounceable common name yet – which then arrives through the post. The temperature of the soil must be at least 5°C for the nematodes to work, which limits their application to between mid-March and October, roughly speaking: if in doubt, check how cold the soil is with a soil thermometer, which can be bought for a few pounds from garden centres. If you can't use the nematodes immediately, you must keep them cool. They can last up to two weeks in the fridge, unopened. (When my nematodes were delivered, I put them in the fridge, as per the directions, until the weekend, although I was worried that Rick would assume they were a new form of hummus and eat them on some toasted pita bread.) When you have fifteen minutes to spare, mix the powder with water and sprinkle it onto the area you want to treat. The nematodes fan out through the soil, 300,000 of them jostling for space in every square metre. When they come across a slug, they home in on it, wriggle their way inside its body and release bacteria that make the slug stop eating and eventually die.

Once the slug is dispatched, the nematodes leave the body and hunt out another victim. The beauty of this system is that it's quick to apply, harmless to pretty much everyone else, including pets, birds and children, and effective for around six weeks. It is, however, rather more expensive than a pack of slug pellets, and you must be sure to follow the instructions to the letter. The nematodes should start to work within about three days. Other varieties of nematodes have also been developed as biological controls for other pests, including vine weevils, leatherjackets and chafer grubs (the fat white larvae you might find damaging the roots of your lawn that emerge as menacing-looking but harmless June bugs). It's worth mentioning that not all nematodes are beneficial. The nematode family – also known as roundworms – is a large one, containing thousands of different species in all sorts of environments. Some nematodes cause elephantiasis in humans, while one species is a parasite of the placenta of sperm whales and can reach nine metres long. The damaging nematodes you're most likely to come across in your garden are eelworms, which eat plant roots and attack tubers.

And what of snails? There seems to be less of a problem with snails on allotments than in gardens. It's probably because snails love stone walls, which tend to feature more in gardens than allotments. Nevertheless they can still be a menace on the plot, particularly if you have raised beds where they can lurk. Nematodes are reported to have some impact on the snail population as well as on slugs, but a catch-and-dispatch regime is still advisable. There is something particularly repellent about hearing a snail shell crushed under your welly, though. If you can't bear the thought of that, Bob Flowerdew has a rather Heath Robinson way of putting captured snails to work. He suggests making a home for them – a 'snailery', if you will – using some pots stacked on a plastic tray surrounded by water so they can't slime away. You then gorge the gastropods on old lettuce and cabbage leaves and swill out the droppings to use in liquid feed. I suspect you have to be very fond of snails to give that one a try.

Allotment diary
July 2005

Never, ever decide to find out where the snails that are eating your prized sedums are living, discover a dozen juicy gastropods behind a wall and crush them with your shoe, only to realise that what you're actually wearing on your feet is not your garden clogs but a pair of fluffy blue slippers. Let's just say I am glad they're washable…

Gooseberry fool

Nematodes are unusual as an organic alternative to pesticides in that they're quick to use, even if it takes a while for them to take effect. Unfortunately other wildlife-friendly, organic approaches to ridding your plot of bugs are pretty labour-intensive, involving removing the pests by hand.

Take the method for dealing with gooseberry sawfly, for example. Sawfly lay their eggs on the leaves around the base of gooseberry and red and white currant bushes. Once hatched, the larva crawls into the juicy leaves of your precious plants and munches its way out from the centre, getting bigger and bigger just like the hungry caterpillar in the children's story – although this one's not cute and it doesn't like cherry pie. Leave this pest unattended for a few days, and the lovely lime-green foliage on your gooseberry bush will be chomped into oblivion – and no leaves equals no fruit. There can be several larva cycles within one season, and the final generation of sawfly will spend the winter in the soil around the bush as cocoons.

All the books on organic pest management will tell you that there are things you can do about this: pruning the bush into an 'open goblet' or fan shape, for instance, because the larvae like sheltered territory. Unfortunately although this may reduce your sawfly count somewhat, you'll still end up with a bare bush if they do strike. So the answer is to engage in frequent checks for the eggs or larvae. Pick them up and squish them one by one when they appear from the middle of spring until early autumn. (If you can't bear to squish, you could put the larvae in a bowl and feed them to your goldfish or garden birds.) The trouble is, the larvae are hard to spot as they often lie along the line of the leaf veins to camouflage themselves. And this method's all very well if you have one or two gooseberry bushes, but what if you have ten?

If you're desperate, you can try derris dust, which is sanctioned as a last resort for organic gardeners because it originates from plant extracts. But do take great care to follow the instructions to the letter, and apply in the evening after the bees are back in their hives, as it can kill them too. It really depends on how keen you are for a good crop of gooseberries, and how willing you are to use a pesticide that can harm beneficial insects which help keep other pests on the allotment under control. Disturbing the ground around your soft fruit bushes in winter can also help to expose the pest's cocoons to the birds, who should follow on to gobble them up.

Allotment diary

Despite my love of beasties generally, the larvae of the gooseberry sawfly are top of my hit list at the moment. They can munch their way through a bush and destroy any chance of enjoying luscious gooseberries within days, if not hours. So in the lexicon of evil, they're on a par with the Borg, or the Daleks, or a BNP canvasser ringing my doorbell.

Companion planting

You may have seen rows of marigolds interspersed with cabbages or tomatoes on an allotment, or a ring of chive plants around a block of carrots. While this may be an attempt to make the plot look pretty, there are other reasons for mixing flowers and edible plants on your plot. The catch-all name for this technique is companion planting, and it's a method for deterring pests from colonising your crops.

Certain pairs of plants, when grown next to one another, are said to benefit from each other's company in some way. There's a lot of folklore associated with companion planting, and I don't take all of it seriously. For instance, beans and onions are supposed to 'dislike' each other, but I'd grown both very successfully cheek by jowl during several seasons before I read about their supposed enmity. However, scientific research is starting to confirm at least some of the old gardeners' tales. Certainly the strong odour of leeks, chives and garlic can confuse the carrot fly and prevent it from seeking out your carrots, and research has shown that French and African marigolds contain chemicals that are thought to reduce infestations of wireworms in tomatoes, potato cyst nematodes, and slugs.

My approach has been to resist worrying about the rather complex specifics of which flowers grow well with what, and to simply enjoy a mix and match approach, allowing serendipity to take at least some of the planning out of my hands. And whatever the flower, it will attract lots of useful insects to the plot such as hoverflies whose larvae eat aphids. The poppy seeds that stowed away in some compost from my garden produced a rash of blooms in their first year, and they've been self-seeding all over the place ever since. And I always allow a few sunflower and cornflower seeds (two of my favourites) to drop to the ground. Some inevitably germinate the following year in unexpected places, but if any start to encroach on a valued crop, they're pulled up and usually end up in a vase on the windowsill. Otherwise, I let them flourish and enjoy their blowzy beauty each summer. I do likewise with fennel, which can self-seed everywhere, but the insect pollinators love it.

The absentee allotmenteer

One of the problems with an allotment is that unless you've got a lot of time to spare, for most of the week there's no one around to keep an eye on what's happening on your plot. So I'm always glad to see a cat patrolling around my storage box. For one thing, they will be hunting for the mice that might be making a home in my compost heap or nibbling at my newly planted peas. And they will also deter the birds that like to uproot freshly planted onion sets. The Victorians, who had a rather less than enlightened way of looking at their domestic creatures, would attach a cat or kitten to a wire strung across a strawberry patch or other vulnerable border, forcing them to pace back and forth and see off marauding mice and birds.

Any form of barrier that will exclude pests whether you're in attendance at the plot or not is a great idea. It might simply be some netting to stop pigeons reaching your purple sprouting broccoli – which they love to come and peck at early in the morning, probably before you're around to shoo them away – or mesh over strawberry plants to keep the mice out. Or take the carrot fly. Despite the name, it isn't actually that great at flying, although it does have an incredible sense of smell. It prefers to skim along just above the ground, sniffing out from a distance of up to a kilometre away any area planted with carrots to sow its eggs in. So if you don't fancy trying to confuse the carrot fly's sense of smell by mixing in onions, chives or garlic among the carrots, try putting up a barrier at least seventy-five centimetres high all the way around your carrot patch, made of horticultural fleece, fine mesh, or simply an old sheet. No need to add a roof as the flies won't be able to fly high enough to get over the top of the barrier and so will be prevented from laying their eggs in the soil around the carrots. And no eggs means no maggots eating holes in your carrots.

Flea beetles are a particularly annoying pest that my plot seems to suffer from badly, and this problem is also best cured with netting. I never seem to have enough netting to cover my rocket, which is particularly prone to flea beetle, so I work around the problem by planting this crop in the spring and autumn and not bothering in the summer, when the beetles seem to thrive. Another clever trick I've heard is to wave a piece of cardboard coated in molasses above the affected crop while you disturb the leaves with your hands, so the flea beetles leap to a gooey death.

The pea moth is one creature I don't do a lot to control, mainly because the only real deterrent is covering the whole row of plants with mesh, which isn't practical when picking peas every day in the summer. So I live with the fact that when I pod peas I have to look out for tiny holes that signal there are pea moth larvae inside. The infected pods usually make up about five per cent of my pea crop, and are simply dumped straight back on the compost heap. Planting early and late varieties that won't be flowering during the moth's flight times helps to keep numbers down, as can rotating the crop around different parts of your plot – see chapter three for more details on how crop rotation works.

Allotment diary

August 2005

I love visiting my allotment at dusk, once all the other plot holders have packed up and gone home and it's just me, and the local cats out hunting for field mice. There's something beautiful, if a little melancholy, about watching the sun disappear behind the horizon and the rickety sheds blot together in the fading light.

It does have its downsides, however. Tonight I was removing the stones that weigh down the cover on my compost heap. I lifted off one, then another, then another, then another. And then I thought: hang on, that's not a stone, that's a particularly large brown slug I'm holding.

Giving the soft soap

Yes, prevention is the best cure, and barriers are all very well, but pests often creep up on you when you're least expecting them. I remember visiting my plot on a bitterly cold day when the thermometer hadn't risen above freezing. One of the only plants not under cover but still thriving was a single purple sprouting broccoli, the sole survivor of a particularly poor attempt at germinating a row of brassicas. And yet, when I took a closer look, I realised that nestling on the tender inner stems of the plant were colonies of aphids, sucking the sap like mini vampires. Aphids will rarely completely kill a plant, but they will stunt its growth and weaken it.

If you don't fancy rubbing the aphids from every growing tip on every single plant, you can use an insecticidal soap solution – which is acceptable to organic gardeners as a last resort – to spray them off. The fatty acids in the soap will kill the aphids and other pests such as whitefly and spider mites on contact, but they will also kill other useful insects. You can buy this solution ready-made or make your own version. I mix a teaspoon of environmentally friendly washing-up liquid into a two-litre plastic bottle of water. A solution of boiled rhubarb leaves or even the invasive weed horsetail is also reputed to help, although I've never tried either of these options.

One thing that never enters my mind is the idea of completely eradicating a particular pest. Instead, my rationale is that I'll control a pest only to the extent that allows me to harvest a decent crop. Ultimately, by using an organic approach to your allotment, you should find that you achieve some kind of balance, where the pests are still present but are controlled by the burgeoning population of predators such as ladybirds, lacewings and hoverflies. The balanced approach does take a change of mindset for anyone who is unacquainted with creepy crawlies, but the 'ugh' factor soon passes. In fact, I now find that shop-bought vegetables seem strangely sterile without the usual splattering of mud and occasional slug hole or stowaway earwig.

Diseases

Diseases are another cause of much gnashing of teeth among allotmenteers. The three culprits are much the same as those that cause disease in humans: fungi, bacteria and viruses. As with pests, prevention is much better than cure, largely because if you are gardening organically, there may not be a cure. If you can keep your plants healthy, they're more likely to be able to fight off whatever is thrown at them. Hygiene also helps, so keep your tools and pots clean in between outings to the plot, if you can.

The particular diseases you're plagued with will largely depend on what you grow and where you grow it. Look for disease-resistant varieties – it is possible to find ones that are organic as well – and try to spot and identify diseases as soon as you can. Read any guide to plant diseases and how to deal with them, and pretty soon you'll notice a common thread. The advice for when almost any kind of disease strikes is to remove every single one of the affected leaves and either burn them or put them into your domestic rubbish bin. If you are gardening organically, there isn't a lot else you can do other than nip the infection in the bud before it spreads to other, healthy plants. Make a mental note to improve conditions by all means possible. Crop rotation and a healthy soil will always help, as will generous spacing of plants to encourage air circulation.

Blight is probably the most talked-about allotment disease, because it can wipe out two of the most valued harvests: tomatoes and potatoes. The first you'll know of the arrival of this particularly harmful fungus is the collapse of your plants, though this is sometimes preceded by brown or black patches on the leaves. It often strikes in warm, humid weather, when the spores are most likely to proliferate and spread. In the case of potatoes, tubers may not be affected: cut away the foliage and wait a couple of weeks before harvesting the crop, by which time any spores of the fungus left on the surface will have died off. Before you get started buying seed potatoes, talk to your neighbours and find out if blight is a routine problem on your site. If you know your potatoes are likely to be vulnerable, pick blight-resistant varieties, and don't bother with the more susceptible types of potato that are likely to perform poorly. There are a few varieties of blight-resistant tomatoes available, too, and it helps to space your plants widely, grow them under protection and avoid wetting their leaves when watering.

Onion white rot is another troubling disease that can affect any allium, including shallots, leeks and garlic. The first year I grew onions I harvested a bumper crop. The next year I dutifully rotated my onion sets to another area of the plot only to find that half of them had been reduced to a mushy mess by a fluffy white fungus; the rest, which had seemed healthy, rotted to hollow skins in storage. A quick look in a gardening book confirmed my diagnosis of the soil-borne disease onion white rot, which had also affected my garlic. The crop was chucked in the bin. The shallots fared better, so more of them survived than onions, and my leeks have not fallen prey. The disease will stay in the soil for anything up to fifteen years, so there isn't a lot I can do. Every year since, I have been trying different parts of the plot with varying success. Next I am going to try growing onions from seed, which is meant to help, as the root system is not so developed when the fungus strikes. I wouldn't exactly say I have developed a Zen-like calm about such setbacks, in fact it's heartbreaking to see a good onion harvest turn to an inedible mush, but it does make me appreciate my successes all the more.

Spotlight on...

THE PURPLE PODDED PEA

This heritage variety is one whose origins seem shrouded in mystery. It must have been around for more than a hundred years because Charles Darwin wrote about it in *The Effects of Cross and Self-Fertilisation in the Vegetable Kingdom*, describing experiments he carried out crossing the purple podded pea and another variety called the maple pea. Regardless of its history, this pea is worth growing for its ornamental value, and the sheer novelty of its appearance. The two-tone lilac and dark cerise flowers are followed by purple pods, as the name suggests. These can grow up to twelve centimetres long, although they are best picked when smaller. The plant can grow to around two metres tall, and the dark green foliage makes a stunning backdrop to the purple pods.

I've found the pods are best eaten like mangetout: when small, they can be used raw to liven up the salad bowl, or added to a stir-fry, although the peas can be shelled and cooked in the usual manner once the pods are mature, or left to dry and used in soups and stews. Not everyone agrees with me about their culinary possibilities, however. *The Heligan Vegetable Bible* notes rather sniffily: 'Peas cook to a brown colour and are virtually inedible. Just possibly if the pods were harvested when still flat they could be cooked as mangetout.' The US Seed Savers Exchange lists a blue podded pea that looks very similar to the purple podded pea I know. It describes it as a soup pea so presumably it is meant to be used dried.

Seed sources: Robinson's Mammoth Vegetable Seeds, Heritage Seed Library.

Eleven
Harvesting

> As is usual when I can't get my head round
> momentous events, I headed down to the allotment
> today and pulled up potatoes and onions while
> listening and singing along to 'Prince Charming'.
>
> **Clare, _Pumpkin Soup_ blog**

The moment when an allotment crop reaches fruition is the end of many months of toil: winter weekends spent perusing the seed catalogues for the perfect variety; bitter spring days devoted to digging in compost and sowing seeds with frozen hands; and summer evenings of pulling weeds, lugging watering cans and squashing bugs. But the job of harvesting brings mixed feelings, because it can be a daunting task. Stripping the occasional crisp pea pod from a plant and popping it in your mouth is one thing, but running the gauntlet of a dozen spiky gooseberry bushes or beginning the backbreaking task of digging up a hundredweight of potatoes can bring out the procrastinator in the most dedicated allotmenteer. As allotment blogger Human Bean put it: 'When are the breeders going to develop self-harvesting vegetables (along with weed-eating slugs)?'

Nevertheless, the payoff is a grand one: truly fresh food – something few of us have a chance to experience unless we grow our own fruit and vegetables. I am a freshness freak. Once I'd been converted to the delights of ultra-fresh, ultra local food straight from the allotment, I started coming up with ever more fiendish ways of optimising the freshness. For instance, I've considered setting up a camping stove right next to my sweetcorn plants, bringing a pan of water to a steady rolling boil, then picking the cobs and cooking them without a moment's delay, before any of the sugar has had the chance to turn to starch. And I've thought about bringing some cream with me so I can wash and then eat the strawberries the moment they're picked.

Many gardening books go into huge detail about sowing and cultivation, but very little is written about the process of harvesting, perhaps because it's seen as too obvious to discuss. In fact, how you harvest individual crops can have a significant effect not only on how the produce will keep, but also on whether the plant will continue to thrive and whether you can expect a second harvest. Take rhubarb, for instance. You'd think it would be hard to go astray here; just cut if off any old how when you have the secateurs handy, right? That's what I'd been doing until I read Monty Don's detailed description of the art of harvesting rhubarb in his book, *The Complete Gardener*, and realised I'd been doing it all wrong. I should have been pulling and twisting each stalk while holding it at the base, to make sure there were no remaining fragments that would encourage the crown to rot. And I should have only taken half the stems on any plant, to make sure next year's crop would be just as good. Well, who knew?

That kind of information can make the difference between a summer of rhubarb fools and a sickly plant that confounds its grower by failing to match the umbrella-sized leaves being sported on neighbouring plots. So in this chapter I'll try to share some of the best tips I've garnered, both on how to get the most out of the crops you've worked so hard to produce, and on how to deal with the inevitable gluts that can turn a good harvest into a chore, as anyone who has ever grown more than one courgette plant at a time will know.

Tools of the harvest

Harvesting is best left to the end of any plot visit so that your produce spends as little time as possible languishing in the heat before it is eaten or stored. If it's particularly hot, you're a freshness freak like me and your home is some distance away, you may want to consider bringing a cool box and an ice pack or bag of ice cubes, or you could pre-chill your plastic boxes in the freezer. I tend to make a mental list of how much I'll need of each crop that day, then pick double the amount. In the case of lettuce, for instance, that means I can disregard all the leaves that are anything but perfect and put them straight on the compost heap. And with potatoes and beetroot, I can keep a few back for the following day, make up some soup or give a few away to friends, if I'm feeling generous.

My arsenal of harvesting equipment consists of:

🍅 **A small sharp knife with a plastic handle:** pinched from my kitchen drawer and now a permanent resident in my allotment bag, this is ideal for cutting the stems of pumpkins, courgettes and globe artichokes.

- 🍅 **A pair of scissors:** also a refugee from my cutlery drawer, scissors are handy for snipping off cut-and-come-again lettuce, flower stems and Swiss chard.
- 🍅 **Plastic bags, cardboard boxes and baskets:** I use these for collecting harvested crops – the bags are useful for salad leaves while the boxes are ideal for carrying heavier vegetables. If you can afford it, though, invest in a gardener's trug.
- 🍅 **A digging fork:** for teasing root crops from the ground.
- 🍅 **A few old plastic and metal trays:** for laying out onions and garlic to dry. Oven trays work fine.
- 🍅 **Some old plastic containers:** for picking soft fruit.

Courgettes and cucumbers

I always get nervous when I see another plot holder approaching me with a pleading look in their eye and a bulging plastic sack in their hands. It can only mean one thing: they have a load of courgettes they're desperate to offload on me. Courgettes are the plants most likely to produce a glut on a scale that not even the most dedicated vegetable-munching household can manage. A family of four can probably live on the fruits of a single plant, yet most allotmenteers grow several, either just in case they get eaten by slugs, or because they want to try several different varieties. The upshot is that everyone, from close friends to distant relatives, gets offered the surplus. Elaine Borish has even written a recipe book called *What Will I Do With All Those Courgettes?* And a momentary lapse in picking can result in an even bigger problem. As I write there's a large marrow – a sneaky squash that grew from courgette to monster out of sight in some long grass at the edge of the plot while I was away on holiday – sitting on my kitchen worktop that's just crying out to be stuffed.

Like rhubarb, courgettes are plants that need to be picked in the right way. I spent a whole summer getting prickled by the spiky leaves as I wrestled to pick my courgettes by twisting them off the plant, a method that usually left half the fruit still attached to the stem. It's not something I suggest you try. I learned my lesson, and now find it far easier to use a sharp knife to cut them off at the base – the ribbed bit where the fruit joins the plant. The same is true for cucumbers, although another top tip from Monty Don suggests that particularly pendulous cucumbers can be cut in half while on the plant; you harvest one end and leave the other on the plant, where it forms a callus and waits to be picked at a later date. Genius. No more mushy cucumber in the bottom of your fridge.

If you're after the delicacy of the courgette flowers, which are wonderful when battered and deep-fried, or stuffed with ricotta, time really is of the essence. One year I picked dozens of the things only to leave them languishing in the hot sun for an hour and then find the flowers had turned limp. Instead, pick the flower still attached to its mini-courgette just before you're ready to leave and then hotfoot it home to cook. The recipe in *Antonio Carluccio's Vegetables* is perfect.

Picking the flowers can help to prevent a courgette glut, but the truth is I always end up with roughly five times more than I can eat. My eye is repeatedly lured by unusual varieties so I always end up with too many seed packets for courgettes. I pick them while small so they're flavoursome enough to make into a very simple salad when grated or sliced and mixed with olive oil and vinegar. The slightly larger ones are used to make potato, courgette and mint cakes, and the biggest specimens are made into chutney. The chutney recipe I use is one I've adapted from Hugh Fearnley-Whittingstall's *The River Cottage Cookbook*. I add some prunes, and substitute muscovado sugar for about a third of the granulated sugar and balsamic vinegar for the white wine vinegar. I started including prunes as a result of tasting some divine chutney on the Isle of Arran in Scotland, at the Machrie Bay Golf Course tea rooms. I'm not a golfer but it was worth going for the home baking and the delicious chutney. And the muscovado sugar and balsamic vinegar give extra flavour.

Soft fruit

The best way to harvest any soft fruit is little and often. If I attempted to pick all the blackcurrants from my five bushes in one go I would end up with a slipped disc. I tend to go bush by bush, stripping away the fruit with my fingers and dropping them into a plastic box, not worrying particularly if a few leaves end up in the mix. Back at the house, I give them a quick rinse in cold water and pick out any leaves or stems, then allow them to drain before laying the currants on an old plastic tray.

The tray then goes straight into the freezer, usually balanced on top of a precipitous pile of other harvested crops frozen earlier in the season. Once the currants are frozen, which will take a few hours, I whip the tray out of the freezer and scrape the fruit – now as hard as bullets – into the small, lidded, plastic containers you get from takeaways. Each one is just large enough for a couple of servings of fruit, and this method works for any currant as well as for blackberries. I picked it up from my mother, who struggled heroically to harvest the fruit of several mammoth blackcurrant bushes each year. It prevents the frustrating scenario of a block of frozen-solid fruit staring you in the face every time you want just a handful to liven up some yogurt or porridge oats. If I am making jam, things are even easier. Soft fruit shouldn't be washed before making jam as that dilutes the pectin, so it all goes straight into the pan.

The challenge with both raspberries and blackberries is trying to pick more than you eat. I am not one of those killjoys who forbids snacking as you harvest; indeed, what better way to experience fruit as it should be, straight off the plant? Raspberries are among the softest of the soft fruits, and should be layered as thinly as possibly in the bottom of a plastic box or dish, to prevent the berries from being crushed under their own weight. I haven't bothered with a blackberry bush on my plot because, like many allotment sites, the fences are draped with them. It always amazes me how few people bother to pick blackberries, especially when they seem to be as elusive and expensive as caviar on the shelves of most supermarkets. When I harvest the particularly plump fruits from one pathway near my house, I get strange looks from people, presumably wondering what on earth I am doing standing in a nettle patch and fumbling about in a bush. The ultimate blackberry dish is, of course, blackberry and apple crumble. I include a handful of blackcurrants, as they add a tart note that complements the other fruit. I've always sworn by Delia Smith's recipe in her *Complete Cookery Course* series, but I sometimes add some porridge oats, chipped almonds or crushed brazils to liven up the topping.

And strawberries? I don't think you'll need much help on this one, but there's one recipe that provides the perfect plot-side picnic option. Why not invite some friends round to join you, provided you're prepared to share your produce. It comes courtesy of the allotment blogger Human Bean and serves two to four, depending on how greedy you're feeling. Take twelve good-sized strawberries and remove the tops. Dip them first into 20ml balsamic vinegar and then into 2tbsp of sugar, until they are thoroughly coated. String the strawberries onto skewers (soak wooden ones in water first to prevent them from burning) or lay them on a baking tray if you prefer to grill them. Grind some black pepper over the fruit and bung them on the barbecue for a minute or two (or under a pre-heated hot grill for about the same amount of time). The addition of balsamic vinegar and pepper may sound like an unusual combination, but, trust me, it works a treat.

Allotment diary

July 2005

I just tasted my first blackberry of the year. It looks as if it's going to be a bumper crop, judging from the amount of fruit on the brambles. This particular blackberry bush offers the plumpest, sweetest berries I have ever tasted. I have already cleared space in my freezer and am dusting down my preserving pan ready for the picking season. I could tell you the location of this bush, but then I'd have to kill you.

Root crops

There's not much to harvesting the likes of beetroot, carrots and radishes. It's a good job to give your allotment assistant, small child or keen but clueless friend who is not to be trusted with the skilled jobs, like picking (or eating) strawberries. Simply douse the ground with water to ensure it isn't rock hard, apply a judiciously placed fork or trowel to help the roots out of the ground, and then grab and pull. But if you're worried your technique's not up to scratch, carrot enthusiast John Stolarczyk – owner of the World Carrot Museum website – advises grabbing the greens at the crown of your chosen root, and pulling and twisting gently until it pops out. If the worst happens and the greens break away in your hand, insert a small fork under the root and lift it free. (It's important when picking carrots to remove the harvested ones from the area as soon as possible as the smell of crushed foliage will attract carrot fly.) I've found Stolarczyk's harvesting tactic also works well for other root crops such as parsnips, swede and turnips.

I've always been addicted to pickles of all kind. But it wasn't until I grew my own beetroots that I came around to the idea of eating them in their unvinegared form. The flavour of boiled fresh beetroot was a revelation: sweet and yet somehow earthy. It's also extremely good grated raw on top of a salad, although my favourite beetroot recipe is self-sufficiency guru Hugh Fearnley-Whittingstall's beetroot and roast tomato soup in his *River Cottage Cookbook*. I try to use home-grown produce for both of the main ingredients, but if your beetroots are ready earlier than your tomatoes, I've found you can chop, sauté and freeze them ready to continue the recipe when your tomatoes come on stream.

Peas and beans

First, a useless pea fact, courtesy of top chef and vegetable lover Antonio Carluccio in his book *Antonio Carluccio's Vegetables*: 'pisello', which is Italian for pea, is also 'a rather juvenile slang word for the male configuration, so to speak'. Somewhat more useful, however, is Carluccio's assertion that it was Italian gardeners in the sixteenth century who first thought of eating peas fresh rather than drying them as had been done since the Stone Age. I salute their good sense; there's little on the allotment sweeter than a pea eaten straight from the plant. Speed is the key with picking peas and beans. Within hours the sugar turns to starch and the sweetness is lost. Try to pick your peas just before you're due to leave the plot. Take them home and pod them straight away, blanching and freezing any you can't eat that night. I aim to pick peas when they're still young and not bullet-hard. Start from the bottom of the plant and work up, as the lower flowers will mature first, and once grown into pods these are also the most vulnerable, becoming dinner for hungry mice.

Allotment diary

June 2005

This weekend I managed to have a trio of new taste experiences courtesy of my allotment. I tasted sorrel for the first time and was instantly hooked. I was worried I'd hate it as much as I hate chicory, but its lemony sharpness hit the spot for me. I ate my first immature pea pod of the year, straight off the plant. Freshness defined. And I ate my first ever immature broad bean pod – and realised that it's not the same as eating an immature pea pod. I think I'll wait until the beans ripen and try again.

Tubers

Digging potatoes is something I have to admit to being rather bad at. My fork always seems to act like a spud-seeking missile, spearing every other tuber as I attempt to lever up the soil around the plant and bring up the crop. And whenever I see pictures in gardening books of mammoth lines of newly harvested potatoes sitting in the sunshine, I try to recall the last time I dug up a potato without having to stare at the sky with narrowed eyes, willing it not to start raining.

But the theory, at least, is that you should insert your fork into the soil a safe distance – maybe twenty-five to thirty centimetres – from the haulm (a horticultural term for the stem) of the potato plant and gently lift out the tubers. Inevitably you'll end up slicing into some of them. It saves a lot of time and heartache if you separate out these damaged ones as they appear, because left in storage they'll rot and ruin the rest of your crop. Once you've chucked the haulms onto your compost heap, do make sure you have a good rummage around in the soil for any stragglers. If you're careless like me you'll end up with potato plants appearing like weeds just where you don't want them the following year. Ideally, the tubers should be left to dry off in the open air for a couple of hours before they're bagged up in paper sacks for storage. Assuming the sun isn't shining, you can stick them on a tray or piece of cardboard in a cool, dry place – a garage or unheated lobby or hallway is ideal. (If visitors comment, just explain that it's a rustic decoration as featured in *Country Life*.)

But back to those rejects: time is of the essence. Get them straight back to your kitchen and turn them into something good. I usually cut away the damage and chop them up for potato salad à la allotment, which consists of the potatoes, boiled until you can just penetrate them with a fork and gently tossed in a little olive or hemp oil and a couple of spoons each of natural yogurt and good quality mayonnaise, plus a very generous sprinkle of finely chopped parsley, red onion and French sorrel. The flavours – particularly the lemony bite of the sorrel – make for a fantastic combination that is light years away from the slimy concoction that comes in plastic tubs in supermarkets.

Allotment diary

May 2004

I've got purple (and white) sprouting broccoli coming out of my ears. Well, not quite, but I have so much that I offered some of my prized stash to selected office colleagues (those who I believe will actually cook it rather than leave it to rot in the fridge – one has to be ruthlessly selective with such prime goods). It's a wonderful vegetable that encourages smugness in all true allotmenteers as it just can't be grown out of season to supply the mass-retailing, cookie-cutter demands of the supermarkets.

Dispatching the glut: red lentil soup

One of my favourite recipes for using up bits and pieces of allotment excess is a quick and simple lentil soup that is robust enough to incorporate pretty much whatever leftover vegetables you throw at it. It's one of the first things my partner ever cooked for me, in the high-ceilinged kitchen of the sprawling old former vicarage where he lived, a place that had been home to PhD students since the sixties.

The beauty of using red lentils is that they need no soaking, and they complement the slightly spicy flavours of the cumin, cardamom and coriander; you can make it a little hotter by adding

Red lentil soup

Ingredients (serves four to six)

1 medium onion, chopped
1 medium carrot, diced
1 medium leek, chopped
1 clove garlic, sliced
1 tsp ground cumin
1 tsp ground coriander
2 cardamom pods
1 bay leaf

225g red lentils, rinsed
1 litre vegetable stock
400g chopped tomatoes, tinned
    or fresh (if fresh, peeled and
    deseeded)
1 tbsp tomato purée
3 tbsp olive oil for frying
Salt and pepper

Gently heat the olive oil in a saucepan and add the chopped vegetables and garlic. Sweat the vegetables (fry without colouring) by cooking on a low to medium heat with the lid on until the onions appear soft and translucent. This should take a few minutes.

Add salt and pepper to taste, plus the cumin and coriander, and fry on a medium heat with the lid off for another four to five minutes. Keep moving the vegetables around the saucepan so that they don't stick to the bottom. Add the rinsed red lentils and cook for a further two to three minutes, again stirring frequently.

Add the vegetable stock, tomatoes, tomato purée, cardamom pods and bay leaf. Bring to the boil and then simmer on a low to medium heat until the red lentils are soft. This should take about twenty minutes. Remove the cardamom pods and bay leaf and allow the soup to cool. Blend the soup to desired thickness, then re-heat, check the consistency and seasoning, and eat.

a fresh or dried chilli. It's a wonderful dish to serve with a hunk of buttered granary bread to hungry allotment volunteers following an afternoon spent digging. If you like your soup smooth, just

Spotlight on...

LETTUCE FORELLENSCHLUSS

I'm a sucker for varieties with odd names, and for anything speckled, so this beautiful lettuce is top of my list. (Perhaps the only better lettuce name I've heard is the Italian variety *Ubriacona Frastagliata,* or Drunken Woman, although I've yet to try that one.) Its leaves are splashed with red, which liven up the salad bowl and make the plant pretty enough to hold its own in an ornamental bed, although it tastes delicious too. The name *Forellenschluss* is German and refers to the fact that the colouring recalls the speckles on a trout's back; it's a romaine-type heritage variety that originated in Austria. The plant has performed impressively for me. Even when I sowed some seed one October and then forgot to give the row any protection from the winter weather, the seeds still germinated and were thriving when I finally spotted them during a spring weeding session.

Seed sources: The Real Seed Company, Seeds by Size.

whizz it with a blender wand once it's done: if you prefer it chunky, leave it as it is. Either way, it's a thick consistency, so increase the amount of stock if you like your soups thin. It also freezes very well. It's suitable for lacto vegetarians and vegans and takes about forty-five minutes to prepare and cook.

Rick says that you can experiment with the vegetables you use, adding or substituting the onion, carrot and leek for what you have handy – celery or chard leaves, for example – but it's a good idea to retain two out of three of them. If you want to make the vegetable stock yourself rather than buying one, Rose Elliot's book *Learning to Cook Vegetarian* has a cast-iron recipe.

Twelve
Storing your harvest

It may sound grandiose, but in many ways the history of civilisation is the story of our progressive mastery of food preservation. After all, to be wild is to eat on the hoof.

Nick Sandler and Johnny Acton, *Preserved*, 2004

I have an old gardening manual from the 1950s that is full of lists of what to do when, but some of the instructions on storing vegetables were confusing to me as a beginner. In September, for example, it told me to 'store parsnips against a wall or fence' – but was that in the ground, propped up against the wall, what? Nonetheless, however opaque the instructions, storage was clearly seen as a crucial part of the allotment routine. A lot of modern gardening books don't say much about how to store vegetables, perhaps because the arrival of the fridge and freezer are assumed to have ended the need for other more traditional methods of preserving allotment crops.

I find my freezer invaluable for storing soft fruit from my allotment and tomato sauces made at the height of the summer glut, but I don't use it a great deal for vegetables. That's partly because I only have a small freezer, but also because I'd rather eat what is in season than frozen vegetables, which never seem to taste as good.

There are different storage methods for each crop, and if you intend growing more than you can eat of anything, it's worth knowing how to get the most out of the harvest. Of course there are some crops that simply won't keep more than a few days. Lettuce and other salads will last several days in a sealed plastic bag or box in the fridge, but can't be effectively stored elsewhere. Others, given the right conditions, will store for months at a time, providing you with a constant supply of veg throughout the year.

The best storage place for most produce is somewhere cool, dry and frost free. Sheds are often pressed into service as convenient places to put vegetables, particularly heavy crops such as potatoes and pumpkins. But unless your shed is completely free of damp, it's often better to store crops at home, where you can keep an eye on them for signs of deterioration. And having easy access to your vegetables will also encourage you to use them before they go bad. Try to find the coolest part of your home to use as a storage area. It could be a spare room, an unheated porch or even under your bed; I use my garage.

Here's a potted summary of the various methods and which crops you can use them for. You'll notice that some vegetables, such as carrots, appear in two lists. It's a matter of personal preference which storage method you choose.

✎ Leave in the ground

Any winter vegetable that can remain in the earth until it is needed gets a gold star in my book. It's the ultimate no-work storage method, and means that you can harvest crops as and when you need them. The drawbacks are potential damage from slugs and insects, and from exposure to harsh weather such as heavy frosts and waterlogged ground, though Jerusalem artichokes seem to survive these setbacks without significant problems.

If your plot is very exposed but you still want to take advantage of outdoor storage, you can dig up root crops and replant them shallowly in dry, sheltered soil, ideally up against some kind of protection from the elements such as a shed or hedge – a process known as heeling in. If you live in an area that suffers from regular subzero temperatures, you'll probably be better off opting for one of the other storage methods below.

Carrots	Parsnips
Celeriac	Potatoes
Celery	Swedes
Jerusalem artichokes	Turnips
Leeks	

✎ Hang in a cool, dry place

The pumpkin experts at the Real Seed Company recommend 'curing' winter squash by putting them in a warm place (around 25°C) such as a kitchen for ten days. This is reputed to help the skin dry out and make them last longer. Once cured, they go into cool conditions of around 12°C. I usually just take my pumpkins straight from the plot to my garage, which is dry and frost free, and hang them up for storage without bothering to cure them; they usually last several weeks that way. But it may be worth considering the curing process if you have a large pumpkin stash that you want to eat over a long period.

Either way, there are things you can do to maximise their shelf life. To start with, don't store them on a shelf. Pumpkins and other winter squash should be hung up in anything that allows the air to circulate around the whole of the fruit. The thicker the skin, the longer the fruit will last, and this will depend on which variety you grow. One year I had one particularly tough squash that was just beginning to rot as the following year's pumpkin harvest was being picked.

Once your crop is hung up, check the skin regularly. Small marks on the surface are signs of decay, so when these appear there is no time to delay: use it or lose it. If a pumpkin is starting to go over, the easiest option is to cut it in half, scoop out the fibrous centre and any damaged material and roast the remaining flesh in the oven with a few crushed cumin and coriander seeds and a drizzle of olive oil. If I have time for something a little more elaborate, I call on a pumpkin, chilli and coconut soup reverse-engineered by Rick following a visit to a restaurant. The resulting soup freezes very well, so you can make a large pan and store it in small batches.

Onions, shallots and garlic are also hung up to allow air to flow around the skin. The traditional way is to hang them from strings, but you can use netting instead. There are many ways to string an onion, and instructions usually include impossible-to-follow diagrams. My method can best be described as quick; the resulting strings won't win any beauty contests, but at least you don't need a PhD in knots to get the hang of it. First, make sure that the onion stems are absolutely dry, and remove any bulbs that show the slightest sign of disease or damage. I leave mine to dry out for a few days after I've lifted them, either on a tray in the sun, or inside if the weather's rotten. Once the stems are like paper, I divide the onions into threes, then roughly plait the stems together. Then I plait together three bunches of three onions to create a nine-onion bunch, and tie a bit of string at the top and bottom of each plait to hold the whole lot together. Try to keep the plaits fairly small, as there's nothing worse than a heavy string of onions falling to the floor. Shallots tend to have shorter stems and are more tricky to string, so I just gather them up and tie a knot in the bunched stems, or store them in a string bag hung in a cool place.

Garlic	Shallots
Pumpkins and other winter squash	Onions

Sand storage

Most vegetables will turn soft and wrinkly if left in the open air for more than a few days, so if you need to find a way of making your harvest last a little longer, this method is ideal. Most root vegetables should store for weeks if not months, given the right conditions.

How you treat your vegetables straight after they are harvested makes a big difference to how they will fare in storage. Never wash anything you want to keep in this way: just rub off excess soil and allow them to dry, in the open air if possible. Cut the leaves off to about three centimetres from the top of the root so that the carrot itself is left intact. The remaining stems will help to keep the carrot alive. Put aside any damaged or diseased specimens for immediate consumption: if you store these with the others, they may spread infection to the whole crop.

Scour your local supermarket or fruit and veg market for stacking boxes, then line these with plastic sheeting and fill the insides with layers of sand or sawdust chips between each layer of vegetables so that they are completely covered. Keep each root separate from one another and moisten the storage medium with a little water as you pack. The moisture will be taken up by the carrots to help them stay crisp, but make sure that the sand or sawdust is only just damp – too wet and it will encourage rotting.

The kitchen is usually far too warm to store vegetables in this way. The best place is somewhere airy and cool – a shed or garage is fine, provided it's rodent-free. Keep a close eye on them: you should be able to take one root at a time, as and when it's needed in the kitchen, which will give you a chance to inspect the rest.

Beetroot	Parsnips
Carrots	Swedes
Celeriac	Turnips

⬬ **Store in a cloth or paper sack**

The old adage about one rotten apple spoiling the barrel isn't merely a figure of speech: once you've tried to keep a store of vegetables over the winter, you'll know exactly what it means. A single decomposing potato can spread the rot to the rest of the store, so every time you take some potatoes for cooking, tune in your nose to detect the acrid smell of rotting spud. If you catch the offending rotter early enough and remove it, the rest of the harvest should not be affected.

Potatoes should be kept in the dark to stop them from sprouting, and given plenty of air circulation: a plastic bag is the worst possible environment as condensation will build up. Choose instead cloth or paper bags, which should be well covered and left in an unheated room (not the kitchen). Or you can layer the crop in a box of dry straw. I've also had a lot of success storing spuds in a cardboard box. If you can find a box that has been used to store wine bottles, you can use the cardboard compartments to your advantage, putting a handful of potatoes in each. If one potato does go bad, the rot won't spread to the tubers in the other sections.

Potatoes

🐦 Clamps

The Victorian way of storing winter root vegetables was in a clamp or grave. Should you choose to try it, bear in mind that this earth-and-straw construction is an all-or-nothing method, as you can't just remove a few spuds as and when you need them – something that's always put me off.

Here's the theory anyway, gleaned from various visits to frighteningly perfect walled Victorian gardens such as the Lost Gardens of Heligan in Cornwall. A shallow trench is filled with straw and the potatoes or root vegetables are then piled on top between layers of sand. The pile is covered with more straw and a top coating of about 10cm of earth, and a chimney is inserted in the top to allow air to reach the vegetables (an old piece of piping will work). It's rather hit and miss as to whether your harvest will keep under these conditions, and there's no way of checking how they are doing until the big day when you open up the clamp. But if you have a large quantity of root vegetables to store and nowhere inside to keep them, this could be the answer for you.

Beetroot	Potatoes
Carrots	Swedes
Celeriac	Turnips
Parsnips	

🐦 Soups and sauces for the freezer

Many vegetables are best enjoyed at their freshest, but however much home-grown produce you pack into every meal, there's still a distinct possibility in the summer months that you'll be left with an overflow of vegetables that you can't simply stick on a shelf or in the fridge. If you can, prepare sauces and soups in bulk to take care of the glut. One simple way of preparing tomatoes for the freezer is to roast them on a baking tray, each one sliced in half and topped with a few slivers of garlic. Remove the skins and seeds by sieving the cooked fruit and freeze the pulp for winter pasta sauces and stews. Chillies, aubergines, peppers and courgettes can be prepared in a similar way. Make sure you include the date on the label so you can use them in good time. The frozen packs should last until next year's harvest arrives providing you have a reliable freezer.

Aubergines	Peppers
Chillies	Tomatoes
Courgettes and other summer squash	

Blanch and freeze

Blanching certain vegetables is a good way of ensuring that they retain their flavour and colour in the freezer. Dip them into boiling water for about thirty seconds, then put them straight into very cold water – a pan with some ice cubes floating in it is ideal. Allow them to drain thoroughly, then place them in portion-sized, labelled bags or boxes in the freezer until they're needed. I have to say I only bother with this method for peas and broad beans, which make a real treat outside their season.

Beans, French, runner and broad	Peas
Brussels sprouts	Spinach
	Swiss chard

☁ **Dry and store**

Most French beans can be saved for drying and using in soups and stews, but if you can, choose varieties that have been specially selected for drying. Allow the pods to develop on the plant. In late summer they will go brown and begin to dry out. If it's a particularly wet month, cut down the plants and hang them upside down until the pods are bone dry; otherwise, allow them to stay in situ until they've lost all their suppleness. Pop out the beans from their pods, put them on a china plate for a couple of days to dry, then place them in an airtight container – but be warned that they must be absolutely dry at this point for if there is a drop of moisture left in a single bean, the whole lot will go mouldy and you'll have to throw them away.

Chillies can be dried easily, provided you have a spell of hot, dry weather at your disposal. The chillies can be threaded together using a large needle threaded through the base of the stem with strong fishing line or string. Hang the strings outside and keep a close eye on them, removing any chillies that begin to rot. When the chillies are completely dry (this could take several days), you can hang the string in up in your kitchen and simply snap one off when you need it, placing it in just-boiled water for about half an hour to rehydrate it. Alternatively, grind the chillies up and store them in an airtight jar and they'll keep even longer.

Peppers and chillies with thick skins, such as jalapenos, won't air dry successfully and will need to be dried in a food dehydrator, a piece of kit specifically designed for drying fruit and vegetables ready for storage. If you don't want to invest in one of these, peppers and chillies will also freeze well. Wash and dry your fruits then lay them on a plastic tray in your freezer. Once they have frozen hard you can put them into a plastic box or freezer bag.

Borlotti and haricot beans	Peppers
Chillies	

☁ **A footnote on food storage**

There will be times when, however careful you try to be, you'll fail to keep a close enough eye on your food stores. The first warning sign will be a funny smell that you can't quite track down, until you remember the jar of dried beans tucked away in the corner, now soft and sprouting, or the pumpkin forgotten on the top shelf in the garage, slowly collapsing in on itself in a fuzz of white mould. Don't be too hard on yourself when this happens. For one thing, your compost bin will welcome the extra ingredients. And all of us let things slide once in a while when modern life gets in the way of our attempts to enjoy a slower pace. It will only spur you on to make better use of your crops next time around, and help you to refine your storage methods so that next year nothing will be wasted.

Alternatively, if you can't use it, why not give it away while it's fresh? If you've run out of friends and family to pass on your glut to, why not leave your surplus in a box at the gate of your allotment or in the trading shed for someone to pick up?

Spotlight on...

PINK FIR APPLE POTATOES

These are not apples, although their skin does have a pinkish hue, but gourmet potatoes. You're unlikely to see them on the supermarket shelves, however, probably because of their tendency to produce knobbly tubers that look like alien life forms. But what they lack in looks, they make up for in flavour. Garden writer Elspeth Thompson described them in her book *The Urban Gardener* as 'the caviar of the potato world', and rightly so. It's a waxy salad potato that's best boiled with the skin left on. They also make very fine fried potatoes, and latkes (potato cakes) when grated, as they tend to hold their shape.

Pink Fir Apple is reputedly fussy, producing lower yields than other types, but it seems to suit my plot perfectly and has outperformed every other potato I have tried. It is late to mature, however, and needs to be harvested in late September or early October to get the best results. Pink Fir Apple is unfortunately prone to blight, so if this disease is a problem where you live, you could try another waxy variety that's got some resistance to blight, such as Nicola, Charlotte or Valor.

Pink Fir Apple dates back to 1850 and it is one of the oldest varieties still in cultivation. It has come back into favour in the last couple of decades and even has the seal of approval from Delia Smith. Need I say more?

Seed potato sources: Organic Gardening Catalogue, Carroll's Heritage Potatoes, Mr Fothergill's Seeds.

The plot thickens

When I started writing this book, it was early autumn. I was still picking pumpkins, stringing onions up to dry, and savouring the last of the peas, but as the pace of life on the allotment began to slow, there seemed to be more time to reflect on the year's successes and failures, and to embark on the task of putting my experiences into words. Now it is early summer, my manuscript is almost finished and the next generation of pumpkins, onions and sunflowers are all thrusting skyward. Everything is crying out for attention, from the weed-ridden strawberry patch to the tomato plants threatening to burst through the top of the cold frame, and I am itching to begin spending the long summer evenings pottering about on the plot, putting into place my plans for the season ahead.

After several seasons on the plot, it still amazes me just how different each growing year is. Whether you're a plot holder of one or twenty-one years' standing, there is always some clever tip to learn, a new or unusual vegetable variety to try, and a neighbour willing to share their expertise and a few strawberry plants with you. The allotment is never 'finished' – it's a constant work in progress that will wax and wane with the seasons, and I can't wait to see what new challenges and pleasures the next year will bring.

If you're new to allotments, I hope that this book has given you a taste of the rising anticipation I feel every time I unlock the gate to the allotment site. I hope it has also prepared you for some of the setbacks you might experience when starting out with a new plot, be it marauding slugs, a tumbledown shed or seeds that won't germinate. If you have a year or more on the plot under your belt, it's easy to focus on what went wrong and what remains to be done rather than on your triumphs – the crisp lettuces that livened up your salad bowl all summer, or the tangy chutney you made from your courgette glut. I hope I've reminded you of why you rented your plot in the first place: fresh home-grown food, fitness, and fun with family and friends.

But I really must stop writing now. The sun is shining, it's a perfect day for planting out my French beans, and I can't delay any longer. See you on the plot.

Jobs month by month

Here you can find guidance at a glance as to what, ideally, you should aim to do each month on your plot. For every month I've included a table of recommended crops to sow (either under protection, in pots or trays on a windowsill or in a greenhouse, or directly into the soil), plant (I've indicated whether I mean directly into the soil, or 'plant out' into their final positions, after allowing the seeds to germinate and grow into established seedlings), harvest, or protect (by using horticultural fleece, a cold frame or a cloche), and a fun monthly project to brighten up or improve your plot.

The suggested to-do lists are meant merely as an inspiration rather than a set of commands. The correct time to plant any crop will depend on how far north you live, the weather conditions that year and which variety you are trying to grow. Many crops – including potatoes, cabbages, cauliflowers, broad beans, spinach and lettuce – can be grown at completely different times of year depending on the particular variety you choose. So while a lettuce called Winter Marvel will, as the name suggests, thrive when sown in a cold frame at the end of September and harvested in early December, a summer lettuce such as, well, Summertime can be sown in May and harvested in July. A third variety called All The Year Round will… well, you get the idea.

Read the seed packet carefully (it's amazing how many people – me included – don't) and try to stick to the timetable it suggests. But if you find you're officially too late to sow a crop, sow it anyway! Crops sown later than planned can usually catch up and, with a bit of extra protection from the weather or a particularly fine autumn, can extend your growing season well into the cooler months. A bit of experimentation with sowing and harvesting times will allow you to work out what works on your individual plot – and every one is different.

January

I love the snow. You can't see the weeds. You can't see all the undug bits. Just a soft silent blanket over the world.

Maurice Pennance, *Clodhoppers* blog

January is traditionally a month for fresh starts: perhaps instead of forking out for a gym membership this year, you could spend the money on renting an allotment, or if you already have a plot that you've neglected, committing to getting it back into production. Although the soil is still far too wet and cold for much sowing and planting outdoors, there are jobs you can be getting on with, both inside and outside. Start chitting your early potatoes, clean up your seed trays and pots ready for the planting season, carry out a seed audit of all the packets you already have and figure out what needs using up this year and what should be thrown away, and, if you keep them, make sure your seed feeders and bird baths are full for the winter visitors to your plot. A thick layer of bark chips or cocoa shells between beds will stop you slipping in the mud – some weed-suppressing sheeting below it will also reduce the onset of unwelcome new plant arrivals come the spring.

If you have rhubarb on your plot (and most people do whether planned or not), you can produce a gourmet early crop of stems by putting a bucket over the dormant plant to block out all the light and then, if you can, surrounding that with a layer of manure,

TO DO THIS MONTH

Sow under protection
Broad beans
Leeks
Lettuce

Radishes
Rocket

Plant direct
Currants
Raspberries
Shallot sets

Harvest
Broccoli, purple sprouting
Brussels sprouts
Cabbage
Cauliflower
Celeriac
Jerusalem artichokes
Kale

Leaf beet
Lettuce
Parsnips
Radishes
Rocket
Spinach
Swiss chard

Protect
Cabbage
Cauliflower
Celeriac
Kale
Leeks
Lettuce

Parsnips
Radishes
Rocket
Spinach
Swiss chard

which will let off some heat to fool the plant into springing into growth earlier than normal. By forcing the plant in this way, in a few weeks' time you should have tender, sweet stems that will make a very fine rhubarb fool, ice cream or compote. You can also force sea kale in the same way. It's also time to cut all autumn-fruiting raspberry canes down to ground level to encourage new growth.

Clear winter days are the ideal time to start planning for the year ahead. Dig over weedy beds and incorporate compost or well-rotted manure. When you have swathes of bare soil, don't leave it exposed: cover the ground with black plastic sheeting held in place with pegs to stop weeds from sprouting and to begin to warm the soil in preparation for the sowing season. Or get some much needed post-Christmas exercise by raking up leaves (if you don't have a garden, try your local park) to make into leaf mould. Just pop them into a plastic sack with some holes in it and leave the bag somewhere inconspicuous and damp for a year, after which time you'll have a bagful of one of the best soil improvers.

The only fresh vegetables you're likely to be harvesting now are crops that have been grown under some kind of protection, or tough crops such as leeks, kale, cabbage and Brussels sprouts. Make sure cold frames, cloches and fleece are securely pegged down, and check the plants underneath regularly for slugs seeking refuge from the cold and to be sure that the soil hasn't completely dried out.

And there's no better way to fend off the winter chill than tackling a stubborn patch of brambles or nettles with a pair of gloves and a fork – get stuck in and you'll soon warm up.

✍ **This month's project**

START AN ALLOTMENT DIARY

Once you've had a plot for a year or two, it becomes hard to recall what you've grown, when it was sown, transplanted and harvested, and what worked and didn't work. An allotment diary is a great way of recording all this information in a single place. Just get a hardback notebook that will withstand your muddy paws and start noting down planting dates, successes, failures, and so on. If you're comfortable with computers and the Internet, another option is to create a blog or online diary, which will also provide a home for your photographs, and is searchable — handy if you can't remember when you did something. There are various easy-to-use blog-hosting websites, including Blogger, which is free, but I use Typepad, which costs around £3 a month for the basic version. The additional advantage of a blog is it's a great way to get in touch with other allotmenteers: I've met dozens through my blog, Horticultural, and have received great advice and encouragement from them. If you would like to explore allotment blogs further, try visiting some of the ones listed in the directory at the back of this book.

February

There is no such thing as bad weather, just bad clothing.
Norwegian proverb

The evenings are starting to lengthen, but February can still be a bitter month, so don't assume that a mild day is a signal to plant all your seeds. There are a few crops you can get cracking with, however, either in pots on your windowsill or sown on your plot with a covering of fleece: have a look through the list below to see what's possible. If you haven't done so in January, it's time to plant shallot sets and garlic, which will tough out the worst of the weather and start to sprout in time for a crop in June or July. Jerusalem artichokes can also be planted now, but put them in a patch of earth that you can spare year after year – once established, they're impossible to get rid of from that spot.

But the keyword now is preparation: why not kickstart your compost heap for the coming year by adding manure, urine, or a shop-bought compost activator – or all three. If you don't have a compost heap yet, this is not necessarily a bad time to start one, although it probably won't really get going until the weather warms up a little. In the meantime you can prepare the earth for hungry crops such as runner beans and courgettes by trench composting: make a trench under the spot where they are to grow, line it with cardboard and mix in some kitchen waste. Top it off with the soil you've removed to make the trench and it will soon

TO DO THIS MONTH

February

Sow under protection

Cabbage
Cauliflower
Celeriac

Rocket
Swede

Sow direct

Broad beans
Onions (from seed)

Parsnips
Radishes

Plant direct

Garlic
Jerusalem artichokes
Raspberries

Rhubarb crowns
Shallot sets

Protect

Cabbage
Lettuce
Parsnips
Radishes

Rocket
Spinach
Swiss chard

Harvest

Cabbage
Broccoli, purple sprouting
Celeriac
Jerusalem artichokes
Kale
Leeks
Lettuce
Parsnips

Radishes
Rhubarb crowns (you have
   to force them at this time
   of year)
Rocket
Spinach
Swiss chard

begin to break down (do remember to mark its location with a couple of sticks for future reference).

Start digging in green manures such as field beans before they begin to flower, so that there's time for the nitrogen they've been storing up – which is great plant food – to be released into the soil. Prepare seed beds for the first sowings of the year by making sure the soil is broken down into fine crumbs, then covering it in black plastic if you haven't already done so. And, finally, if you haven't ordered seeds yet, get out the catalogues and start planning.

⌖ This month's project
CREATE SOME ALLOTMENT ART

Allotments don't have to be utilitarian places where the focus is entirely on producing food. Bring some artistic inspiration to your allotment by creating a sculpture: it could be a piece of twisted driftwood springing from the earth, surrounded by a pattern of pebbles and shells collected from a holiday beach; a mobile made from painted terracotta pots hung from a tree with raffia; or a decorative weathervane made from recycled wood for the top of your shed. If there are a few like-minded fellow plot holders, you could even set up an allotment art trail so you can admire each other's work.

March

Is there something in the Bible that says 'Thou shalt
not covet thy neighbour's plot'?

Emma Kitteridge, *Losing the Plot* **blog**

One of the finest seasonal treats to be had from the allotment –
purple sprouting broccoli – should be ready to harvest this month:
pick the central heads first and the plants should throw out lots of
secondary growth for later harvests. As the weather – and therefore
the soil on your plot – begins to warm up, so will your sowing
schedule, requiring more and more of your time. Provided
conditions are mild, the seeds of tough customers such as leeks,
spring onions and cabbages can be sown in the seed beds you've
already readied for the season; or, if slugs are a menace, sow them
in trays or modules first and then wait until they are sturdy enough
for planting out next month. Plant your shallots now, if you haven't
done so already, and onion sets and broad beans can go into the
ground now, too.

Spring also heralds a boom in the population of those less-than-
welcome visitors, pests and weeds. Begin to tackle them before
they take hold. Check for slug damage to young plants and have
your anti-slug armoury at the ready: slug-controlling nematodes can
be applied once the soil reaches 5°C. It's also time to check on any
vegetables you still have in storage, such as potatoes, onions and
pumpkins, for signs of deterioration: use them up while you can.

TO DO THIS MONTH

Sow under protection

Aubergines
Celery
Celeriac
Lettuce
Tomatoes

Sow direct

Beetroot
Broad beans
Brussels sprouts
Cabbage
Carrots
Cauliflower

Leeks
Onions
 (from seed)
Parsnips
Peas
Radishes

Rocket
Spinach
Spring onions
Turnips
Swiss chard

Plant direct

Asparagus crowns
Currants
Jerusalem artichokes

Onion sets
Potatoes
Raspberries

Rhubarb crowns
Shallot sets

Plant out

Cauliflower
Lettuce

Protect

Cabbage
Celeriac

Lettuce
Spinach

Swiss chard

Harvest

Broccoli, purple
 sprouting
Brussels sprouts
Cabbage
Cauliflower
Celeriac

Jerusalem
 artichokes
Kale
Leeks
Lettuce
Parsnips

Radishes
Rhubarb (forced)
Rocket
Spinach
Swiss chard

☙ **This month's project**

A PLACE TO REST

It's all too easy to spend all your time on the plot toiling away, never taking a moment to sit down and survey what you've already achieved, chat to your neighbours or simply enjoy the peace and quiet. A way of making time out a little more attractive is the installation of a comfy place to sit. At its very simplest and cheapest, this could be a wide plank of wood supported on two piles of breeze blocks, or an old kitchen chair stored in your shed, ready to bring out when the sun shines. It's worth thinking about where to put a seat before the summer arrives, because it's just as important to have somewhere to sit and warm your hands around a cup of hot tea on a chilly spring day when the grass is too wet to sit on. If you prefer something more ornamental, what about a patch of fragrant camomile lawn or a turf seat, so you can enjoy allotment picnics all summer?

Towards the end of the month you can also begin sowing seeds for Mediterranean favourites such as aubergines, chillies, peppers and tomatoes on a warm, sunny windowsill, preferably in a heated propagator so that they reach the required temperature for germination – at least 15°C. Keep a close eye on them for signs of damping off, a fungal condition that can kill off young seedlings: good ventilation, using clean pots and fresh compost, and watering little and often should help to stave off this problem.

If your seed potatoes arrive in the post this month, start them chitting ready for planting by laying them out somewhere bright and they should start sprouting. March is also a good time to plant out blackberry plants, so do buy a bush or two – they are such an easy fruit to grow and so hard to obtain in the supermarket. Now is also your last chance to plant bare-rooted raspberry canes and currant (red, white and black) bushes to ensure plenty of summer puddings next year. If you want an early strawberry harvest, place a few plants under a cold frame or cloche to cosset them into fruiting more speedily.

April

Your shed is an essential multi-task carapace, a shelter not only for all your gear and for yourself, but also serving as a one-stop meeting point for your less well-endowed, shedless mates.

Michael Rand, *Close to the Veg:*
A Book of Allotment Tales, 2005

It's spring, the sap is rising, and even the most fairweather allotmenteer begins to turn their attention to their plot. Even if dismal weather has meant you've neglected your patch all winter, there's still plenty of time to get things going again. Start on a small scale, renovating a single bed or area of the plot to get it ready for sowing. Once one patch is looking neat and tidy, it will give you the enthusiasm to plough on with the rest.

If you're more organised and already have seedlings of summer cabbages and cauliflowers ready to transplant from trays or pots, now is the time to put them in their final growing position. If not, you can buy plug plants of your chosen vegetables at the garden centre and catch up in no time. The weather may be warm and dry enough for the first sowings of quite a few vegetables, but keep an eye on the forecast and test the soil: freezing temperatures and young seedlings aren't compatible. You can still sow, but cover your young charges with a cloche or fleece if in doubt.

On areas being saved for later crops, concentrate on enriching

TO DO THIS MONTH

Sow under protection

Aubergines	Chillies	
Celeriac	French beans	Sweetcorn
Celery	Peppers	Tomatoes

Sow direct

Beetroot	Chard	Radishes
Broad beans	Kale	Rocket
Broccoli, purple	Leeks	Spinach
sprouting	Lettuce	Spring onions
Brussels sprouts	Onions	Swiss chard
Cabbage	(from seed)	Turnips
Carrots	Parsnips	
Cauliflower	Peas	

Plant direct

Globe artichokes	Onion sets
Jerusalem	Potatoes
artichokes	

Plant out

Cabbage	Cauliflower

Harvest

Asparagus	Radishes	Spring onions
Broccoli, purple	Rhubarb	Swiss chard
sprouting	Rocket	
Leeks	Spinach	

259

✒ **This month's project**

TART UP YOUR SHED

If you're lucky enough to have a shed on your allotment, why not make it the focal point of the plot? Paint a mural on the side wall or simply stain it a funky colour: there's no reason why you can't have a purple or blue shed, or a white-and-pastel-striped colour scheme to create a beach-hut effect. Then have a tidy up inside, close up any cracks and check your padlocks and windows are as secure as possible. Curtains may seem like unnecessary frippery, but they will prevent potential thieves from checking out what you have stored inside. If you need inspiration for what's possible, take a look at the website readersheds.co.uk to see what other people have done.

If, like me, you have to get by with a storage box, or perhaps no storage at all, focus your attention on streamlining the haul of gardening equipment you take to the plot each visit. Empty out your gardening bag and leave anything surplus to requirements behind. And make sure you have somewhere at home to store tools between trips: treat yourself to a new shelf or a set of hooks if needs be.

your soil by sowing green manures such as alfalfa, fenugreek and phacelia, and start making your very own plant tonic by steeping nettle, borage or comfrey leaves in water.

Your compost heap should be beginning to hot up now, so make sure you add a good mix of both 'brown' and 'green' materials. Rather than adding huge mounds of cuttings to your composter from the first lawn mowing of the year, consider applying them around the bases of onion or shallot sets, or as a mulch to your soft fruit bushes, ideally on top of a thick mulch of newspaper. Speaking of which, keep an eye out for new pest attacks that could thwart your plans: examine gooseberry bushes for the first signs of gooseberry sawfly larvae and pick off every last one, and be extra vigilant in your search for slugs.

It's now peak time for sowing seeds of tomatoes, aubergines and peppers indoors, and you can start sowing sweetcorn this month too. Buy some globe artichoke plants ready to put in the ground and you'll be on course for a cornucopia of Mediterranean vegetables.

May

> To the amateur gardener's eternally repeated question
> 'When should I?' and 'What's the best time to?' I've
> concluded that nine times out of ten the answer is
> 'When you're thinking about it; when you're in the
> mood'.

Christopher Lloyd, *The Well-Tempered Garden*, 1985

Spring may be in full swing this month, but don't let warm days
fool you: temperatures can still drop significantly at night, and
frosts are still a distinct possibility for most of the UK in May. So
if you do plant out tender plants you've grown in trays or
modules, such as celery, celeriac, lettuce, leeks, summer
cabbage, Brussels sprouts, aubergines and runner beans, make
sure that you offer them some protection in the form of a cloche,
cold frame or fleece covering. At the start of the month, sow some
sunflower seeds in pots or direct into the soil. It's always worth
growing a few things with no culinary use, just because they look
majestic, and children love to watch them grow and compete to
see 'whose' sunflower has grown the tallest, and birds adore
picking out seeds from the seed heads. Allotment holders fall into
two camps on the issue of birds. Some love to attract birds to their
plot, to eat pests such as caterpillars, and because they love to
watch them. Others prefer to banish them because of the damage
they can do to brassicas, newly-planted onion sets and so on. If

TO DO THIS MONTH

Sow under protection

Aubergines
Celeriac
Courgettes,
  marrow and other
  summer squash
Chillies
Cucumbers
Peppers
Pumpkins and other
  winter squash
Sweetcorn

Sow direct

Beetroot
Broccoli, purple
  sprouting
Cabbage
Carrots
Cauliflower
Florence fennel
French beans
Kale
Lettuce
Leeks
Parsnips
Peas
Radishes
Rocket
Runner beans
Spinach
Spring onions
Swedes
Turnips

Plant direct

Potatoes

Plant out

Cabbage
Cauliflower
Celeriac
French beans
Kale
Lettuce
Sweetcorn

Harvest

Asparagus
Broad beans
Cabbage
Celeriac
Jerusalem artichokes
Lettuce
Peas
Radishes
Rhubarb
Rocket
Spinach
Spring onions
Swiss chard
Turnips

you're in the latter camp, you can cut off the sunflower heads and take them home to place on your bird table.

Now is the time for sowing sweetcorn, pumpkins and courgettes in pots so they will be ready for planting out next month; French beans can either be sown direct in the spot where you want them to grow, or in pots where you can keep a closer eye

⧆ This month's project

CREATE A WILDLIFE POND

Most plots have them: a boggy, scrubby corner where nothing ever seems to grow except the weeds. Why not put it to good use by building a pond? Such a feature on an allotment may seem unnecessary, but it will attract huge amounts of wildlife to the area, including beautiful dragonflies and first-class slug chompers such as frogs, as well as providing a drink and a bath for the local birds and hedgehogs.

Before you start, check with the site owner that ponds are permitted. Once you have the go-ahead, you'll need to find a container or buy a liner for your pond. It needn't be huge: you can simply sink a large plastic box, an old bath or plastic dustbin into the ground and surround the edge with flat stones. Fill it with water, but make sure the depth is at least sixty centimetres so that the water won't freeze to the bottom in winter, providing a safe place for amphibians to hibernate. Populate the water with a few native pond plants and the creatures should turn up of their own accord, given time. And do make sure there is at least one gentle slope so that errant hedgehogs don't drown. You can create this by leaning a plank into the water to provide a getaway, or building up one of the pond's sides with some spare soil.

on them until they have established themselves and are ready for planting out in their final growing position.

If you already have rows of beetroot, lettuce, spinach, Swiss chard and carrots on your plot, keep down the weeds by running a sharp hoe in between the rows, and thin the seedlings so that each has enough space to grow. As your potatoes start to reach for the sky, remember to draw earth up around the stems to protect them from the frost and to stop the developing tubers being exposed to the light. Cover soft fruit with nets to stop mice and birds from lunching on them, and place straw around the base of strawberry plants to provide a dry bed for your burgeoning crop to rest on. Make sure your peas are well supported with sticks or netting to stop them from flopping over.

If you're struggling to keep up with an explosion in the weed population on your plot, try to get into the habit of making short visits to target particular areas rather than spending all day battling the problem. A useful shortcut is to roughly chop down the weeds then cover the area with a mulch of straw, black plastic or cardboard. You can part the mulch to plant crops such as potatoes or squash while the weeds rot down below the surface.

June

After a fortnight or so of struggling with what to do
and feeling guilty, I have come to the conclusion that,
despite swearing I never would, I fell into the beginner's
trap of thinking that I could do it all the first year.

Anna, *Plot c81* blog

There's no way of knowing what will be your busiest month on the
allotment: weather conditions will determine how well plants
progress. But my money is on June as one of the most hectic
allotment periods. There's so much to plant and so many crops
becoming ready to harvest that you may feel overwhelmed. Take a
step back, look at what you've already achieved, and don't panic
if you feel you're lagging behind your neighbours. There's still time
to sow many of the central crops, and if you haven't managed to
raise your own vegetable seedlings, don't feel ashamed to buy
some in from the garden centre.

Whether grown yourself or shop bought, crops such as
tomatoes, aubergines, sweetcorn, leeks and purple sprouting
broccoli are best transplanted into their final position in early
summer, once all threat of late frosts has evaporated. If in doubt,
wait, or protect the transplants with fleece or cloches. Give them a
head start by adding some compost or a sprinkling of seaweed
fertiliser into the bottom of the planting hole. The more you pick
peas and French beans, the more pods they will produce, so

TO DO THIS MONTH

Sow direct

Beetroot
Carrots
Courgettes, marrows
  and other summer
  squash
Cucumbers

Florence fennel
French beans
Lettuce
Peas
Pumpkins and other
  winter squash

Radishes
Rocket
Runner beans
Spring onions
Turnips

Plant direct

Potatoes

Plant out

Aubergines
Broccoli,
  purple sprouting
Cabbage
Cauliflower
Celeriac

Chillies
Courgettes, marrows
  and other summer
  squash
Cucumbers
Kale

Leeks
Peppers
Pumpkins and
  other winter
  squash
Tomatoes

Harvest

Asparagus
Beetroot
Broad beans
Cabbage
Carrots
Currants
French beans
Gooseberries

Lettuce
Onions (from sets)
Peas
Potatoes
Radishes
Raspberries
  (summer fruiting)
Rocket

Rhubarb
Spinach
Spring onions
Strawberries
Swiss chard
Turnips

harvest little and often to prolong the harvest.

It's also the soft fruit season, so you may be enjoying blackcurrants and strawberries. Save your soft fruit from birds and mice by netting the bushes if you haven't done so already, and try to pick and use each crop while it's at its prime, even if that means freezing some or turning them into pies, ice cream or jam. Once your strawberry plants have finished fruiting, give them a bit of TLC by trimming off straggling leaves and runners. If you want more strawberry plants next year use a tent peg to secure a runner to the soil to root and create a new plant. If you don't have any strawberry plants yet, you can plant out newly bought plants any

⊘ This month's project
MAKE AN ALLOTMENT GIFT BOX

One of the best ways of protecting Britain's remaining allotment sites is for every single patch to be occupied by an enthusiastic plot holder. And once you have become passionate about allotments, it's natural to want to wax lyrical about the benefits of growing your own fruit and vegetables to others. Rather than boring them by preaching the wonders of your own patch of green, you can convert friends and family to the cause much more effectively by giving them an allotment gift box or basket. If you're lucky enough to be enjoying your first harvest, include something you've grown and perhaps some jam made from your strawberry or blackcurrant crop. You could also add a book on allotments. Even if it doesn't make them rent a plot of their own, it will help to explain why you devote time to tending yours, and they might even offer to help you out in exchange for a regular cut of your crops.

time between now and late September, but will have to wait until the following year to reap a harvest.

Water thirsty crops such as squash and tomatoes as regularly as you can, preferably in the early morning or evening. You can help to conserve moisture by applying mulch around the base of the stems. When potato plants begin to flower, they benefit from extra watering to help the tubers swell, so a few additional trips with the watering can will pay off later in the year.

Above all, remember to spend a few minutes on each visit just enjoying your plot, smelling the delicate odours and snacking on fresh fruit or leaves as you pass by. Consider it a reward for all your hard labour.

July

The air is heavy with the scent of flowers and earthiness. I'll just sit down for two minutes. The soil is warm and cushioned with dry compost, and it pillows my shoulders and head. Mmm, bliss.

Victor Osborne, *Digger's Diary:*
***Tales from the Allotment*, 2000**

July is a month I mostly associate with toting watering cans up and down the path, quenching the thirst of the various plants that should be providing me with a steady flow of food. Don't forget to rest, particularly in the middle of the day when the sun is at its fiercest, and try to water your plants in the early morning or later evening when the water won't evaporate so quickly.

By now your comfrey plants should be big and bushy: cut them back and put the leaves on the compost heap or steep them in water for a wonderful, if smelly, plant tonic. And do keep an eye on your compost heap. It should almost be shrinking before your eyes at this time of year, particularly if the weather is hot, but it may also dry out, which will slow down the decomposition process. Shove your hand inside, or if you're not so brave, stick a fork in it. Dig deeper than about ten centimetres and the material should be moist, but not wet. If it's too dry, pour on some water: if wet, remove the cover for a few days to let the moisture evaporate.

It's also time to transplant your sweetcorn plants into their final

TO DO THIS MONTH

Sow direct

Beetroot	Lettuce	
Carrots	Peas	Swiss chard
Florence fennel	Radishes	Turnips

Plant direct

Potatoes (for an autumn/ winter crop)	Strawberries

Plant out

Broccoli, purple sprouting	Cabbage	Kale
	Cauliflower	Leeks

Harvest

Beetroot	Globe artichokes	Runner beans
Currants	Gooseberries	Shallots
Broad beans	Lettuce	Spinach
Cabbage	Onions (from sets and seeds)	Spring onions
Carrots		Strawberries
Celery	Peas	Swiss chard
Courgettes, marrows and other summer squash	Potatoes	Turnips
	Radishes	
Cucumbers	Raspberries (summer fruiting)	
French beans	Rocket	
Garlic	Rhubarb	

growing site: remember to arrange them in a block to encourage pollination. And keep training your cordon tomatoes that don't grow on bushes, and have a single stem by tying the main stem to a sturdy stake and pinching out side shoots, so that the plants concentrate their energies into producing flowers and fruits.

As everything from peas and beans to lettuces and courgettes reach the peak of ripeness, you may feel overwhelmed by a glut.

⌖ This month's project

MAKE A SCARECROW

As anyone old enough to remember the children's television series *Worzel Gummidge* will know, there's a certain magic about scarecrows. Although they've long since been abandoned by farmers as a way of keeping birds off crops in favour of more scientific means such as automatic bird scarers, scarecrows still hold a place in our imagination, providing the focus for village festivals across the country.

You can construct one for your allotment using old clothes stuffed with straw or balled-up tights and socks. Attach the 'body' to an upright stake and insert a horizontal support through the armholes. Use your imagination: your scarecrow could be modelled after yourself, or a celebrity, or be dressed in the strip of your preferred football team. Whatever you choose, your scarecrow will be a talking point, a landmark for your plot and something fun for children who may find digging and weeding boring. It may even scare away the birds that are uprooting your newly planted onion sets and pecking at your broccoli.

See this as an opportunity to share your crops with family, friends or work colleagues, and don't feel guilty about only eating the very finest of the crop: those holey lettuces will be a great addition to your compost heap. By the middle of the month, you should take your last rhubarb leaves for harvesting, then leave the plant alone for the rest of the year to rebuild its strength for the following season.

And don't forget to keep sowing! 'Early' carrot, beetroot, turnip and pea varieties sown early in the month will extend your harvest season, while planting an early variety of seed potato will provide you with new potatoes for your Christmas lunch.

August

What is it tonight, then? The pub, the cinema, early to bed for a bit of 'this and that', or a spot of slug hunting by torchlight? It's got to be slug hunting, hasn't it? Slug hunting by torchlight. Great fun.

Patrick Vickery, *Garden Blethers* website

It's just as well at this time of year to remind yourself that allotment work is a marathon, not a sprint. It's hard to think ahead to the end of summer, but if you don't plan ahead you may find that your supply of vegetables runs out faster than you expected.

One of the key jobs this month if you're a fan of pumpkins and other winter squash is to pinch out the growing tips of the plants once they already have several fruits growing. This will force the plant to channel its energy into the existing fruits rather than trying to produce more which ultimately won't have time to mature.

You should also be thinking about winter vegetables by now, and transplanting cabbage, Brussels sprouts and kale into their final growing positions. And by sowing more lettuce, radishes and winter spinach, you can keep your salad bowl full throughout the autumn. If you don't have any seedlings to put into beds left empty by newly harvested crops, you can sow green manures in them to stop nutrients being leached from the ground and so prepare the soil for a forthcoming crop.

TO DO THIS MONTH

Sow direct
Cabbage
Lettuce
Onions (from seed),
  overwintered

Radishes
Spinach
Spring onions
Swiss chard

Turnips

Plant direct
Strawberries

Plant out
Broccoli, purple
  sprouting

Cabbage
Leeks

Harvest
Aubergines
Beetroot
Cabbage
Cauliflower
Celery
Chillies
Courgettes, marrows
  and other summer
  squash
Cucumber
French beans

Garlic
Globe artichokes
Lettuce
Onions (from sets
  and seeds)
Peas
Peppers
Potatoes
Pumpkins and
  other winter
  squash

Radishes
Rocket
Runner beans
Shallots
Spinach
Spring onions
Sweetcorn
Swiss chard
Tomatoes
Turnips

If you aren't sure whether your potatoes are ready to harvest, you can cheat and scrape away some of the soil to have a peek at the tubers. If they aren't big enough, just carefully replace the soil and leave them be for a few more weeks.

Jerusalem artichokes may start flowering if it's a hot summer. Some gardeners recommend cutting off the flower buds to improve the crop, but they're rather pretty sunflower-like blooms, so I leave them be – there are always more than enough tubers to be busy harvesting.

✑ This month's project
HOLD AN ALLOTMENT PICNIC

Most of your friends and family probably know that you have an allotment, but have they ever seen it? Invite ten people to your plot one weekend afternoon to show them around. Tempt them with a picnic or barbecue that features vegetables from your plot, then rope them in to help you with a particular project, such as putting up a new shed, repairing a fence or harvesting potatoes. Make sure you aren't going to be breaking any of your site's rules about visitors, and don't get in the way of any of your neighbouring plot holders – whom you can invite too, of course.

September

After all the leafy turmoil and extravagance of high summer, it is something of a relief to see some bare soil again at the allotment.

Elspeth Thompson, *The Urban Gardener*, 2000

It's crucial to gather in as many crops as possible before the weather turns and they are ruined by the rain and cold. Towards the end of the month, pick tomatoes, even if they are green. Put them in a paper bag with a banana and they should ripen, or if not they'll make a very fine green tomato chutney. It's important to dry out crops you plan to store, such as onions and shallots. If the sun is shining this can be done outside; otherwise, find a cool dry place indoors and lay them out on netting to allow the air to circulate. Leave pumpkins and other winter squash for as long as you can, but when frosts threaten, detach them along with a good thirty centimetres of stem and move them inside. As with all stored crops, use any specimens that are damaged immediately.

Cut back summer-fruiting raspberry canes to ground level and tie in new canes to your supports, after thinning them to three to six canes per plant, and remember to remove netting from your strawberry bed to do some tidying up and weeding.

You should start thinking about saving seeds for next year (peas and beans are easy ones to start with) and preparing the soil for

TO DO THIS MONTH

Sow direct

Lettuce	Rocket
Radishes	Spinach

Plant direct

Onion sets, overwintered	Strawberries

Plant out

Cabbage

Harvest

Aubergines	Florence fennel	Raspberries
Beetroot	French beans	(autumn fruiting)
Cabbage	Globe artichokes	Rocket
Carrots	Leeks	Runner beans
Cauliflower	Lettuce	Spinach
Celeriac	Onions (from sets	Spring onions
Celery	and seeds)	Sweetcorn
Chillies	Peas	Swiss chard
Courgettes, marrows	Peppers	Tomatoes
and other	Potatoes	Turnips
summer squash	Pumpkins and	
Cucumber	other winter	
	squash	

winter. Sow green manures such as Hungarian grazing rye, phacelia and field beans to stop nutrients being lost from the soil during the winter and to improve soil structure. Begin trench composting on cleared ground where you're planning to plant pumpkins and beans next year, and keep up the squish patrol for caterpillars on brassicas.

As the days begin to shorten, think about bringing out the cloches and fleece to protect overwintering vegetables such as Swiss chard. If you want fresh herbs to harvest all winter, dig up some chives, mint, basil and sage and pot them up for your kitchen windowsill. And it's your last chance this month to plant out newly-bought strawberry plants.

If you are especially keen to get an early crop of onions next year, buy specially prepared overwintered onion sets, which can be planted now and will grow throughout the winter, and be ready for harvest several weeks earlier than spring-sown sets.

✑ This month's project

ADOPT A VEGETABLE

Aside from obtaining and growing heritage vegetables yourself, you can get friends and family interested in the cause by buying them the gift of an adopted vegetable from the Heritage Seed Library. Choose a suitable variety from the more than 150 on offer, picking a name to suit the recipient – sadly the Lazy Housewife bean is one of the more popular choices. They will get some seeds and growing pots, along with information about their heritage cultivar, and could be inspired to get into helping preserve our vegetable heritage. See the directory at the end of the book for more details.

October

What of October, that ambiguous month, the month
of tension, the unendurable month?

Doris Lessing, *Martha Quest*, 1964

I'm not sure why Doris Lessing found October unendurable,
though it can be depressing when the realisation dawns that
summer is finally over. But although things might be slowing down
on your plot, if the weather holds out you may find you're still
harvesting summer vegetables. You should try to pick and store as
much as you can now in preparation for the winter ahead.

Top priority for me at this time of year is making sure that my
potatoes are out of the ground and stored, and my pumpkins and
other winter squash are safely hung up. Cut down the tall stems of
Jerusalem artichokes, but leave a few centimetres sticking out of
the ground so that you can find them when you want to do some
harvesting; they should last all winter in the ground.

It's never too early to start thinking about the future. Plant
overwintered varieties of broad beans and onions, sow winter
radish and lettuce seeds and send off for next year's seed
catalogues. Plant garlic bulbs now for an early summer crop next
year, and make sure any remaining onions are harvested and dried
by the end of the month. Resist the temptation to tidy up the plot
too much: a bit of plant debris provides a welcome home for lots of
valuable insects, including aphid-eating lacewings and ladybirds,

TO DO THIS MONTH

Sow under protection
Lettuce
Radishes

Spinach

Sow direct
Broad beans

Plant direct
Garlic
Rhubarb crowns

Onion sets,
    overwintered

Plant out
Cabbage

Protect
Lettuce
Radishes

Spinach
Swiss chard

Harvest
Beetroot
Brussels sprouts
Cabbage
Carrots
Cauliflower
Celeriac
Chillies
Courgettes,
    marrows and
    other summer
    squash

Florence fennel
Leeks
Lettuce
Onions (from sets
    and seeds)
Parsnips
Peas
Peppers
Potatoes
Pumpkins and
    other winter squash

Radishes
Raspberries
    (autumn fruiting)
Rocket
Swiss chard
Turnips

although it is worth raking up a few plastic sacks of fallen leaves to convert into leaf mould, a marvellous soil conditioner. Cut French and runner bean plants down at ground level, but leave the roots in the earth to release nitrogen into the soil. Pack away wooden stakes and supports so they don't rot in the rain.

✍ This month's project
MAKE A HOME FOR A HEDGEHOG

Everyone loves hedgehogs. Despite their prickles, they're the most cuddly looking of allotment visitors, and do-gooders into the bargain, chomping on slugs and caterpillars, although they also eat beneficial insects such as ground beetles. As development wipes out many urban and suburban green spaces, allotments are becoming crucial territory for Britain's dwindling hedgehog population, which is declining at a rate of about a fifth of the population every four years. There's no better way to help hedgehogs than making sure they have plenty of hidey holes between November and March, when they generally go into hibernation. You can buy fancy hedgehog houses made of wood from sustainable sources and these need to be sited carefully in a corner where any prickly visitors won't be disturbed: at the foot of a hedge, partially obscured by leaves is ideal. If you don't want to shell out on a specially made box, just make sure that there are plenty of dry leaves piled up somewhere, because hedgehogs use these to construct their nests. I keep a large pile of branches behind my compost bins, which make an ideal home. Finally, if you're planning a bonfire for Guy Fawkes night, do construct the pyre just before you're ready to burn it, or, if it's been in situ for a few days, give it a good shake to ensure no hedgehogs have made it their home.

November

Too damned cold to do a damned thing and all I've managed for weeks is to dig stuff and shove in some garlic and onions.

Carina O'Reilly, *Plot Holes* blog

Don't be too hard on yourself at this time of year. You've probably got used to bringing home a basket of goodies every time you visit your plot, but frosts have likely killed off anything not winter-hardy by now, and inclement weather and the switch to GMT may mean you only get to your plot weekly or fortnightly. Don't be racked by guilt, but do stay in the habit of making regular visits, even if it's only to batten down the hatches on your shed, tidy away stray beanpoles and pots or have a chat with your neighbours.

Clear days can be ideal for getting some maintenance work done, so this is a good time to give your shed or storage box a lick of paint, renovate an old raised bed or build a new one, and clean and oil your tools. Add mulch to empty soil on your allotment to stop nutrients draining away during heavy rain, and close down your compost heap for the winter by topping it off with an old woollen blanket, or plastic or cardboard sheeting. Kitchen and garden waste can still be saved, of course: just add it to a composting trench.

Don't forget to start using the stores of vegetables and fruit you've so carefully preserved in the freezer or on the shelf. Now is

November

TO DO THIS MONTH

Sow under protection
Rocket

Sow direct
Broad beans   Peas, overwintered

Plant direct
Currants   Onion sets,   Raspberries
Garlic   overwintered   Rhubarb crowns

Protect
Broad beans   Peas, overwintered   Spinach
Lettuce   Radishes   Swiss chard

Harvest
Brussels sprouts   Kale   Spinach
Cabbages   Leeks   Swedes
Carrots   Lettuce   Swiss chard
Cauliflowers   Parsnips   Turnips
Celeriac   Potatoes
Jerusalem   Radishes
  artichokes   Rocket

the season for crumbles made from soft fruit frozen earlier in the year, hearty stews containing dried beans and pumpkins from your store, and chutney cooked up with the last of the courgettes and tomatoes. November is also the perfect time for planting newly bought bare-rooted raspberry canes and currant bushes, although

꧁ This month's project

ATTEND A SEED SWAP EVENT

One of the delights of having an allotment is the experience of sharing your bounty with others: friends, family, neighbours and work colleagues will welcome your excess harvest at times of glut. But it doesn't stop there, for you can expand your repertoire of plants and exchange seed surpluses with fellow growers, too, helping them and you to be thrifty. There's no point in hoarding seeds, after all, as many have a limited lifespan of only a few years. Since about the mid-1990s, seed swapping has become an organised community event, with the invention of what's known as the Seedy Saturday or Sunday. These events bring together allotment holders and gardeners to exchange their excess seeds – both from commercially-bought packets and from seed they've saved themselves – as well as seed potatoes, young plants, and spare tools and pots. It's a great way of keeping heritage varieties alive, getting to know other growers and knitting together an allotment community. Dozens of seed swap groups have been set up across the country: there is no specific seed swap organisation in the UK but the Heritage Seed Library and local allotment or gardening groups should be able to help you track one down. You'll be welcomed even if you don't have much to offer, as most Seedy Saturdays will accept a small donation in lieu of a swap.

you can get away with leaving this job until as late as mid-March if weather conditions are inclement in the winter.

It's also peak season for sowing overwintered broad beans and peas. Make sure you choose a variety that is described as 'autumn sown' or 'overwintered', though. Broad beans and peas will benefit from some protection during the winter months, so cover the newly sown rows with horticultural fleece now to save time later. You should now be enjoying a good harvest of winter vegetables, including leeks, kale and Brussels sprouts. Help the leeks develop long white stems by earthing them up with extra soil and strip away some of the lower leaves from your celeriac plants to encourage large roots to form.

December

How I value my allotment in the run-up to Christmas as a priceless breathing space away from crowds and consumption.

Antonia Swinson, *Scotsman*, December 2005

As the year winds down, so too does the allotment. It's time to take stock of the past twelve months' successes and failures, tidy up loose ends and batten down the hatches for winter. Make sure your shed, storage box and fencing are secure enough not to blow down in a heavy storm, put away canes and stakes, and check that any tall plants are well tied in to sturdy supports (a pair of old tights makes an excellent tie for bigger specimens). If you have a greenhouse that you plan to use during the winter, get it ready by giving it a good clean, and insulate the insides with bubblewrap.

If you insist on keeping busy, you can lift and divide rhubarb crowns, dig manure into beds and give your tools the once over. If you haven't needed to protect winter crops such as cabbages and Swiss chard before now, start thinking about it before it's too late and your crop is reduced to a pile of mush.

But if the weather's bad, why not settle down in an easy chair to peruse the gardening catalogues and plan next year's allotment campaign? It's never too early to sketch out a draft of what you will grow where next season, and it will help you to keep a track of

December

TO DO THIS MONTH

Sow under protection
Rocket

Plant direct

Currants	Raspberries
Garlic	Shallots

Protect

Lettuce	Spinach	Swiss chard

Harvest

Brussels sprouts	Kale	Swedes
Cabbages	Leeks	Swiss chard
Carrots	Lettuce	Turnips
Cauliflowers	Parsnips	
Celeriac	Radishes	
Jerusalem	Rocket	
artichokes	Spinach	

crop rotation. Keep half an eye on your stores and use pumpkins and potatoes before they're beyond their prime.

Use a bright winter's day to prune blackcurrant bushes, removing a third of the stems from each bush. Pick the older stems to cut back – these can be identified by their colour – the wood will be much darker than newer growth.

If you can, try to incorporate a couple of home-grown treats into your Christmas dinner menu: onions for the stuffing, roast potatoes from your store, Brussels sprouts straight from the plant, or some carrots kept in damp sand until the big day. It should show your dinner guests just what a year-round provider an allotment can be.

ᘓᵛ **This month's project**

DECORATE A CHRISTMAS TREE FOR YOUR PLOT

Seen from the perspective of a December day on the allotment the idea of chopping down a tree and dragging it inside your house as a way of celebrating Christmas seems utterly ridiculous. Why not decorate a living tree on your allotment instead, which will give you a lift on the dullest winter day and can also be put to practical use.

You could turn an established apple tree into a Christmassy bird scarer to protect winter cabbages and broccoli by hanging silver streamers, bits of tinsel too tatty for your home and old CDs or DVDs (the kind you get free on the front of magazines) from red and green ribbons tied to the branches. Of if you are more interested in attracting birds than driving them away, what about buying balls of fat studded with seeds, peanuts or even freeze-dried mealworms to hang from the branches? It's cheaper, if a little more labour intensive, to make your own bird feeders. Melt some suet or lard in an old saucepan, then add seeds, nuts, cheese and dried fruit at a ratio of around one third fat to two thirds seed mix. Get a plastic yogurt pot – you can paint the outside if you're feeling artistic – punch a small hole in the bottom and thread some string through, tying knots in the end on the inside of the pot so that you can hang it up. Then pour the fat mix into the pot and let it harden. Once cooled, the feeder is ready to hang from your tree. If you don't have a tree on your plot, you can stick a branch in the ground instead and decorate that, or jazz up blackcurrant bushes or raspberry canes.

An allotmenteer's glossary

Aeration: a way of increasing the quantity of air pockets in the soil, either by digging or by adding materials such as perlite or humus (see below).

Allium: any member of the allium genus of plants, which includes onions, shallots, leeks, chives and garlic.

Annual: a plant whose life cycle – from seed germination to the death of the plant – only lasts one year.

Biennial: a plant that grows over two seasons, usually flowering and/or fruiting in the second before dying off.

Biodiversity: the abundance and range of animals, plants, fungi and micro-organisms present in any environment, as fostered by organic gardening.

Biological control: using another creature to attack a pest infestation, such as introducing ladybird larvae to feast on aphid-covered leaves.

Blanching: in horticultural (rather than culinary) terms, this means shielding a plant – usually celery, but also cardoons and endives – from the light so that the green chlorophyll fades and the stems have a more delicate flavour.

Brassica: any member of the brassica genus of plants, such as cabbage, rocket, cress, cauliflower, Brussels sprouts and kale.

Bolting: a term used to describe a vegetable crop that has become worthless because it has started to flower and set seed. Can be a problem with salad crops as warm weather causes some varieties to flower. The word 'seedy', meaning unwell or off-colour, derives from the description of a plant that is full of seeds and therefore past its best.

Chitting: encouraging seed potatoes to sprout before planting them in the ground. Achieved by placing in a light, cool place.

Clamp: an outdoor structure made out of soil and straw used to store root vegetables like carrots and potatoes. Largely out of favour as it's tricky to maintain. Also known as a grave.

Cloche: a clear glass or plastic cover, traditionally bell-shaped, used to cover individual plants or groups of plants to protect them from frosts or temperature extremes.

Cold frame: a wooden or aluminium-framed structure with a hinged glass or clear plastic lid that is used to protect plants from extremes of weather. See *hardening off*.

Comfrey tea: comfrey contains high levels of nitrogen, so a solution of comfrey leaves, having sat for some weeks in water, works as an organic liquid feed when watered on plants. Nettles can be used as an alternative to comfrey.

Companion planting: a planting scheme where plants that provide some benefit to an allotment crop are grown close to that crop. For instance, the strong odours of onion, chive and garlic plants are believed to mask the smell of carrots, thereby throwing the destructive carrot fly off the scent.

Compost activator: any substance used to speed up the process of decomposition: human urine, comfrey leaves and shop-bought preparations all work.

Cordon tomato: see *indeterminate tomato*.

Cotyledon: the first leaf to appear after a seed has germinated. This usually looks completely different from the plant's 'true' leaves.

Crop rotation: a growing regime that groups plants into several categories according to their needs; usual groupings are the potato family, legumes, brassicas and roots. In the first year, each group is grown on a particular area of the allotment; the following year the beds are 'rotated' in a specific order so that the plants always receive the best possible soil conditions and no group grows on the same soil in consecutive years.

Crown: the part of a plant where the stems meet the roots; usually positioned at soil level when planting.

Cucurbit: any member of the *cucurbitaceae* family of plants, which includes melons, courgettes, cucumbers and pumpkins.

Cultivar: shorthand for cultivated variety: a strain of plant that has been developed by gardeners through selective breeding.

Cut-and-come-again: a leafy salad crop – lettuce, corn salad, Chinese greens and so on – that is picked as individual leaves when the plant is still young, and expected to continue to grow, providing a continuous harvest.

Damping off: a fungal disease that kills seedlings, making them collapse from the stem. Prevalent in damp conditions.

Deadheading: removing the flower heads from plants as they fade in order to prolong the flowering period.

Determinate tomato: a tomato plant that grows in the form of a bush. See also *indeterminate tomato.*

Dibber: a pointed stick, usually wooden, used to make holes in the earth for sowing seeds and planting bulbs or seedlings. Can be crafted from the broken handle of a digging spade or fork.

Double digging: a particularly taxing method of preparing a bed for planting, generally used for compacted or poorly drained soil, in which sections of soil are dug into trenches and the bottom of the trench is broken up with a fork.

Earthing up: piling up earth around the base and stem of a plant. Mostly used to prevent light from reaching potato tubers and celery stems and to deter weeds.

Fanging: root vegetables, particularly carrots, can develop this condition, where the body of the vegetable is split into two or more 'fangs' as a result of having been sown in soil too rich in nitrogen, or through being grown in stony soil.

Fertiliser: any material added to soil to provide varying amounts of soluble nitrogen, phosphorus and potassium, all of which are nutrients that help plants to grow. Includes manure, comfrey tea and commercially available brands.

Fleece: a thin, white, lightweight material that protects plants from harsh weather while allowing light to reach them, also used to exclude pests. Also known as horticultural fleece.

Forcing: putting a plant – usually rhubarb or sea kale – into the dark, usually by means of a bucket or a tall lidded terracotta pot specially designed for the purpose, in December or January so that it produces delicate, tasty shoots.

Friable: a term used to describe soil that has just the right consistency for growing: crumbly but not too light.

Green manure: a crop, such as field beans or rye grass, that is grown to improve the quality and fertility of the soil rather than for eating. Often left to stand over the winter and dug into the ground in the spring. Also known as cover crops or living mulches.

Hardening off: the process of gradually exposing seedlings grown indoors or in a greenhouse to the harsher conditions of the outside in preparation for planting them out on the plot.

Hardy: any plant that can survive without cover or other protection throughout the year, including the winter.

Haulm: officially this term refers to the stem of any plant, but most allotmenteers use it specifically for the stems of potato plants.

Heeling in: a method of storing root crops outside by digging them up and replanting them shallowly in a dryish, sheltered, frost-free spot – against a shed or building wall is ideal. Heeling in is also used as a method of keeping newly purchased rose plants or trees alive until conditions are right to plant them out in their final positions.

Heritage vegetable: a variety of plant that is pollinated by natural means (the wind, insects, birds and so on) and was introduced before 1951 but has ceased to be grown commercially because it doesn't conform to the requirements of industrial-scale agriculture. Heritage vegetables are prized by some gardeners for their unique qualities, history and flavour. Also known as an heirloom vegetable.

Hot bed: a cold frame that is positioned over a layer of fresh manure which, as it breaks down, releases heat to warm the structure. Used as a mini-greenhouse to raise crops when temperatures outdoors are too low for growing crops.

Humus: the organic material contained within soil, created when organisms such as worms and bacteria break down dead plant matter.

Indeterminate tomato: tomato plants from which the side shoots are removed to allow the plant to grow as a single stem. Also known as cordon or vine tomatoes. See also *determinate tomato*.

Kitchen (or compost) caddy: a lidded container with a handle that's kept in the kitchen to collect vegetable waste for the compost bin.

Lazy bed: a form of raised bed not bounded by boards or bricks but marked out using trenches. The margins of the bed are dug out and the excess soil is piled up in the middle to create a ridge upon which vegetables – most popularly potatoes – are grown.

Leaf mould: decomposed leaves that can be used as a medium for seed sowing and as a way of adding humus to soil.

Leggy: a word used to describe plants that have grown too fast or without enough light, leaving them tall and with sparse foliage.

Legume: any member of the *Leguminosae* (also known as *Fabaceae*) family, especially peas and beans. Includes runner beans, fenugreek, broad beans and lupins.

Lime: a calcium compound spread onto soil as a dressing to raise its pH (make it less acidic and more alkaline).

Loam: a rich soil that's ideal for cultivating fruit and vegetables. Contains equal quantities of sand, clay and silt and is full of organic material.

Microplant: a small plant that has been propagated under laboratory conditions and is usually sold in trays. This technique is often used as a way of keeping rare potato varieties alive.

Mulch: material that is layered thickly on the surface of the soil to retain water, suppress weeds and prevent the leaching of nutrients. Many different materials can be used for mulch, including black plastic sheeting, wads of newspaper, cardboard and grass cuttings.

Nematode: a family of tiny parasitic worms. Some nematodes, such as *Phasmarhabditis hermaphrodita,* can be used to control pests, such as slugs. Others can damage plants, for example eelworms, which eat roots and potato tubers.

New Zealand box: a compost bin system dreamed up in New Zealand that uses square wooden bins to store the decomposing material.

Nitrogen fixer: plants from the legume family that can help to enrich the soil with nitrogen. Bacteria that live in the plants' roots take nitrogen from the air and convert it into a form that plants can use as an essential soil nutrient. The nitrogen is then stored in the plants until they are incorporated into the soil and decompose, gradually releasing the nitrogen into the soil where it can once more be taken up by subsequent crops. Many green manures are also nitrogen fixers.

Nodule: a growth on the roots of certain plants that hosts bacteria which take nitrogen from the air and store it.

NSALG: National Society of Allotment and Leisure Gardening.

Offset: a young plant that grows out from the body of a mature plant and develops its own root system. It can be removed and transplanted to create a second plant.

Organic gardening: working with nature to boost the productivity and natural health of the soil in order to grow plants without the use of synthetic chemicals.

Overwintering: in allotment terms, overwintering means planting specially prepared seeds or sets in the late summer or autumn which will start growing, survive the winter and supply you with an early spring harvest. Specially 'overwintered' or 'overwintering' varieties of peas, garlic, broad beans, lettuce and onions are some of the most popular crops for overwintering. (In more general gardening terms, overwintering means protecting tender plants from the winter weather by moving them to a sheltered spot such as a cold frame or conservatory.).

Perch: see *rod*.

Perennial: a plant that will survive for several years.

Perlite: a lightweight, white, granular substance used in potting-compost mixes because it holds water and helps aerate the soil.

Permaculture: a movement that champions following nature's patterns to live in a sustainable way that does not use up the earth's resources. Short for 'permanent agriculture', the term was coined by Australian ecologist Bill Mollison.

Pinch out: to remove a plant's shoots in order to check its growth or train it in a certain way.

Plug plants: young plants that are too old to be classed as seedlings but are not yet fully grown. Usually sold in module trays and ready to plant out immediately on the plot.

Pole: see 'Rod'.

Pollination: the transfer of pollen – either by wind, insects, birds or human hand – between the sexual organs of plants as a precursor to the fertilisation of seed. Cross-pollination occurs when the transfer is between two different plants; self-pollination is when the pollen is moved either between two different flowers on the same plant, or between the sexual organs of a single flower.

Prick out: to transplant young seedlings from a seed tray or pot into individual pots.

Propagating: growing new plants by using various techniques, such as taking cuttings, sowing seeds or removing offsets.

Pruning: removing stems from a plant in a bid to make it more productive. Commonly used on soft fruit such as raspberries and blackcurrants.

Raised bed: a growing bed edged with wood, plastic or some other material and filled with extra soil to lift it above the level of the surrounding paths. Favoured by many allotmenteers as a less labour-intensive way of growing.

Rod: an archaic British unit of measurement used to mark out allotment plots. One rod equals thirty and a quarter square yards or just over twenty-five and a quarter square metres. Also known as a pole or perch. Most British allotments measure ten rods, or about 253 square metres, although many sites now offer plots of half that size.

Root ball: the cluster of roots and the soil clinging to it that remain attached to a plant when dug out of the ground.

Rust: a fungal disease that can affect broad beans, onions, leeks and garlic. The symptoms are rusty red pustules on the leaves and stems in the summer months.

Seed potatoes: specially-treated potato tubers that are bought by growers and prepared for planting by being sprouted (or chitted as it's also known). When placed in the ground the sprouts will grow upwards and each tuber will produce a single potato plant, which can yield dozens of potatoes.

Sets: small, specially prepared bulbs of either onions or shallots that can be planted instead of sowing seed and will grow into full-sized bulbs.

Slip: a rooted plant cutting. The term is often used for sweet potatoes.

Soil improver: any organic material added to the soil to improve its fertility and general condition, including leaf mould, mushroom compost and rotted manure.

Soil pH: a measure of how acid or alkaline a patch of soil is. The pH scale goes from 0 to 14: soil with pH 7 is neutral, pH 0 to 7 is increasingly acidic, and pH 7 to 14 is increasingly alkaline. Most soil in the UK falls between 4 and 9. Soil pH can dictate what plants you can grow, as some won't thrive in acid or alkaline conditions.

Square-foot gardening: a method of growing fruit and vegetables where the crops are grown in a grid of one-foot (thirty-centimetre) squares.

Station sowing: sowing seeds in their final growing position, far enough apart that little or no thinning is required. Often used for larger seeds such as squash and beans, where two seeds are planted together to ensure that at least one seed germinates in each spot – if two seedlings grow, the weaker one is removed.

Sterile: when describing a plant, this means that the plant is unable to reproduce sexually, in other words by setting seed. Some sterile plants can however be propagated from cuttings, or by separating clumps of roots into new plants. When used in reference to compost, it means that any micro-organisms or fungi have been killed off, making sterile compost an ideal medium for sowing seeds.

Succession planting or sowing: a little and often approach to sowing seeds, resulting in a crop that matures over a number of weeks or months rather than all at once.

Thong: a section of root planted in the ground to cultivate a new plant. Often used in reference to horseradish plants.

Three sisters planting: a method of planting devised by Native Americans whereby sweetcorn, beans and squash are grown together in a single bed. The beans grow up the corn stalks and add nitrogen to the soil, and the squash leaves provide shade for the beans and corn, prevent weeds from moving in, and deter pests from reaching the crops.

Tilth: soil that has been prepared for growing; should be crumbly and fine, free from large stones with plenty of organic material.

Trenching: a technique used either to protect delicate plants during the winter by placing them in a trench filled with quick-draining compost, or a method of blanching celery stems by excluding the light. The plants are grown in a trench a spade's depth and twice as wide and the stems are covered with earth – blanched – as they grow to prevent light from reaching them.

Trench composting: a shortcut way of composting that entails burying green and kitchen waste in the ground and covering with soil, several months before the start of the growing season. Particularly useful when preparing the ground for growing crops that thrive on rich soil, such as pumpkins, courgettes and beans.

Truss: a stalk that ends in a cluster of flowers or fruit. Most often used to describe the flowering stems of tomato plants.

Vermiculite: a lightweight, flaky mineral used in potting-compost mixes for its water retention and aerating qualities.

Volunteer plant: a seedling that has grown from a parent plant which has unintentionally been allowed to spread its seed.

Wormcasts: piles of fine, humus rich soil that are excreted by worms. Can be harvested from wormeries or bought and applied to your plot as a soil improver.

Wormery: a bin containing worms that's used as a faster, more efficient way to compost kitchen waste and generate organic fertiliser.

Bibliography

Allotments: A Plot Holder's Guide (Department for Communities and Local Government)

Andrews, Sophie, *The Allotment Handbook* (Eco-Logic Books/Worldly Goods, 2001)

Appelhof, Mary, *Worms Eat My Garbage* (Eco-Logic Books/Worldly Goods, 1982)

Biggs, Matthew, McVicar, Jekka and Flowerdew, Bob, *The Complete Book of Vegetables, Herbs and Fruit: The Definitive Sourcebook for Growing, Harvesting and Cooking* (Kyle Cathie, 2004)

Borish, Elaine, *What Will I Do With All Those Courgettes?* (Fidelio Press, 2002)

Bourne, Val, *The* Daily Telegraph *Seeds of Wisdom* (Cassell Illustrated, 2003)

Carluccio, Antonio, *Antonio Carluccio's Vegetables* (Headline Book Publishing, 2000)

Clayden, Paul, *The Law of Allotments* (Shaw & Sons, 2002)

Crouch, David and Ward, Colin, *The Allotment: Its Landscape and Culture* (Five Leaves Publications, 1997)

Crouch, David, Sempik, Joe and Wiltshire, Richard, *Growing in the Community: A Good Practice Guide for the Management of Allotments* (LGA Publications, 2001)

Darwin, Charles, *The Effects of Cross and Self-Fertilisation in the Vegetable Kingdom* (Adamant Media Corporation, 2001)

Don, Monty, *The Complete Gardener* (Dorling Kindersley, 2003)

Don, Monty, *My Roots: A Decade in the Garden* (Hodder & Stoughton, 2005)

Elliot, Rose, *Learning to Cook Vegetarian* (Weidenfeld & Nicolson Illustrated, 1998)

Fearnley-Whittingstall, Hugh, *The River Cottage Cookbook* (HarperCollins, 2001)

Fearnley-Whittingstall, Hugh, *The River Cottage Year* (Hodder & Stoughton, 2003)

Foster, Clare, *Compost* (Cassell Illustrated, 2005)

The Future for Allotments (Select Committee on Environment, Transport and Regional Affairs, 1998)

Gurdon, Martin, *Hen and the Art of Chicken Maintenance: Reflections on Raising Chickens* (The Lyons Press, 2005)

Hickmott, Simon, *Growing Unusual Vegetables* (Eco-Logic Books/Worldly Goods, 2004)

Lacey, Roy, *Cowpasture: The Everyday Life of an English Allotment* (David & Charles, 1980)

Lloyd, Christopher, *The Well-Tempered Garden* (Viking, 1985)

Opperman, Chris, *Allotment Folk* (New Holland, 2004)

Osborne, Victor, *Digger's Diary: Tales from the Allotment* (Aurum Press, 2000)

Pears, Pauline (ed.), *HDRA Encyclopedia of Organic Gardening* (Dorling Kindersley, 2005)

Pollan, Michael, *Second Nature: A Gardener's Education* (Grove Press, 2003)

Poole, Steve, *The Allotment Chronicles: A Social History of Allotment Gardening* (Silver Link Publishing, 2006)

Rand, Michael, *Close to the Veg: A Book of Allotment Tales* (Marlin Press, 2005)

Sandler, Nick and Action, Johnny, *Preserved* (Kyle Cathie, 2004)

Shelton, Robin, *Allotted Time: Twelve Months, Two Blokes, One Shed, No Idea* (Sidgwick & Jackson, 2006)

Smit, Tim and McMillan Browse, Philip, *The Heligan Vegetable Bible* (Cassell Illustrated, 2002)

Steel, Jenny, *Bringing a Garden to Life* (Wiggly Wigglers 2006)

Stewart, Amy, *The Earth Moved: On the Remarkable Achievements of Earthworms* (Algonquin Books, 2004)

Tarpley, Webster Griffin and Chaitkin, Anton, *George Bush: The Unauthorized Biography* (Progressive Press, 2004)

Thompson, Elspeth, *The Urban Gardener* (Orion, 2000)

Thompson, Ken, *An Ear to the Ground* (Eden Project Books, 2003)

Turner, Carole B, *Seed Sowing and Saving* (Storey Books, 1998)

Tzu, Sun, *The Art of War* (Penguin Books, 2005)

Uglow, Jenny, *A Little History of British Gardening* (Chatto & Windus, 2004)

Williams, John B and Morrison, John R, *A Colour Atlas of Weed Seedlings* (Manson Publishing, 2003)

Allotment and gardening blogs

Allotment Lady
kooringa.com

Allotment No 21
allotment21.blogspot.com

...And I hate Worms!
ihateworms.blogspot.com

Anything But Sprouts
anythingbutsprouts.blogspot.com

At Last I've Got My Plot!
plotblog-lilymarlene.blogspot.com

Bexsallotment
bexsallotment.blogspot.com

Clodhoppers
sirlancsallot.blogspot.com

Dave's Allotment
davesallotment.blogspot.com

Down on the allotment
digwell.blogspot.com

Duck Dinner Dash
duckdinnerdash.blogspot.com

Fluffius Muppetus
fluffymuppet.blogspot.com

Greenfuse
foodtrain.typepad.com/greenfuse

Garden Blethers
geocities.com/gardenblethers

Losing the Plot
losingtheplot.blogspot.com

Mike's Allotment Diary
surelythisisntinteresting.blogspot.com

Moonbells' Allotment Diary
www.moonbells.com

My Allotments
myallotments.blogspot.com

My Tiny Plot
www.mytinyplot.co.uk

Our Allotment's Blog
ourallotment.blogspot.com

Plot Blog
plotblog.blogspot.com

Plot c81
plotc81.blogspot.com

Plot Holes
plotholes.blogspot.com

Pumpkin Soup
allotment.humanlint.com

She Who Digs
shewhodigs.blogspot.com

Directory

Allotment and gardening organisations

Allotments and Gardens Council (UK)
www.theallotmentsandgardenscounciluk.org.uk

Allotments Regeneration Initiative
www.farmgarden.org.uk/ari

Allotments UK
www.allotments-uk.com

Federation of City Farms and Community Gardens
www.farmgarden.org.uk

Garden Organic (formerly the Henry Doubleday Research Association)
www.gardenorganic.org.uk

National Society of Allotment and Leisure Gardeners (NSALG)
www.nsalg.org.uk

Permaculture Association (Britain)
www.permaculture.org.uk

Royal Horticultural Society (RHS)
www.rhs.org.uk

Scottish Allotments and Gardening Society
www.sags.org.uk

Soil Association
www.soilassociation.org

Seeds, plants and equipment

Beans and Herbs
www.beansandherbs.co.uk

Carroll's Heritage Potatoes
www.heritage-potatoes.co.uk

Chiltern Seeds
www.chilternseeds.co.uk

Crocus
www.crocus.co.uk

DMT Dia-Sharp
www.dmtsharp.com/products/diasharp.htm

DT Brown Seeds
www.dtbrownseeds.co.uk

Edulis
www.edulis.co.uk

Freecycle
http://uk.freecycle.org

Mr Fothergill's
www.fothergills.co.uk

Gardenopoly
www.gardenopoly.co.uk

Green Gardener
www.greengardener.co.uk

Implementations copper tools
www.implementations.co.uk

Johnsons Seeds
www.johnsons-seeds.com

King's Seeds
www.kingsseeds.com

Marshalls Seeds
www.marshalls-seeds.co.uk

The Millennium Seed Bank at the Royal Botanic gardens, Kew
www.kew.org/msbp

The Organic Gardening Catalogue
www.organiccatalogue.com

The Real Seed Catalogue
www.realseeds.co.uk

Robinson's Mammoth Vegetable Seeds
www.mammothonion.co.uk

Seeds By Size
www.seeds-by-size.com

Seeds of Italy
www.seedsofitaly.com

Suffolk Herbs
www.suffolkherbs.com

Tamar Organics
www.tamarorganics.co.uk

Thomas Etty Esq.
www.thomasetty.co.uk

Seed saving and swapping

Association Kokopelli
www.kokopelli-seeds.com

Heritage Seed Library (UK)
www.gardenorganic.org.uk/hsl

International Seed Saving Institute
www.seedsave.org

Primal Seeds
www.primalseeds.org

Seed and Plant Sanctuary for Canada
www.seedsanctuary.com

Seedy Saturday (Canada)
www.seedysaturday.ca

Seed Savers Exchange (US)
www.seedsavers.org

Wiggly Wigglers
www.wigglywigglers.co.uk

Composting

Centre for Alternative Energy
www.cat.org.uk

Community Composting Network
www.communitycompost.org

Recycle Now guide to home composting
www.recyclenow.com/home_composting

Acknowledgements

Many people have helped or inspired me in the writing of this book. In particular, I'd like to thank:

Rick, my partner on the allotment and in life, for his unerring ability to make me laugh at myself, and for his very fine red lentil soup; my mum and dad, and Louise and JJ, for their love and assistance, both long-distance and in person; Frieda Mestinsek, who showed me just how much fun gardening can be; the Flying Caberoony, for encouragement and seed packets from afar; my editor Lisa Darnell for her sage advice and backing at every stage of the writing process; all at Atlantic Books for making this book a reality; everyone at Guardian Unlimited news and politics for adopting vegetables, and coming up with many alternative titles for this book; Tom Happold and Susie Steiner for setting the ball rolling; Orlah Shiels for her gardeners' apple pie recipe; Sarah Norwood and all the other allotmenteers and gardeners I've met online and in person who have inspired and challenged me; my friend and journalistic exemplar Jack Hamilton for his wisdom in all matters (I think I kept to your unwritten rules on acknowledgements), and my pal Kash Prashad – I hope this is another entry for the cuttings book. Finally, I must thank John Admiral Byng, who was a far more accomplished allotmenteer than I'll ever be.

Index